BARCODE IN BACK

At the Font of the Marvelous

The Iroquois and Their Neighbors
Christopher Vecsey, *Series Editor*

OTHER TITLES IN THE IROQUOIS AND THEIR NEIGHBORS

Archaeology of the Iroquois: Selected Readings and Research Sources
JORDAN E. KERBER, ed.

Big Medicine from the Six Nations
TED WILLIAMS

The Collected Speeches of Sagoyewatha, or Red Jacket
GRANVILLE GANTER, ED.

The History and Culture of Iroquois Diplomacy: An Interdisciplinary Guide to the Treaties of the Six Nations and Their League
FRANCIS JENNINGS, ed.

In Mohawk Country: Early Narratives of a Native People
DEAN R. SNOW, CHARLES T. GEHRING,
and WILLIAM A. STARNA, eds.

Iroquoia: The Development of a Native World
WILLIAM ENGELBRECHT

Iroquois Medical Botany
JAMES W. HERRICK and DEAN R. SNOW, eds.

The Mashpee Indians: Tribe on Trial
JACK CAMPISI

Oneida Iroquois Folklore, Myth, and History: New York Oral Narrative from the Notes of H. E. Allen and Others
ANTHONY WONDERLEY

The Reservation
TED WILLIAMS

Seven Generations of Iroquois Leadership: The Six Nations since 1800
LAURENCE M. HAUPTMAN

At the Font of the
Marvelous

Exploring Oral Narrative
and Mythic Imagery of the
Iroquois and Their Neighbors

Anthony Wonderley

 SYRACUSE UNIVERSITY PRESS

Syracuse University Press
Syracuse, New York 13244-5160

First Edition 2009

09   10   11   12   13   14   6   5   4   3   2   1

The paper used in this publication meets the minimum requirements
of American National Standard for Information Sciences—Permanence
of Paper for Printed Library Materials, ANSI Z39.48–1984.∞™

For a listing of books published and distributed by Syracuse University Press,
visit our Web site at SyracuseUniversityPress.syr.edu

ISBN-13: 978-0-8156-3207-8   ISBN-10: 0-8156-3207-X

Library of Congress Cataloging-in-Publication Data
Wonderley, Anthony Wayne, 1949–
    At the font of the marvelous : exploring oral narrative and mythic imagery of the Iroquois and their neighbors /
Anthony Wonderley. — 1st ed.
        p. cm. — (The Iroquois and their neighbors)
    Includes bibliographical references and index.
    ISBN-13: 978-0-8156-3207-8 (hardcover : alk. paper)
    ISBN-10: 0-8156-3207-X (hardcover : alk. paper)
    1. Iroquois Indians—Folklore.   2. Algonquian Indians—Folklore.   3. Indian mythology—New York (State)
4. Indian mythology—Ontario.   5. Oral history—New York (State)   6. Oral history—Ontario.   7. Folklore—
New York (State)   8. Folklore—Ontario.   9. New York (State)—Social life and customs.   10. Ontario—Social
life and customs.   I. Title.
    E99.I7W84 2009
    398.2089'9755—dc22
    2008051732

Manufactured in the United States of America

To Anthony D. and Lucas R.,

—*two fine young men*
who make their parents proud

Anthony Wonderley is curator of the Oneida Community Mansion House in Oneida, N.Y. He was educated at the University of Michigan (B.A.), the University of Nevada/Las Vegas (M.A., Historical Archaeology), and Cornell University (Ph.D., Anthropology). He is the author of *Oneida Iroquois Folklore, Myth, and History: New York Oral Narrative from the Notes of H. E. Allen and Others,* also published by Syracuse University Press. His articles on Iroquois archaeology, folklore, and history have appeared in *American Antiquity, Bulletin of the New York Archaeological Association, Mohawk Valley History, New York History, Northeastern Anthropology,* and *Ontario Archaeology.*

Contents

Illustrations

Maps

Acknowledgments

I'VE DONE WELL by Syracuse University Press and appreciate their professionalism and support throughout this labor. Special thanks to editors Linda Cuckovich, Mary Selden Evans, Christopher Vecsey, and Glenn D. Wright and to manuscript readers, including Jordan Paper.

I became interested in the subject matter resulting in this book while I was a historian in the Oneida Indian Nation's legal department. I will always be grateful to that employer for giving me a job and for the incomparable opportunity to be meaningfully engaged in my work.

Chapters 1, 4, and 7 originally were given as talks at the Annual Conference on Iroquois Research at Rensselaerville, N.Y., from 1998 to 2005. To the scholars of that event, past and present, I recognize an immense intellectual debt. Specific thanks are due to Bill Engelbrecht and Mike Foster for clarification on a number of points in Iroquois archaeology and linguistics.

Earlier versions of chapters 1 and 7 were published in the journals *American Antiquity* (Wonderley 2005a), *Northeastern Anthropology* (Wonderley 2006b), and *Ontario Archaeology* (Wonderley 2005b). I appreciate the assistance and helpful criticism received from the editors (Michael Jochim, Sean Rafferty, Andrew Stewart) and reviewers of the three articles (those whose names I know are: Tim Abel, Susan Jamieson, Kurt Jordan, Jordan Paper, Michael Spence, and Joan Vastokas). The peer-review process worked for me and made my work better. Thank you.

Chapter 7, an archeological look at Iroquois mythic imagery, is a visual topic dependent on quality artifact drawings done by Julia Meyerson (ills. 5, 6c) and Daniel L. Faulkner (all the other illustrations). I created the four maps.

I am grateful to several individuals who made available material crucial to me in a wonderfully timely fashion: Blair Rudes (University of North Carolina, Charlotte), George Hamell (then of the New York State Museum, Albany), and Valerie-Ann Lutz and Mary McDonald (American Philosophical Society, Philadelphia). And thank you, Patricia Hoffman, for contributing a flattering photograph of the author.

Introduction

Oral Narrative of the Iroquois
and Their Neighbors

ON A VISIT to Cherokee country about the year 1812, a literate Mohawk chief named John Norton was intrigued by an unusual aspect of the landscape. Norton loved the oral traditions of the north and, when he asked his hosts to tell him about the feature, he expected to be entertained by a tale explaining how the oddity came to be. The Cherokees, however, only shrugged, saying they knew no stories about it. Now here were people, the astonished Norton confided to his journal, who clearly were *not* "addicted to the marvelous" (Klinck and Talman 1970, 62).

Norton knew. The folktales, legends, and myths of the Iroquois or Haudenosaunee (in upstate New York and adjacent Ontario) and their Algonquian neighbors (all around Iroquois country) rank among the most imaginatively rich and narratively coherent traditions in North America. Mostly recorded around 1900, these oral narratives preserve the voice and something of the outlook of autochthonous Americans from a bygone age— prior to the dominance of radio, cinema, television, and Internet—when storytelling was an important fact of daily life. The folklore comprises an enormous body of material, one largely neglected by native and nonnative scholars alike.

Such wondrous tales informed and inspired this set of essays about oral narrative in the Native American Northeast. The anthropological studies that follow focus on the nature of the stories as inferred, chiefly, from their plots. What do they say? What are they about? My answer is that some encapsulate cultural truths important to understanding Iroquois religion and worldview. Among the oral narratives testifying to older beliefs are several that clarify mythic imagery observable in the archaeological record. Other stories stand as irrefutable proof of bonds established between distant peoples, connections otherwise undocumented. Folktales and myths illustrate what people share, but they also furnish clues about what makes groups culturally distinctive. Finally, and in a few of the better-documented instances, one can follow plot development over time to recover a piece of the past of the people who told the story.

The research grew out of an earlier book in which Iroquois oral narrative was interwoven with history and prehistory to tell the story of the New York Oneidas for whom I worked at the time (Wonderley 2004). The present studies explore and expand on questions raised in that earlier work. For example, I found that stone giants, popular creatures in Iroquois folklore, were similar to "various races of northern cannibal monsters familiar to neighboring Algonquian groups including windigo" (100). In this book, I make windigo's acquaintance to get a clearer picture of the relationship between Algonquian and Iroquois mythic creations. Or again, in the earlier book I suggested that representational imagery found on certain archaeological objects might be reified oral narrative understandable from later folklore and myth. Humanlike depictions on ceramic cooking pots could be mythological cornhusk people. Faces and figures on certain smoking pipes of fired clay might relate to stories about mythic origin. The hypotheses are developed here in greater detail.

I use a generally accepted tripartite classification for oral narrative that remains, after a century and a half of folklore usage, ambiguous and vague. By convention, oral narrative comprises three genres: myths, folktales, and legends. All are regarded as true, but myths, a people's most important stories, are the truest of all. Myths tend to be regarded as older and more sacred and serious than other kinds of narrative. Usually they explain how the world came to be ordered, how something significant came about, or where a people came from (for example, the Iroquois tradition of emerging from the earth, discussed in chapter 7). Myths tend to begin in primal time and often include cosmic activities. They feature supernaturals and such culture heroes as Manibozho or Gluskap among speakers of Algonquian languages and Sky Holder among the Iroquois (chapter 4).

Legends describe human action "locally bound and historically rooted" (Grantham 2002, 3). They claim special and usually explicit credibility by alluding to what is regarded as historically true (for example, Iroquois accounts of the Kahkwa War considered in chapter 2).

Folktales are less historically minded than legends and more secular than myths. Many seem more clearly designed to amuse and entertain. Among Iroquoian and Algonquian speakers in the Northeast, folktales are often animal stories or human adventures. Examples of folktales in this book are legion and include such story types as the "Killer Lizard" (chapter 3) and the "Friendly Visitor" (chapters 5–6). As nonmyth and nonlegend, the category is more residual than anything else. A point repeatedly made is that some folktales carry a suggestion of age and thematic importance redolent of myth (chapters 1, 3).

Oral narrative is that part of traditional expressive culture comprising a people's verbal art or lore (also called oral literature). For all humans, life is shared symbolic existence, a common social experience of abstraction and language. "People learn the perception of the world as it comes to them in the talk of people around them and is encapsulated in the categorization of reality and the presumptions about time, space, and causation in the world. The rich complexity of the narrative about reality that each of us gets sets the tone and character of our lives" (Goldschmidt 2000, 802). In a nonliterate setting, a culture's narratives are an especially important medium for conveying premises of belief and perception. The concepts often are expressed in mythopoetic language favoring memorable comparison and evoking vivid imagery. Such stories serve as signposts for people navigating together through the richly symbolic landscape that is the human condition.

As medium and means for making cultural sense of the world, oral narrative is explanatory. The key insight of anthropologist Bronislaw Malinowski (1984, 199) in the 1920s was that myth fulfills "an indispensable function: it expresses, enhances, and codifies belief . . . it vouches for the efficiency of ritual and contains practical rules for the guidance of man."

Some oral narratives serve as social charters legitimating the present order and asserting its naturalness and rightness. Others explain in the sense that they comment on problematic aspects of social reality and, perhaps, provide the symbolic tools to resolve or think through dilemmas (Drummond 1981). Some stories of this sort may well supply a psychological palliative for difficulties that cannot be resolved or even openly stated.

Oral narrative's explanatory bent makes for a retrospectively oriented gaze—these stories "anchor the present generations in a meaningful, significant past, functioning as eternal and ideal models for human behavior and goals" (Vecsey 1988, 24; cf. Cruikshank 1994, 407). Trying to make sense of the past, some oral narratives not only talk about history, they also "attempt to reconcile a view of 'what really happened' with an understanding of 'what ought to have happened'" (Hill 1988, 10). Oral narrative can transform the experienced past and guide one's experience of history (Bricker 1981; Erickson 2003). Far from opposing one another, history and oral narrative work together as "a unified strategy for coping with new problems" (Gossen 1986, 4).[1]

The oldest narratives considered in this book are early seventeenth century in date. Among speakers of Iroquoian languages in the Northeast at that time were the Susquehannocks in present Pennsylvania, the Iroquois proper of present upstate New York, and the Hurons and Petuns of Ontario near the Georgian Bay (see map 1).

The Iroquoians had the largest and most sedentary concentrations of population in the Northeast. They lived in more or less permanent villages of a thousand or more inhabitants and composed of houses made from elm-bark shingles set on a framework of saplings and logs. Almost twenty feet in height and width, such a residence resembled an enormous Quonset hut sixty to two hundred feet long depending on how many families lived within. The greater part of the building was divided into apartments twelve to twenty-five feet long. On one side, the living area was open to the central

---

1. Oral narrative doubtlessly does other things as well. For one thing, it entertains and provides aesthetic satisfaction. More or less formal creations polished in the retelling, stories please in the art of their figurative and poetic expression. Oral narrative also is an important agency for educating and socializing a society's young people. The stories of a group "teach more indirectly by means of a consistent and coherent set of underlying assumptions about the nature of reality which in one way or another is repeated in them again and again" (Overholt and Callicott 1982, 140).

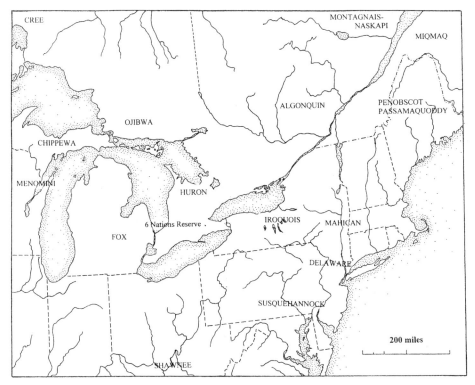

1. The Northeast.

aisle running the length of the house. On the other, it was furnished with a bench or sleeping platform attached to an exterior wall. Each apartment was occupied by a nuclear family sharing a hearth or cooking fire with a similar family across the central corridor.

The larger settlements were surrounded by a barrier of upright stakes. Stockades were defensive works testifying to the threat of violence from intervillage feuding. The goal of such fighting was to incorporate into the home group an enemy for each individual lost from one's own community. An enemy's scalp counted in such a tally but one could also bring home a living prisoner. Such a captive might be figuratively adopted, then tortured and executed in a public rite in which the community absorbed the captive's spirit by eating his or her flesh. Alternatively, the prisoner really was adopted to replace a deceased family member by assuming that person's name, rights, and responsibilities.

Iroquoians obtained food by gathering wild plants and fruits, by hunting (especially deer), and, most of all, from harvesting domesticated agricultural foods, including beans, squashes, and, especially, maize. Unlike the European system of extensive and labor-intensive agriculture, the Iroquoian method of horticulture was to burn clear a garden-plot area, then plant the three kinds of food together. Over time and as the yield declined, the plots were rotated. Farming was a female task requiring perhaps six weeks of a woman's time annually.

A gender-based Iroquoian division of labor assigned duties of the village and immediate clearing to women, those of the forest and foreign lands to men. Women, in this scheme, were responsible for collecting firewood and gathering such wild foods as berries and nuts. In addition to tending the gardens, women cooked the meals consisting chiefly of corn gruels. Men, in contrast, were the hunters, diplomats, and warriors.

Since this way of life necessitated the absence of males for long periods of time, it appears that the fundamental social unit was not the nuclear arrangement but the extended family reckoned through the mother's line. Such a matrilineage typically comprised a grandmother and her daughters and grandchildren along with various spouses. Most bark houses probably were home to such a family and under the supervision of the senior matron.

These female-centered families belonged, in turn, to a matrilineal clan, a grouping of families presumed related through the female line. Clan groupings were important in ceremonial, social, and political life. Each clan probably had deliberative councils, one composed of senior women and the other of senior men or counselors. Most of the leaders hailed from certain prestigious families looked up to as a kind of aristocracy, and many of the important men held their positions by virtue of appointment by the senior matron or clan mother. The ruling committee of a village or of a tribe or nation (several villages regarding themselves as one people) was basically the clan council extended and writ larger.

Throughout the Northeast by 1600, clusters of tribes commonly allied with one another to coordinate military efforts against a common enemy. Combatants waging war at this level were capable of destroying whole enemy confederations, as we shall see in chapter 2. The best known and longest-lived of these associations was that of the Iroquois alliance, consisting originally of five tribes (east to west across upstate New York: Mohawk, Oneida, Onondaga, Cayuga, and Seneca). Although no consensus exists as to the precise age and origin of the Iroquois Confederacy or League, archaeological evidence, traditions, and ethnohistorical data pertinent to these questions are explored in chapter 7.

Iroquoians probably had the most complexly developed political institutions in the Northeast. Nevertheless, obedience could never be compelled. Among the Iroquoians as well as all the peoples mentioned in this book, there was a strong tendency toward egalitarianism and the ethos of individuality.

Surrounding the Iroquoians were speakers of Algonquian languages. To the east were Mahicans (Hudson River valley in eastern New York) and Delawares (or Lenapes of southeast New York, eastern Pennsylvania, Delaware, and New Jersey). They also possessed matriclans and lived in villages composed of bark houses and dedicated to maize agriculture. However, Delaware and Mahican settlements generally were smaller (about two hundred) and less permanently inhabited than those of the Iroquois. During the winter, the villages broke up into smaller groups that moved to their hunting territories.

To the west were such peoples as the Shawnees (southern Ohio), Foxes (southern Michigan), and Menominis (northern Michigan and Wisconsin), all characterized by clans reckoned patrilineally (through the father's line). Here again, village life with maize crops tended to be more seasonal than it was among the Iroquoians. With the coming of cold weather, villages dispersed into smaller groups to pursue hunting in the forest.

Hunting increasingly took precedence over horticulture as one proceeded north. Closely related groups of people—variously called Chippewa-Ojibwa and, further east along the St. Lawrence River, the Algonquin proper—inhabited boreal forests on both the American and Canadian sides of the Great Lakes. Calling themselves some variant of "Anishnaabeg," most lived in small (several hundred), patrilineal bands widely scattered across the landscape. Their hunting-gathering-fishing economy focused on seasonally shifting foods that, in turn, required a seminomadic way of life. Their largest settlements were composed of dome-shaped wigwams, made of birch bark or cattail, congregated at favorable fishing locations during the summer. With winter came a dispersal into smaller family groups for hunting (see chapter 5).

Miqmaqs, Penobscots, and Passamaquoddys lived similarly in their boreal settings ranging from Maine to New Brunswick. Their bands, however, were structured bilaterally—that is, reckoned through lines of both parents. Farther north, the subarctic zone, extending west from Manitoba to the Labrador Peninsula on the east, was home to fewer Algonquians and smaller groups. These Crees, Montagnais, and Naskapis depended almost exclusively upon hunting and were the most nearly nomadic of all.

Overall, Algonquian peoples probably depended more than the Iroquoians on gathering wild foods and hunting. Algonquians tended to be more diffusely distributed across the landscape pursuing lifeways requiring greater mobility.[2]

By European standards, both Algonquian and Iroquoian societies seemed nonhierarchical (essentially equal in social standing and material possessions), socially undifferentiated (lacking specialized political, religious, economic, and educational institutions independent of general kinship arrangements), and technologically simple (all items created by hand of stone, wood, hide, and other naturally occurring substances). More often than not, the ethnocentric Europeans regarded native people as uncivilized and savage.

Most seventeenth-century documentation of native folklore and myth was recorded by French missionaries belonging to the Roman Catholic Society of Jesus (Thwaites 1896–1901). For them, native people presented the additional difficulty of being pagans who told what the Jesuits viewed as devilish fantasies and illogical fables. Few Christian chroniclers took native stories seriously, and even fewer would risk perpetuating them by writing them down. Yet, bits and pieces of oral narrative did get recorded.

---

2. This cultural and geographical summary, admittedly superficial, is offered as nothing more than a general introduction to the peoples and scope of this work. The interested reader could begin to access the vast literature on this subject through the most recent encyclopedic treatment, *The Handbook of North American Indians,* especially volumes 15 (Trigger 1978) and 6 (Helm 1981).

Such documentation comprises the oldest body of Native American lore in North America (Hultkrantz 1981, 189–90).

The Northeast also is home to some of the earliest folkloric material coming more directly from native sources. The journal of the adopted Mohawk chief, John Norton, for example, bears the date 1816 (Klinck and Talman 1970). An Iroquois writer named David Cusick produced, in English, a history of his people as early as 1827 (Beauchamp 1892). (The works of Norton and Cusick are discussed further in chapter 2.)

Iroquois *annalistes* also developed a distinctive genre of mythic documentation later in the nineteenth century, especially on the Six Nations Reserve in Ontario. Both John Arthur Gibson and Seth Newhouse, for example, synthesized bodies of tradition relating to the Iroquois League—how that confederacy came about and how it was supposed to function (Fenton 1998, 80–97; Parker 1916; Scott 1912; Woodbury 1992). Their efforts surely sprang from a desire to record important knowledge for succeeding generations. At the same time, the texts they produced reflected the traditional claims of factions then competing for political legitimacy on the reservation (Fenton 1949 and 1998, 39; Weaver 1984). Such works are valuable compilations of oral materials, of course, but, as attempts to codify, they also introduce some measure of innovation. (A Tuscarora instance of this halfway house between transcribed speech and literary composition is examined in chapter 2.)

The idea that Indian folklore was interesting was introduced to American readers by Henry Schoolcraft (1999) as early as 1828. His oral narratives—chiefly Great Lakes Algonquian but including considerable Iroquois material as well—derived entirely from the Northeast. Likewise, the first American ethnography of Native American life—Lewis Henry Morgan's *League of the Iroquois or Haudenosaunee*—contains useful information about northeastern oral narrative in the middle of the nineteenth century (1962, originally published 1851). The Northeast, in sum, is a region whose oral narrative offers exceptional scope for investigating time depth in folklore and myth.

However, the overwhelming preponderance of documented oral narrative in the Northeast was recorded between 1880 and 1925. Among the Iroquois, for example, William Beauchamp (1922), Elias Johnson (1881), Arthur Parker (1989), and Erminnie Smith (1983) published reasonably serious compilations of folktales. More substantial collections taken at least partly in the native languages were assembled by Jeremiah Curtin (2001), J. N. B. Herwitt (1918; Rudes and Crouse 1987) and Frederick Waugh (n.d.; Randle 1953). Similar and related folklore from Hurons and Wyandots was made available at the same time by other researchers (Barbeau 1915; Connelley 1899; Hale 1888, 1889).

The Northeast is hardly unique in that respect. Throughout North America, most native folklore was documented around the turn of the twentieth century. This was the heroic age of anthropologist Franz Boas, the time when Boas and his colleagues and students (native as well as non-native) feverishly labored, in concert with Native American traditionalists, to record every facet possible of Native American life. Committed to understanding each culture or tribe on its own terms, anthropologists were drawn to myths and folktales as mirrors reflecting aspects of culture ranging from details of daily life to symbols and values. And because such content was, in effect, chosen by the people themselves, oral narrative appealed to anthropologists as a kind of tribal autobiography providing an insider's view of the culture (Boas 1916, 393). Insofar as myths and folktales preserve memories of activities no longer practiced, they also were important documents in cultural reconstruction.

These indefatigable workers documented what is probably the largest body of indigenous folklore and myth in the world. Since the information is not embedded in esoteric or theoretical discussion, most of it is accessible to nonspecialist readers. Much of it remains unstudied to this day.

The data consist of texts written in a European language, usually English. Each presents a sequential set of incidents. The stories are brief, their brevity suggestive of attenuated speech in the days before sounds could be recorded. They are spare, typically providing few details and little personality development. They are not autobiographical or eyewitness accounts. They say little about causality or explanation, or about the body of assumptions once held in common by tellers and listeners alike. Conveying virtually nothing about linguistic complexity, verbal performance, or social setting, they cannot be studied as social activities or foreign-language phenomena (Cruikshank 1998; Hymes 1981). The plots and story lines themselves are, perforce, the objects of inquiry.

Though I do not pursue it, these narratives could well be materials suitable for a structuralist analysis. Such an approach is exemplified in the work of Claude Lévi-Strauss (1983, 1990a, 1990b), an anthropologist who has interpreted perhaps a thousand folktales and myths (he does not distinguish between them), mostly from South America. The human mind, for Lévi-Strauss, takes the measure of the world through such metaphors of oppositional relationship as hot-cold, male-female, and culture-nature. Having phrased the matter discontinuously, the mind somehow seeks deliverance from contradiction and paradox through symbolic operations mediating opposites into something else. Oral narratives are one way the mind works through such symbolic problems (Lévi-Strauss 1963).

If, therefore, a story is really an associational arrangement the collective mind finds congenial at some unconscious level, its meaning should be sought in those deep structures unknown to the storyteller and not in such superficialities as plot. A specific "myth" is treated as "but one fragment of a veritable torrent of similar stories, transformations of the originals, with innovations, inversions, and various oppositions of different parts of the myths" (Mindlin 2002, 272). But the themes so revealed "have no end and turn into other stories." It is better, that student of Amazonian folktales sadly concludes, "to stick with the narratives themselves" (280).

I agree. Content obviously matters. While one may attribute to a story an infinite number of meanings, the one most irreducible and undeniable inheres within the narrative itself—specific plot with proximate incidents, actors, setting, and so on. No story exists without narrative, and none can be understood without reference to the story it tells. A tale always "means what it says" (Thompson 1965, 177).

I approach these data comparatively, trying to determine whether story plots of reasonable coherence can be documented and, if so, where. Simultaneously, I try to understand where the narrative does not occur and, if a different tale is told in its place, whether overlap or commonality can be discerned. The star tales examined in chapter 1 and the story type called Friendly Visitor surveyed in chapter 6 illustrate this methodology. Then one goes pattern-hunting, inductively seeking to clarify the phenomenon with reference to perceived commonalities and differences (for examples, the windigos in chapter 5).

In addition to comparing contemporaneous things, there is also time's arrow to take into account. Each time a story was told, the teller and audience were linked in a social act expressively and conceptually meaningful to both parties. But a story told has no physical reality. As something ephemeral, it is subject to modification in each circumstance and over time. Literally speaking, a story is only as old as the moment it is told.

Exploring what happens over time is another form of comparison, one that really is the most rudimentary exercise in historical research. To draw a conclusion about the temporal dimension, one must understand something about a phenomenon as it was at, minimally, two points in time. The evidence is lined up chronologically, and what was said earlier is compared to what was said later. I perform basic historical comparison of this sort when examining Iroquois legends about conquering western New York (chapter 2) and evidence pertaining to the principal Iroquois deity, Sky Holder, in chapter 4.

As for dating, the Northeast furnishes a rich-enough historical record that one can sometimes compare securely dated variants as is done with war legends and descriptions of Sky Holder. Other mythic plots have material correlates to which archaeological dating can be applied (chapter 7).

More frequently, the age of oral narrative is unknown. Being a historian and prehistorian, I am curious about the antiquity of a thing (obsessively so, some have said). I crudely gauge the probability of age by applying a form of common-sense reasoning called the age-area hypothesis, an invention of Franz Boas (1940, 425–45) and his colleagues of the American Historical School.

Those researchers carefully noted the geographical distribution of such cultural traits as a style of moccasin, or a way of classifying relatives, or a type of folktale. If the trait was complex in its constituency (the classic example being the complicated ideational construct called a story), it was unlikely to have been created out of nothing more than once (Edmonson 1971, 45). Once in existence, the trait would spread outward. Its oldest occurrence, logically, would be sought in the center of the trait's distribution. More importantly, a trait of continuous and wide distribution would have required time to spread over a large area. In very general terms, therefore, the age of a trait is proportionate to the size of its distribution (Sapir

1994, 57–60; Wissler 1938, 315). The age-area hypothesis becomes, in this fashion, a way of thinking about time depth.

Age-area is not a very muscular explanation or theory. In the absence of chronometric fact or archaeological correlate, it is a vague indication of antiquity. The concept happens to be consistent with the data of oral narrative, and I use it to acknowledge that some oral narrative is "a very old pattern, woven into the terrain over the course of thousands of years" (Bierhorst 1985, 1).

I do not question that folktales, legends, and myths may convey multiple meanings or different meanings to different individuals. For me, however, Malinowski's insight is key to comparative and historical research. I take it as axiomatic that some oral narrative is "not an idle rhapsody, not an aimless outpouring of vain imaginings, but a hardworking, extremely important cultural force" (Malinowski 1984, 196). Because it is important in social existence, sense can be made of it.

Interested in the past, my concern is with the evidence of oral narrative as it was documented early on, chiefly in the form of brief stories. I proceed comparatively and historically in inductive fashion. I do not skate far from the empirical evidence or the narrative content.

I try to approach the data critically. Most commonly, this is itself a comparative exercise in which one asks: Are the sources similar in content and tone? A ballpark of credibility results from such agreement and, conversely, what stands out as different should be regarded with suspicion.

For example, mixed up with ethnological reportage of the age is a genre of Victorian parlor literature purporting to convey Native American stories, often to a young reading audience. Such works typically combine authorial embroidery and fabrication to such an extent that, if there was any authentically native basis to the plot, the story has been rendered worthless for any comparative purpose.

Canfield (1902), Converse (1908), and Powers (1923) exemplify such problematic sources of Iroquois folklore. Much of Arthur Parker's *Skunny Wundy* (1994), a 1926 children's book of "Seneca Indian tales," is fiction. A later effort along the same lines, *Rumbling Wings and Other Indian Tales* (Parker 1928), is entirely and explicitly so. Works of this sort obviously are untrustworthy.

Of course, one also tries to be honestly self-critical. I am not aware that I have an ideological ax to grind. My professional life is unlikely to be advanced or validated by the labor. I feel pretty certain this book will not profit me financially.

The Essays

Tales about stars hold a special interest for they seem to relate products of the mind to real things in the physical world. If there is an empirical or scientific basis to mythic thought, it ought to be discernible in this subject matter. Chapter 1 examines Iroquois star stories, almost all of which are about the Pleiades and Big Dipper constellations. Even though such tales tend to be brief, there is reason to regard them as serious oral narrative. The Pleiades, for example, were once regarded as the land of the dead.

These narratives, however, turn out to be oddly redundant (the Pleiades have two names and two stories) and weirdly nonspecific (one of the Pleiades stories also attaches to the Big Dipper). Further and comparatively, both conditions occur frequently elsewhere in North America. This suggests the tales do not reflect phenomena that were closely observed. Star stories, as Boas observed (1914, 407), are products of the cultural imagination.

Regarded as myths, the stories evince surprising links to distant mythic traditions of intercontinental occurrence. Presumably, this phenomenon is very old. But what was the meaning of such tales to actual storytellers at one time and place? The explicit Iroquois answer is that the stories express a local, contextual truth about identity.

Incidentally, sky phenomena lay at the heart of nineteenth-century attempts to interpret Native American myth. The idea was that folklore and myth represented attempts by "prescientific" or "primitive" peoples to explain the natural world, especially the apparent movements of celestial objects (Thompson 1929, 237–38, 312). Empirically, however, the sky does not seem to loom large in oral narrative (Lowie 1908; Thompson 1929, 384). This does not mean that the Iroquois were ignorant about what went on in the heavens. It means that such knowledge was not reflected or encoded in Iroquois oral narrative around 1900.

The Seneca Iroquois believed they owned what is now western New York because they had conquered its resident people, the Kahkwas, in the relatively recent past. It was a war or wars probably related to conflicts with Eries and Neutrals described by European chroniclers during the 1630s–50s. At any rate, the Kahkwa War was important to Iroquois storytellers whose interest in the subject resulted in the best documented legend in the Northeast. The copious record also provides the means for discerning how oral narrative expresses and interprets a people's past.

In chapter 2, I examine a number of accounts of the Kahkwa War, chronologically lining them up and paying close attention to who says what. Two different historical traditions are clearly distinguishable. Seneca storytellers consistently emphasized how their people had been victimized by a Kahkwa sneak attack. After repulsing the invasion in a great battle near the Genesee River, the Senecas went on the offensive and dispersed the enemy. For Tuscarora writers, in contrast, the Kahkwa War was largely the story of a perfidious female leader named Wildcat. That queen's office had been created by the Iroquois Confederacy, and she lived in or near what later became the Tuscarora Reservation. Kahkwa War narratives, I suggest, were performing major mythic work for Senecas and Tuscaroras, both hard-pressed during the nineteenth century. For both, but in different ways, the war story provided a means to connect past with present. Its effect was to render the here and now more meaningful and more palatable.

Chapter 3, another comparative survey of stories or story types, charts the occurrence of three more tales of the marvelous, all of wide distribution. In the first, a group of hunters disturbs a monstrous reptile that methodically runs down and kills each of the party save one. The survivor is championed by a beneficent supernatural, usually a lion, who overcomes the Killer Lizard in a titanic fight to the death. In the second, travelers encounter strange fish swimming around in the basin of a tree stump. Against all advice, one insists on eating the find and, in consequence, is transformed into a water snake. In the third, a human crossing a body of water on the head of a horned serpent must induce the creature to continue its efforts.

All have fairly complex plots that could not have been invented independently and identically over and over again. All imply interaction took place between the areas of occurrence. In the first instance, the Killer Lizard story is confined to two widely separated areas: Iroquois country and the Southeast. This pattern may have resulted from the emigration of Tuscarora people from North Carolina to New York in the eighteenth century. They brought with them their own oral traditions that, apparently, affected those of their Iroquois hosts.

The second and third narratives are found, spread out fairly continuously, over enormous distances. The geographical expanse suggests considerable time lies behind the distribution, attested about 1900. In consequence, the stories called "Snake-man" and "Crossing-water-on-a-snake" may come to us from a distant past. Folklorist George Lankford (2007a) offers a historical hypothesis of common heritage to explain these stories. He interprets them as survivals of ancient mythic/religious constructs once known throughout the Eastern Woodlands.

With the exception of Seneca prophet Handsome Lake—the visions he experienced around 1800 and the now-traditional Longhouse faith that resulted—little historical research has been conducted on the Iroquois religion. In chapter 4, I integrate mythic and historical evidence to shed light on religious beliefs prior to the nineteenth century. The primary god was once Sky Holder who, in tandem with his malicious grandmother, presided over human affairs. As Iroquois god of war, Sky Holder probably was referenced by several other epithets or titles. Sky Holder was also the patron of crops who slew his brother Flint, the archetypal hunter. I see this allegory as meditation on how society makes its living. Sky Holder's act of murder mythologically chartered the dominance of agriculture in Iroquois life.

Windigos were cannibalistic beings of both human and nonhuman aspect known to storytellers in the boreal forests from Saskatchewan to Labrador. They were major figures in Algonquian oral narrative who also played an important role in anthropological thinking during the twentieth century. "Windigo psychosis," for example, was long regarded as a culturally specific malady associated, in some fashion, with folktales about windigos. Yet the content of windigo stories has never been examined. What do they actually say?

In chapter 5, I survey the plots of fifty windigo tales, classifying them by subject matter or theme. Windigos in stories recorded nearly a century ago are wicked creatures inhabiting either a timeless mythical space or a naturalistic setting familiar to human beings. The narrative zones are connected and mediated by a third category of story connected with spiritually powerful humans capable of transformation from one state to another.

One of the most complex plots defined in chapter 5 concerns a windigo who befriends a human family, then defends his new relatives from the onslaught of another windigo. In his genuine kindness, the eponymous "Friendly Visitor" stands apart from windigos in other Algonquian stories. Chapter 6 comprises another comparative study of content, this one charting the occurrence and content of the Friendly Visitor story type in an area far larger than that of the Chippewa/Ojibwa examples cited in the sample of windigo stories.

The tale was a particular favorite of the Iroquois, who featured their own windigo-like cannibal monster, the stone giant, as protagonist. The Iroquois form of the Friendly Visitor is interesting as one of the few stories incorporating a feminine perspective and perhaps even advocating a feminist point of view.

I pause here to clarify what may be a controversial view. Among the Iroquois, significant rights of affiliation and inheritance were vested in the female line, and some women exerted substantial political influence. Further, the sexual division of labor was a major fact of social life that especially encouraged the long-term association of women with one another. Men and women probably developed more or less distinct outlooks, and perhaps there were even gender-specific subcultures. That is a logical possibility, and something of the sort is indicated in the archaeological record (chapter 7).

Documented oral narrative, however, does not speak to this issue. Instead, Iroquois folklore, dominated by male concerns with hunting and forest living, seems largely indifferent to women (the basis for this characterization is discussed in chapter 6). Far from unique to the Iroquois, the same situation is commonly remarked of Native American folklore from the Great Lakes to Peru (Barnouw 1977, 48, 51, 92; Bierhorst 1995, 14–15; Taggart 1983, 7; Urton 1985, 9–10).

Some scholars assert that the absence of the female voice is evidence that such a thing existed. It was not recorded, they reason, because the chroniclers were foreign males biased against or ignorant of oral traditions belonging to the women. My view is that records spanning four centuries do not substantiate such an opinion but also provide no means to refute it. If a distinctly feminine genre of folk material did exist, it must have been like knowledge of the stars—something that did not find mythic expression.

But, however unusual the Friendly Visitor was in its apparent feminine emphasis, the Iroquois story was also of a piece with its social fabric. It was congruent with other themes characteristic of Iroquois folklore. As the Iroquois told it, the narrative was internally consistent in matters of plot and in most details. Among neighboring Algonquians, in contrast, the Friendly Visitor was more variable in its content, probably less frequently documented, and seemingly less comfortable in its cultural fit.

These circumstances, in tandem with an apparent geographical center in Iroquois country, suggest an Iroquois origin. The story may have diffused outward during the 1600s–1700s, a time when the Iroquois were intensely and often violently active in the Algonquian areas where the narrative was later documented. The spread of a complicated, philosophical story implies cultural interchange of a more peaceful nature. Such influence is detectable chiefly, possibly solely, from the evidence of oral narrative.

The final essay explores material correlates of oral narrative in archaeology. Beginning about the year 1450, certain pottery vessels and smoking pipes of the Eastern Iroquois were embellished with humanlike depictions. These icons are among the most complex representational materials preserved anywhere in the Northeast. For me, the images are haunting and suggestive of mythic and religious import. Chapter 7 is an archaeological study of these intriguing pictures on implements of fired clay. After reviewing the stylistic characteristics and distributions of each kind of artifact, I interweave lines of evidence bearing, in both cases, on context, use, and iconography.

The pots bespeak culinary and domestic activity centered on the hearth, the realm of women. Anthropomorphic representations on cooking vessels in this setting connoted corn and, very possibly, made reference to mythological cornhusk people and bounteous harvests. The pipes attest to male activity probably diplomatic in nature and interregional in scope.

The imagery on these artifacts evoked primordial emergence from the earth and may have asserted the common mythic origin of several groups. Thus, I argue, oral narrative projected appropriately into the past tells us things about ancient religion and politics we did not previously suspect and could not discover through other means.

At the Font of the Marvelous

1

Iroquois Star Lore

What Does It Mean?

HOW DOES a folktale or myth originate? Is it possible to account for a specific plot? One of the rare attempts to explain an oral narrative in the Northeast was made by archaeologist Lynn Ceci (1978) in a study of the Pleiades constellation among the Iroquois. According to Ceci, a brief and risky growing season for maize in the Northeast happens to coincide with the movement of the Pleiades—its apparent disappearance in the spring and reappearance in the fall. Closely tracking these stars, therefore, would have been essential to crop success. And, if observation of the constellation was critical to the maintenance of Iroquois society, it seemed likely these stars would play an important role in Iroquois ceremony and myth.

In apparent confirmation of the hypothesis, Ceci found the Pleiades were employed to schedule the most important annual rite: Midwinter. As for myth, there is a well-known Pleiades story about hungry dancers who become stars. The allusion to hunger in the tale was supposed to evoke the hungry time of the year, while the twinkling of the actual stars served to remind people of ceremonial dancing. Hence, the timing mechanism of Midwinter and the oral narrative of the star group preserved a memory of systematic celestial observation while testifying to the primacy of the Pleiades in the Iroquois worldview.

This functional interpretation is intellectually appealing because it accounts for the existence of a story and, to a certain extent, makes sense of the story's content. Further, it apparently relates things of the mind to social life and, in turn, to a measurable phenomenon in the objective world. The scenario even has interesting archaeological implications: Whenever we see maize and settled village life, we can assume the Pleiades figured strongly in tradition. Finally, this approach points the way toward predicting when and why certain narratives are invented.

Ceci's hypothesis also seems plausible because the Pleiades unquestionably were significant to the Iroquois. Lewis Henry Morgan (1962, 441–42) names the Pleiades as key to direction-finding during the winter, while William Fenton (1978, 300) and J. N. B. Hewitt (1974, 227–28) indicate the importance of these stars for reckoning seasons. The Pleiades certainly were employed to time the Midwinter rite, a link between stars and ritual that may be ancient (Shimony 1994, 174–75; Speck 1995, 50–51; Tooker 1970, 147). An agricultural calendar based on the Pleiades and documented in the present (Foster 1974, 110–11; Shimony 1994, 174–75) could well be very old (Beauchamp 1892, 35).

But is Ceci's interpretation correct? Wondering if there is anything to it, I surveyed the folkloric material on the star group as reported in this chapter. My first discovery was that the Pleiades cannot be studied without reference to a second constellation: the Big Dipper. The finding enlarged my subject matter from a constellation into the topic of Iroquois star lore generally because Haudenosaunee oral narrative on this subject (folklore and myth identified with stars other than the sun) focuses on this pair of asterisms to the virtual exclusion of everything else.

It must also be said, however, that Iroquois tales of the Pleiades and Big Dipper tend to be exceedingly brief and simple. In the form we have them, they are little more than the stuff of children's books. Are such seemingly minor fables worth any attention? My answer is that, if you scratch the surface of these little pieces, you will catch a glint of major mythic traditions, of far–flung connections, and of fundamental cultural themes.

The Pleiades

Regarded as a herald of seasons throughout the globe (Krupp ca. 1993, 86), the Pleiades occur in what we consider to be the neck of Taurus. The number of visible stars usually is said to be six although the group generally is reckoned as seven. Worldwide, the Pleiades "are nearly always imagined as seven sisters" (Thompson 1946, 238) frequently considered to be dancing

(Leach 1949–50, 2:874–75). Often, an accompanying story explains why one star shines less brightly than the others (Olcott 2004, 420).

At Iroquois latitude (approximately 43 degrees north), the Pleiades seem to appear just after sunset on the eastern horizon around October 10–15. Each successive night, they are first visible at a slightly higher and more westerly position until about January 15, when they attain zenith (directly overhead) at dusk. Then they gradually seem to descend toward the western horizon until disappearing about May 5–10 (Ceci 1978, 303). The Iroquois Pleiades, therefore, have associations with the winter and with the west.

The Iroquois story most commonly recorded about these stars describes a group of young males[1] typically said to number seven, who dedicate themselves to some task such as dancing and singing together. Sometimes they receive instruction from an older man who joins them in the endeavor. When their parents refuse them food for a meal they planned to enjoy as a group, the boys form a circle and dance into the sky—often, it is said, to the accompaniment of a water drum. One or more parents remonstrate, begging the youngsters to return. Only one responds, however, and he falls, crashing deeply into the ground—his demise identified with the origin of pine trees or of meteors. The remainder, sometimes with their older mentor, become the Pleiades star group. One, some versions add, shines more dimly than the rest "on account of his desire to return to earth" (E. Smith 1983, 39).

This story was first recorded in 1838 (Severance 1904, 69). Widespread Iroquois agreement about the plot is apparent from at least the 1850s through the present day (Beauchamp 1922, 109; Myrtle 1855, 133–34; A. Parker 1989, 83–85; E. Smith 1983, 38–39; Speck 1995, 50; Tehanetorens 1998, 96–101).

The same story was told around 1900 by Iroquoian-speaking Cherokees (Hagar 1906, 358–59; Mooney 1995, 258–59) and Wyandots (Barbeau 1915, 58–59; Pearson 2001, 29–32). Though the tale is largely Iroquoian

---

1. In some versions, the youngsters are said to be children (Beauchamp 1900, 281–82; Curtin 2001, 507; Randle 1953, 630). In any event, the protagonists of this story are never identified as girls.

in its distribution,[2] Algonquian-speaking Mahicans of Stockbridge, Massachusetts, knew about the Pleiades during the 1730s as seven dancers who ascended into the sky (Dunn 2000, 175).

The claim to explain pine trees or meteors seems peripheral to the Iroquois plot, possibly because it is foreign, a detail borrowed from the neighboring Lenape/Delaware. In their Pleiades story, seven males, seeking power through rigorous fasting, become pines or rocks or meteors (Bierhorst 1995, 47, 62; Speck 1931, 48, 171–73). This may illustrate how distinct mythological traditions seemingly engage in implicit dialogue. By referencing each other at what Donald Bahr (1998, 30) describes as their "arcane intersections," it is as though they take cognizance of each other's plots by incorporating nonessential details of this sort.

The more important point of the story is that when the stars rise directly overhead in January, it is time to schedule the New Year ceremony, the dancers below mirroring the dancers above (Fenton 1991, 83; Speck 1995, 49–50; Tehanetorens 1998, 101).

Yet, it is not dancing but hunger that attracts the attention of interpreters such as Ceci. According to Lévi-Strauss (1990a, 533–34), the Pleiades are linked to refusal of food throughout the Americas, and he contrasts the Iroquois hungry boys to greedy Bororo children who rise into the sky after eating too much (1983, 115, 242). Focusing as it does on food, this explanatory tack fails to take into account a second and different Iroquois story about the Pleiades.

This other tale (A. Parker 1989, 86–87) describes seven young women who descend from the sky in a corn basket to dance nude over the surface of a lake. A young man in hiding is able to seize and then marry one of them. In time, this couple takes up residence in the sky where the wife rejoins her sisters, the Pleiades. Her brightness, however, is diminished from the time she spent on earth. This story also was recorded among the Wyandots of Oklahoma (Barbeau 1915, 56–58) who also, it will be recalled, know the tale of the boys dancing into the sky. Together, these two Iroquoian narratives provide a satisfying symmetry: The boys go up; the girls come down.

2. Miller (1997, 63) references a Chippewa (Anishnaabeg) variant of this Pleiades story in the early twentieth century.

In comparison with the dancing boys, however, the dancing girls are sparsely documented.[3] What would account for the disparity? Folklorists of an earlier generation believed the story was of foreign derivation and therefore comparatively recent in the Iroquois context. Stith Thompson classified the Iroquoian girls as a variant of a well-known motif/story distributed throughout Europe and Asia called Swan Maiden (motif D 361.1 in Thompson 1955, 2:34). The essential plot is that a young man, in hiding, observes a group of geese who descend to the surface of a lake, shed their feathers, and become beautiful, young, and often naked women. The man grabs the feathers of one of them who must remain to become his wife while the others, resuming their forms as waterfowl, make good their escape. When the wife finds her feather garb years later, she and her children leave the husband, flying off as geese (Leach 1949–50, 2:1091–92; Thompson 1929, 356).

Granted a very close similarity in the stories of the Iroquois dancing girls and Swan Maiden, it is also true that the plots are not identical. John Bierhorst (1985, 202) argues the Iroquois story is better understood not as a variant of the Eurasian Swan Maiden but as an example of what he calls the "Sky Maidens," a North American tale in which celestial beings descend from the heavens in a basket or boat to dance or play ball (see Thompson's Sky-basket motif [F51.2] at Thompson 1929, 355–56). "Sky Maidens" was known in the Southeast (Grantham 2002, 189–91; Swanton 1929, 138–39; Williamson 1992) among the Shawnee (Schoolcraft 1999, 9–12), and possibly among the Pawnee (Dorsey 1997a, 44–46).

Although the "Sky Maidens" story is not documented among the Iroquois prior to 1900, there is an intriguing linguistic clue to greater age. The best-documented Iroquois word for this star group is *hatítkwaʔta:ʔ* in Seneca (Chafe 1963, 43), *oot-kwa-tah* in Onondaga (Beauchamp 1900, 281), and *okĕ:nyaʔ* in Cayuga (Foster 1974, 111)—all probably meaning

3. Ceci (1978, 307) cites a version of the Iroquois Sky Maidens story of the Pleiades by M. L. Skye in *The Red Man,* a publication of the Carlisle Institute in 1911. Another apparent variant is given by Mann (2000, 105–6). A Huron form of the "Sky Maidens" appears in Miller (1997, 56).

"cluster" or "group stars" (Hewitt 1974, 227–28; Speck 1995, 49).[4] How-ever, the name Arthur Parker supplied for the Sky Maiden Pleiades story was not one of the cluster names but rather *De hoñnont'gwĕⁿ'*—"They are dancing" (1989, 86). Much the same word (though presumably in Mohawk, rather than Seneca) was given by Joseph François Lafitau in the early 1700s. The Iroquois, he stated, "call the constellation of the Pleïades *Te Jennoniakoua,* meaning the dancers" (Fenton and Moore 1974, 258). Therefore, if the Pleiades word meaning "dancers" is linked to the second Pleiades story, as Parker implies, the Sky Maidens' tale would be at least three hundred years old.[5]

Lafitau's Pleiades was the location of the afterlife—"a happy dwelling place," according to the Jesuit—where the dead enjoy the great pleasure of dancing. The Pleiades, in other words, were specifically identified as the country or village of the dead in the early eighteenth century. Presumably, this spirit land would be situated in the western sky given the Pleiades's westerly association.

Hewitt (1895) thought the western location for departed spirits to be a concept postdating European contact, a suggestion apparently supported by Seneca archaeological evidence. During the late 1500s and early 1600s, Seneca burials tended to be aligned (headed) toward the west, rather than the east (Sempowski and Saunders 2001, 707–8; see also Wray et al. 1987, 245; 1991, 400). This "rather abrupt and dramatic shift" in grave ori-entation (Sempowski and Saunders 2001, 670) strongly implies that the

4. I have not found a word for the Pleiades in the eastern Iroquois tongues, Mohawk and Oneida. In other Iroquoian languages, the constellation is called *huti'watsija* in Wyan-dot (Barbeau 1915, 58–59; Pearson 2001, 32) and *unădatsúgĭ* in Cherokee (Hagar 1906, 32). These, like the Iroquois terms, are said to mean "cluster" or "group." Neither, however, seems obviously cognate with the Iroquois words for the Pleiades given in the text. I consider the celestial referents discussed here to be consensual identifications among the Iroquois around 1900, which is to say that commonly agreed-upon narratives usually were applied to specific stars (Parks 1985, 58). It is beyond reasonable doubt that those stars are what we know in English as the Pleiades and the Big Dipper.

5. However, Lafitau also says the dancers referenced in this word are both female and male (Fenton and Moore 1974, 258). This detail weakens the possible association of the Pleiades name ("the dancers") with a story about exclusively female dancers.

living visualized a postmortem destination in the west—very possibly the Pleiades. At the same time Senecas were altering the directional focus of their burials, they were suffering extremely high mortality among children. Further, the age group most consistently headed to the west at burial was young adults (707). Could Pleiades stories about young people dancing into the western sky preserve some distant memory of these tragic times?

Although Lafitau did not name it, the route taken by the dead to reach the Pleiades was surely the Milky Way—known to Hurons in the early seventeenth century, as well as to Haudenosaunee of today, as the path of souls (Shimony 1994, 229; Tooker 1991, 140).[6] The belief that the spirits of the deceased travel the Milky Way to an abode of dancing in the sky is characteristic of the Northeast (Speck 1935b, 50–51). More generally, the Milky Way is so widely identified as a road of the dead throughout North America and Eurasia (Lankford 2007b; Olcott 2004, 394) as to imply considerable time depth. Munro Edmonson (1971, 58) thought the concept might be part of a Mesolithic creation myth ten thousand or more years old.

Returning to the subject of the Pleiades as oral narrative, I conclude the Iroquois have two stories and two names for the same constellation.[7] This is a seemingly odd redundancy, but one for which an explanation recently has been offered. According to Barbara Alice Mann, "The tradition of the Seven Sisters and the Seven Brothers recalled parallel sky events, mirror-image replicas gendered for balance, as was all else in the Iroquoian

6. Unlike the Pleiades, the Milky Way seems to possess no obvious directional or seasonal associations—no physical referents, that is, that might provide a bridge to other forms of evidence.

7. For two Iroquois names for the Pleiades, see John Armstrong's creation account, recorded at Cattaraugus in 1896, in which the Woman-who-fell-from-the-sky seems to create constellations by gesturing toward the sky (Hewitt 1974, 227–28; McElwain 1992, 268). The two sets of names—one designating a collectivity, the other dancing—might correspond neatly to the two Pleiades stories—dancing boys and Sky Maidens—but that is uncertain. Barbara Alice Mann (2000, 108–9) also discerns two names for the Pleiades, each of which she identifies with a different story of the Pleiades. Her linguistic dichotomy differs from mine, however, in making no reference to the set of words about dancing. Instead, she contrasts the Seneca word for the Pleiades to the Onondaga-Cayuga words (as given in the text)—all of which may mean the same thing: a cluster or group.

world." Iroquois thinking, Mann believes, is dominated by a female-male dichotomy in which every concept must have a counterpart of opposite sexual value—the sky, for example, being divided into gendered halves. The Pleiades group is in the female sector because those stars are female. They are the sisters of the "Sky Maidens" tale, and that story, Mann asserts, is the only tale literally and properly about that constellation. Although the dancing boys provide the necessary male correspondence in oral narrative, they are on the opposite side of the sky because they are male. And, since they are in the wrong (non-Pleiades) place, they must be some constellation other than the Pleiades (Mann 2000, 105–12).

Mann's hypothesis flies in the face of considerable evidence indicating the Iroquois almost always regarded the dancing boys as the Pleiades. In addition, her reading assumes these stories are anchored firmly, one-to-one, to specific star referents. They are not. The most frequently told Iroquois tale about the Pleiades, for example, also can be applied to a different constellation—usually the Big Dipper.

The Big Dipper

Perpetually circling the North Star and visible year round, this constellation is composed of seven easily seen stars: four defining the bowl of the dipper, three its handle. The Big Dipper is the greater part of Ursa Major—commonly identified in Asia and Europe as a bear, often a hunted she-bear (Gibbon 1964, 238, 243; Leach 1949–50, 2:151; Monroe and Williamson 1987, 15; Thompson 1955, 1:157, motif A771: Origin of the Great Bear).

The Iroquois see much the same thing, their most frequently recorded story identifying the four bowl stars as the bear and the three handle stars as pursuing hunters. The middle hunter carries a kettle or is accompanied by a dog, details apparently referring to a double star at that location. Related with reference to the seasonal movement of the Dipper, the Iroquois hunters are said to track their quarry low along the northern horizon during the late summer and early fall. As the Dipper seems to rise into the sky on its handle, the bear is visualized as turning on her pursuers, who shoot her. The moral pointed is that blood from the bear (or grease from cooking the bear) accounts for the colors of the autumn foliage.

This story was first recorded by Lafitau (Fenton and Moore 1977, 235) in the early eighteenth century. It was documented around the turn of the twentieth century (E. Smith 1983, 39) and, like the dancing boys of the Pleiades, remains well known today (Randle 1953, 630; Rustige 1988, 32–34; Tehanetorens 1998, 77–83). The tale is sporadically distributed elsewhere among the Cherokee (Hagar 1906, 357), the Fox (Jones 1911, 868–73), and the Passamaquoddy (Leland 1992, 379). The Mahicans of Stockbridge probably knew it in 1734 (Dunn 2000, 175).

The same narrative was told by descendants of Algonquian speakers living on the Six Nations Reserve in Ontario, who linked it not only to a star referent but to a ceremony. According to Frank Speck and Jesse Moses (1945), the Midwinter rite of the "Munsee-Mahicans" symbolizes the annual death and rebirth of this celestial bear. Unfortunately, the account seems to stand in ethnographic isolation, its relevance to Iroquois practice problematic.[8]

"[It] is quite certain that the Iroquois and most of the Indians know the Great Bear under the same name as we do," Lafitau observed, "and, as the names of the constellations are purely arbitrary and given by caprice, they cannot have agreed with us in comparing the same names except by a communication of ideas which presupposes some actual personal connection through which this knowledge has come" (Fenton and Moore 1977, 136–37). Thus, the great diffusionist question about American cultural traits was posed centuries ago with reference to the Iroquois Big Dipper. While he did not consider celestial lore, Irving Hallowell (1926) concluded that bear ceremonialism was sufficiently similar across the circumpolar reaches of the globe as to imply a common source into America from Eurasia in the distant past. Others assert independent invention to be probable because the shape and movement of this star group suggested bears to northern people around the world (Hagar 1900, 100–103; Parker in Converse 1908, 59–60n. 2).

Neither view explains why many peoples living in the north do *not* see a bear among these stars. In North America, for example, a band of Algonquian speakers stretching from the Cree of Saskatchewan to the

---

8. Perhaps something like the Munsee-Mahican practice can be detected among Algonquian speakers elsewhere. Vecsey (1983, 110), for example, mentions a Chippewa bear rite at Midwinter.

Montagnais-Naskapi of the Maritimes identifies the dipper constellation as a small, weasel-like animal called a fisher or marten (Brown and Brightman 1988, 106; Michelson 1917, 194–97; Schoolcraft 1999, 3–8; Skinner and Satterlee 1915, 471–74; Speck 1931, 107n. 3). Also, neither position—diffusion from common source or invention at multiple locations—comes to terms with variation arising after the time of origin. There is, in fact, a fair amount of variation in the story about the Big Dipper.

Several Iroquois versions of "The Sky Bear," for example, insist that one of the hunters is carried by the others in a litter (Curtin 2001, 503–4; A. Parker 1989, 81–82). Reminiscent of a western identification of the Big Dipper as a litter or stretcher (Dorsey 1997a, 135; Miller 1997, 233–34; Parks 1996, 106–7), this odd detail provides another example of dialogue among different mythological traditions (Bahr 1998).

Fenton (1978, 301) reported a Seneca variant of "The Sky Bear" story in which the bear, identified with all of the Big Dipper, is pursued by a hunter and his dogs, equated with another circumpolar constellation—the Little Dipper or Ursa Minor. A second story about that constellation is the subject of a composition by Seneca artist Ernest Smith called "The Legend of the Little Dipper." Smith's drawing depicts "seven Indian brothers who, while reveling by the campfire one clear night, suddenly rose up into the heavens," where they became Ursa Minor (Converse 1908, frontispiece).

The tale Smith illustrated closely resembles one told at the Six Nations Reserve in which a fatherless boy, Deganawi'da?, asks his seven playmates to gather together a kettle and some food. When the parents will not allow these items to leave their homes, the eight boys begin to sing and dance and rise into the sky. "Deganawi'da? told the boys not to look back. The mothers cried, and one boy did look back and fell, and where he fell a tree grew at the Bay of Quinte. . . . The other six boys and Deganawi'da? continued to heaven and became the Big Dipper" (Shimony 1994, 167n. 15). So now the seven dancing boys of the Pleiades have become the Big Dipper.

Discussion

It seems, then, the Iroquois Pleiades have been assigned at least two names and two stories, at least one of which is applicable to at least one other constellation. It turns out, however, that none of these characteristics is unique to the Iroquois. Two distinct names for this constellation are recorded among the Arapaho (Dorsey and Kroeber 1997, 160–61), Cherokee (Hagar 1906, 358), Penobscot (Speck 1935a, 20), Shawnee (Kinietz and Voegelin 1939, 37), and possibly the Blackfeet (Miller 1997, 246). Two different stories about the Pleiades are documented among the Cheyenne (Miller 1997, 257–59), Navaho (Williamson 1984, 165), and Penobscot (Speck 1935a, 20, 90; Miller 1997, 43), and probably among the Caddo (Dorsey 1997b, 51–52, 64) and Pawnee (Dorsey 1997a, 119–22; Fletcher and Murie 1996, 152). Common sense suggests there are two names *because* there are two narratives, but this remains uncertain for lack of evidence.

Just as two names and two stories for the Pleiades are not unusual, so it happens that, elsewhere, a Pleiades story can be applied to another constellation, notably the Big Dipper (Miller 1997, 259). An oral narrative important throughout the Plains illustrates this principle (Gibbon 1964, 237). The basic plot is that six or seven boys and a sister, chased by a murderous bear, rise into the heavens to become a recognizable group of stars—the Pleiades, say the Arapaho (Dorsey and Kroeber 1997, 152–53), Arikara (Parks 1996, 146–52), Jicarilla Apache (Opler 1994, 113–16), and the Pawnee (Dorsey 1997a, 119–22); the Big Dipper, say the Blackfeet (Wissler and Duvall 1995, 68–70), Crow (Miller 1997, 242), Kiowa (Momaday 1969, 8), and Wichita (Dorsey 1904, 69–74).

Presumably both interpretations are correct but, if so, the story cannot refer to one specific star group. And, if the tale is interchangeable with two different constellations, the celestial referent becomes relatively unimportant. That suggests the Iroquois tales of the Pleiades and Big Dipper must be essentially mythological, not astronomical, in character. Stories about these star groups provide no evidence for the kind of systematic observational astronomy Ceci (1978) envisioned. Apparently, cultural preference determines which stars are of interest and what information is mapped onto them (see Parks 1985, 61–62; Lowie 1908, 125–28; Waterman 1914).

And yet the sky referent does not vary endlessly or even very much. It seems to be limited to just these two constellations over and over again. The Pleiades and Big Dipper certainly were the most storied star groups in North America and possibly throughout much of the world (Hagar

1900, 92; 1906, 357; Monroe and Williamson 1987, 16; Thompson 1946, 237–38). Further, no other asterisms/constellations seem to have been so routinely equipped with multiple and overlapping stories. Why? Are they uniquely recognizable?

Although the Big Dipper is the more clearly visible and identifiable of the two, it is (as Lafitau noted) an essentially arbitrary construct theoretically replaceable by any other combination of stars. Likewise, other circumpolar asterisms or constellations could take its place if the quality of being seen all year is what makes the Dipper significant.

Do these two groups make better clocks or celestial timekeepers than other stars (Williamson 1992, 58)? If you wish to create a seasonal calendar, certainly the Pleiades works well enough, but then any point on the ecliptic—the apparent path of the sun among the stars—can do the same thing (Krupp ca. 1993, 86–87).

What the Pleiades and Big Dipper most obviously have in common is that both are considered to comprise seven stars throughout much of North America (Miller 1997, 259) and, again, throughout much of the globe (Gibbon 1964)—a symbolic construct of vast distribution and, one suspects, of considerable age. The depth and profundity of these issues make the little stories seem like important mythic traditions.

Indeed, these apparently minor tales behave as major myths in other ways: the manner in which they seem to reference other mythic traditions (the meteors and pine trees of the Pleiades, the stretcher of the Big Dipper) and their links, or at least similar subject matter, to stories present in Eurasia (dancing sisters, hunted she-bears). Reminiscent of Luigi Pirandello's play, *Six Characters in Search of an Author,* these narratives seem to gather to themselves motifs and plots of worldwide occurrence.

Iroquois narratives about stars are not, however, abstract in detail or plot. Far from global in occurrence, their relatively limited distribution does not imply age of many millennia. The issue at this scale of analysis is whether meaning and purpose are discernible in specific cultural context. As stories told by real people at particular places and times, these star pieces were and are enjoyed for what they express—but what would that be?

The Pleiades were regarded as the land of the departed three centuries ago but that belief is never explicitly stated in folklore about those stars.

The most obvious message of the Pleiades stories today is not hunger, quest for power, or lessons in proper parenting. Rather, the central theme is dancing (see Monroe and Williamson 1987, 3), as is emphatically stated in the first recorded version of 1838. That account describes a group of young men who dance to revive neglected religious observances. Ignored by those around them, they become the Pleiades, "where they have ever since continued to dance and sing, as may be seen by the constant twinkling motion. . . . Since that calamitous event, which was considered a judgment of the Great Spirit for the wickedness of the tribe in omitting to honor him by dances, they have ever since been religiously kept up" (Severance 1904, 69).

Lewis Henry Morgan (1962, 263n. 1) was told the same local truth as he witnessed the Great Feather Dance: Iroquois people will be Haudenosaunee forever so long as they hold to their dances. This is what I think the Pleiades stories continue to preserve and teach—even committed to paper, even in English, and even marketed as children's stories.

War in the West

Nineteenth-Century Iroquois Legends of Conquest

THE IROQUOIS of western New York frequently alluded to wars fought by their ancestors with a foreign people called Kahkwa living on Eighteen Mile Creek some twenty miles southwest of today's city of Buffalo (map 2). As this watercourse flows into Lake Erie (vicinity of North Evans), it forms a spectacular gorge fully deserving of a marvelous tale. Although John Norton would have approved the existence of stories referencing this landmark, he might have wondered about their number. Tales about Kahkwas comprise what is probably the most plentiful corpus of legendary material in the Northeast.

Indeed, the general topic seems to have riveted the historical attention of Seneca and Tuscarora people throughout much of the nineteenth century. Whenever questioned about their history, they recurred to war with the Kahkwas. Much, therefore, was recorded, and this written record provides a fair amount of material with which to examine how oral narrative treats a people's history: how it expresses, interprets, and preserves their past.

The study begins with a look at the oral traditions recorded about 1816 by the knowledgeable John Norton. Because Norton documented what native storytellers then regarded as the history of the Niagara region, his writings provide a dated starting point from which to survey the subject. They offer, as well, a standard of comparison for evaluating later versions. In light of Norton's importance, I quote him far more extensively than any other source. Subsequently, a half dozen other narratives about the Kahkwa War from Seneca and Tuscarora sources are examined. In each instance, I consider what is said and how it differs from what was said earlier.

14

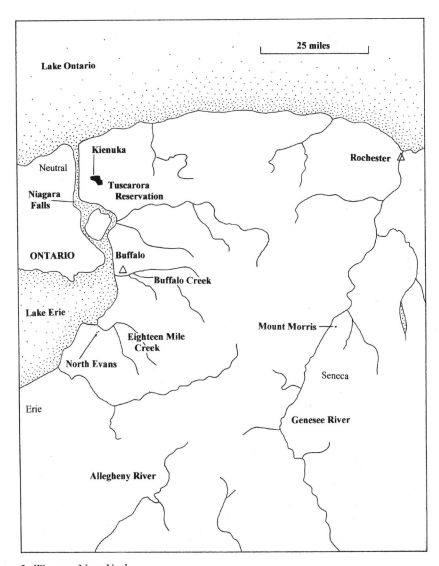

2. Western New York.

But why the Kahkwa War? The Senecas won many other important victories that could have been celebrated in similar fashion—over the Hurons, for example, or over many other peoples during the seventeenth century. Closer in time, they could have recounted battle glories from the French and Indian wars and Revolutionary War, or even the War of 1812. They could have eschewed the topic of war altogether in favor of telling any number of stories about other kinds of events. Apparently, they did not. What therefore was so significant about this specific set of stories?

The general answer is that the Kahkwa War subject was pressed into service to perform certain charter and existential functions. Narratives of the war affirmed Iroquois self-worth during difficult times. Kahkwa War tales asserted Iroquois ownership of a non-Iroquois region at a time when such possession seemed questionable. The stories connected the past to the present and helped to render the here and now meaningful. During the nineteenth century, storytelling focused on the Kahkwas because such legends proved salient to the mythological work that needed to get done.

More than one viewpoint on the Kahkwa War, however, was being propounded. Distinctly different Seneca and Tuscarora approaches to the story presumably reflect the differing circumstances and mythological needs of the two peoples.

In Seneca oral tradition, there seem to have been two fairly distinct versions of the subject, both emphasizing how the Kahkwas invaded their territory then east of the Genesee River. One form of the tale goes on to describe a Seneca counterattack that dislodged the Kahkwas from western New York. The narrative of the Kahkwa War as told by Senecas pointed two morals: Senecas own Kahkwa territory by right of just conquest, and Senecas are superior to other people.

Tuscaroras, through the written word, conveyed a somewhat different story that linked the Kahkwa War to the career of a peace queen. The lady's office was said to have been created by the Iroquois at the time they formed their confederacy. Her precinct, maintained as an asylum from bloodshed, was located in what later became the Tuscarora Reservation. During the 1800s, the ancient title was reinstituted in the person of a Seneca woman who came to live on the reservation. Tuscarora texts implied Tuscaroras are importantly connected with the Kahkwa War and to traditions about the League of the Iroquois.

Tales about the Kahkwa War probably contain some memory of conflicts recorded by nonnative writers during the 1630s through the 1650s.

European chroniclers described Iroquois wars of conquest over peoples named as Eries and Neutrals. The very first order of business here is to summarize this documentary evidence. As the chapter proceeds, I will note possible allusions in oral narrative to historical events. However, the question of historical accuracy—what is true in oral narrative as judged by what was written down at the time—is not my focus. Greater certainty in this matter surely awaits more historical data than are presently available.

The Historic Neutral, Erie, and Kahkwa Peoples

Between the Hurons near Lake Superior's Georgian Bay (Ontario) and the Iroquois east of the Genesee River (New York) were other groups of Iroquoian speakers. Those most frequently mentioned by Europeans were the "nations" of the Neutral and the Erie.

The Neutrals consisted of at least three tribes living among perhaps forty horticultural villages centered in southern Ontario, located north of Lake Erie. Some Neutrals also resided in present New York, and one of their villages could have been an archaeological site called Kienuka, located on the border of the present Tuscarora Reservation in Niagara County (White 1978a, 408–9).

The Neutrals spoke a language similar to Seneca and—even after three years of war, famine, and disease—numbered at least twelve thousand people (Thwaites 1896–1901, 21:191, 33:109). Organized as a confederacy roughly comparable to the unions achieved by the Hurons and the Iroquois, the Neutral alliance proved to be a shifting affair, for at least one tribe was cast out from their fellowship. As a result of that action, the Wenros fled their homeland somewhere east of the Niagara River to seek protection in Huron country about the year 1638 (Fenton 1940, 186–88; White 1978a, 407–11).

The Neutrals were so named by the French because they "keep themselves equally in peace" with the Hurons and Iroquois, who were warring against each other. The country of the Neutrals, however, was also regarded as an asylum, a safety zone in which combatants from both sides could pass one another and even mingle in security (Thwaites 1896–1901,

21:193).[1] Indeed, feeling that one of their number had not been protected properly under this system, the Seneca revenged themselves upon one of the Neutral villages in 1647:

> These Aondironnons are a tribe of the Neutral Nation who are nearest to our Hurons. Not being at war with the [Senecas], they had received them in their villages as friends, and had prepared food for them in all their cabins, among which the [Senecas] purposely divided themselves, the more easily to strike their blow. Their stratagem was successful, for they massacred or seized all who might have resisted, before the latter could perceive their evil design, because they all commenced the massacre at the same moment. (Thwaites 1896–1901, 33:81–83)

The Neutral confederacy was destroyed as a result of war that took place in the years 1650–51. At that time, the Iroquois

> turned their arms against the Neutral nation whither they sent the bulk of their forces. They met with success, and captured two villages on the frontier, in one of which there were over sixteen hundred men. The first was taken toward the end of autumn; the second, at the beginning of spring. Great was the carnage, especially among the old people and the children, who would not have been able to follow the Iroquois to their country. The number of captives was exceedingly large, especially of young women, who they reserve, in order to keep up the population of their own villages. This loss was very

---

1. Morgan (1962, 337–38) reports the existence of similar neutral arrangements else-where: "There was an ancient treaty between the Senecas and the Gä-quä-ga'-o-no, or Eries, who resided upon the southern shore of Lake Erie, to the effect that the Genesee river should be the boundary between them, and that when a hostile band of either nation re-crossed this river into its own territories, it should be safe from further pursuit. An infraction of this treaty was one of the reasons of the long-cherished animosity of the Iroquois against them. A similar compact was once made with the O-ya-dä'-go-o-no, or Cherokees, by which the Tennessee river was the limit of pursuit. If a war-party of the latter had returned and re-crossed the Tennessee before they were overtaken by the pursuing Iroquois, they were as safe from their attack, as if intrenched behind an impregnable rampart. The Iroquois band could still invade, if disposed, the territory of the enemy, but they passed the camp of the retreating war-party without offering the slightest molestation."

great, and entailed the complete ruin and desolation of the Neutral nation. The inhabitants of their other villages, which were more distant from the enemy, took fright; abandoned their houses, their property, and their country; and condemned themselves to voluntary exile, to escape still further from the fury and cruelty of the conquerors. (Thwaites 1896–1901, 36:177)

Far less is known of the Eries. The English recorded their name as Hereckeenes. The French referred to them as the Cat Nation and called them Erie after the Huron word for them: Eriehronnon. At least one Iroquois name for the Eries was Riquehronnon, meaning "people of Riqué"—possibly their capital and one of the only Erie place names known (Thwaites 1896–1901, 45:207; Hoffman 1964, 200; Pendergast 1991a, 16–17; Wright 1974).

The Eries may have been, like the Neutrals and Iroquois, a confederacy or alliance of different tribes and/or villages (Engelbrecht and Sullivan 1996, 25; White 1978b, 412). They were said to speak a language akin to Huron and to number two thousand men "well skilled in war" (Thwaites 1896–1901, 33:63, 41:83). They lived south and southeast of the lake bearing their name until compelled by unnamed enemies to retire inland, possibly about 1645 (White 1978b, 412; Thwaites 1896–1901, 33:237). The Iroquois Confederacy destroyed the Eries as a "nation" sometime about the year 1656 (Fenton 1940, 196–97).

Most documentation on the Eries derives from that final war, much of it recorded by the Jesuit priest, Claude Dablon, writing to his superiors from Onondaga. The Erie-Iroquois war may have begun in the early 1650s, its proximate cause the murder of an Erie diplomatic mission at the hands of the Senecas (Thwaites 1896–1901, 42:177). In 1654, the Eries burned a Seneca village and captured an important Onondaga war leader named Annenraes (41:81). That same summer, the Iroquois mounted a massive attack on the Erie homeland. The Erie retreated but, eventually, some two- to three thousand of them resolved

to build a fort of wood and there await the enemy, who numbered only twelve hundred. Accordingly, they intrenched themselves as well as they could. . . . [The] assault was made and the palisade attacked on all sides;

but the defense was as spirited as the attack, and the combat was a long one, great courage being displayed on both sides. The besieging party made every effort to carry the place by storm, but in vain; they were killed as fast as they advanced. They hit upon the plan of using their canoes as shields; and, bearing these before them as protection, they reached the foot of the intrenchment. But it remained to scale the large stakes, or tree-trunks, of which it was built. Again they resorted to their canoes, using them as ladders for surmounting that stanch [sic] palisade. Their boldness so astonished the besieged that, being already at the end of their munitions of war,—with which, especially with [gun]powder, they had been but poorly provided,—they resolved to flee. This was their ruin; for, after most of the first fugitives had been killed, the others were surrounded. (Thwaites 1896–1901, 42:179–81)

The Iroquois who actually breached the Erie defense were Mohawks, for it was they, supposedly, who "defeated two thousand men of the Cat Nation in the latter's own intrenchments; and, although they were only seven hundred in number, they nevertheless climbed the enemy's palisade, employing against it a counter-palisade, used, in place of shields and ladders, to scale the fortress" (Thwaites 1896–1901, 45:209).

The war dragged on for about two years, then the Cat Nation ceased to exist (Hoffman 1964, 206–10; White 1978b, 415–16). Some of its people certainly fled south, for, in about 1681, six hundred Eries surrendered to the Senecas "near Virginia" (Thwaites 1896–1901, 62:71).

A series of archaeological sites extending from the vicinity of Buffalo south to Eighteen Mile Creek (ca. 1550–1640) is tentatively identified as Erie (Allen 1988, 63, 75; Engelbrecht 1991; White 1971, 26–27; 1978b, 414). Cartographically, however, the east shore of Lake Erie was identified as a territory distinct from that of the Cat Nation.

French mapmakers of the seventeenth century designated this zone as that of a destroyed nation called Akhrakovaetonon (Bourdon map, ca. 1641), Kakouagoga (Bernou maps, ca. 1680), and Rakouagega (Franquelin map, ca. 1689)(Engelbrecht 1991, 3; Pendergast 1991a, 55; 1994, 98–100). All, probably, are forms of the same word (Pendergast 1994; Steckley 1985), one still used by the Senecas in the 1930s to designate a people formerly living west of them: the Kahgwa'ge'o-no (Fenton 1940, 194). Where they lived was no mystery—the Seneca name for Eighteen Mile Creek was Koghquauga (Thwaites 1896–1901, 21:314n. 11), identified in folklore as the place or village of the Kahkwas (as I shall call them).

Because the Kahkwas received scarcely any historical notice, considerable scholarly activity has been devoted to classifying them as either Erie or Neutral. Both Morgan (1962, 41, 337) and Schoolcraft (1975, 164–65) thought the Kahkwas were likely to have been Eries. The earliest statement on the subject is that of Mohawk John Norton, who indicated that a people called the Rad-irakeai ka lived on the shore of Lake Erie. These, he said, were probably those the Europeans call Eries, and one of their villages, Kaghkwague, was on the stream that still bore that name in 1816 (Klinck and Talman 1970, 206).

Norton's Traditions of Niagara Region Wars

Such, in brief, is the evidence of the primary accounts contemporaneous with the events they describe. The transition from history to historical tradition is provided by John Norton, Joseph Brant's adopted son and a prominent Mohawk chief at the Six Nations Reserve, Ontario, during the early 1800s (Benn 1998, 8).

Although Norton's particular sources are not known, they probably included Brant, who spent considerable time around Fort Niagara during the Revolutionary War and, in fact, resided near Kienuka (Turner 1849, 264–65). Norton, however, was an important collector in his right, always gathering the lore of regions through which he passed and especially inhaling Iroquois traditions. In this case, he documented a trio of stories necessary to understanding later variants of the Kahkwa War plot. The three are widely separated in his text and given without reference to one another. To Norton, they apparently were not related.

Attack on the Wildcat's Village

On the eastern bank of Niagara River, at the commencement of the Carrying Place, stood a village, the people of which spoke nearly the same language with the confederate bands [i.e., the Iroquois]. A female chieftain [asterisked notation: "her name was Kakonghsaksea, or Wild Cat"] was at the head of them. They had never engaged in war with the Five Nations, and had always received their armies or war parties with great hospitality. But the latter, having suspected that they had sent information of their movements to the enemy, determined to adopt by force the people of this village into the number of the Five Nations.

For this purpose, a body of warriors assembled from all the Five Fires,—they proceeded to this village of Teyotchirheo, the inhabitants of which, not suspecting their intention, received them with their wonted hospitality. The next morning, when the warriors had formed in a body, apparently with an intention of continuing their route, the chief of the Onniyouthaga or Oneida called out, "My paddle is broken." This was the signal for assault. The inhabitants were immediately surrounded and taken prisoner, without any loss of blood on either side. They were afterwards adopted throughout the different families of the Five Nations. (Klinck and Talman 1970, 210–11)

There is good historical precedent for such an event in the Seneca attack on the Aondironnon Neutral village quoted above. Indeed, certain details specified in the Norton tradition—the premeditated treachery of a war party entertained as guests, the demise of an entire village of people speaking a language similar to an Iroquois tongue—seem so similar to the historical occurrence in 1647 that both could refer to the same incident.

An obvious difference between the versions of the seventeenth and nineteenth centuries is that the earlier account names the victims as Aondironnons. Whether that was the also the name of the village is unclear, but the location of the settlement apparently was near Huron territory in present-day Ontario far from the Niagara region. In Norton's later account, the village receives a different name and is placed east of the Niagara River in today's Niagara County, New York.

Another contrast between the accounts is that the later version provides an important detail not mentioned earlier: the leader of Teyotchirheo village was a woman named Wildcat. This is the earliest attestation of a female peace leader, presumably a Neutral, who, later in time, usually is called by a name similar to the one provided by Norton: Jigansahse.

War with the Kahkwas

Norton knew about the Erie war mentioned by European chroniclers, describing it as a conflict with the Rad-irakeai ka occurring about the middle of the seventeenth century. The Kaghkwagues (or possibly the Rad-irakeai ka as a whole) had killed some Senecas. Retaliating but suffering a setback, the Senecas called on the other Iroquois nations for assistance. The united forces of the Iroquois League "demolished their villages, killed most of the men who bore arms, and distributed the women and children among their tribes and families" (Klinck and Talman 1970, 206).

Norton devoted more ink to an earlier war with the Kahkwas:

It is related of the Caghkwague villages prior to their final destruction, that having gained some advantages over the Ondowaga [Senecas], a cessation of hostilities had taken place, when the latter, suspecting them of evil designs, sent two active men to the village of Tegotchirheon, instructed to ply into their intentions. On arriving there, to prevent suspicion, they pretended to have been hunting, and that their intention, in coming there was to buy tobacco, having expended the stock they had brought from home.

At this village they learned, that the principal part of the inhabitants were gone to Caghkwague, to be present at a festival held there. They took their departure, as if to return to their hunting ground, but as soon as they were out of sight of the village, they changed their course, and took a direction for Teyoghseroro, or Buffalo Creek, which they reached in the afternoon, and found the village almost destitute of inhabitants. They were informed that they also were gone to Caghkwague to the feast. After leaving the village, without being perceived, they took a course for that place, and arrived there after dark.

They remained in the lobby of the town house, where they saw all the people assembled. After a little time, they heard the chief recapitulate in a speech the result of their deliberations. It was resolved to invade the country of the Ondowaga in five days. He concluded by exhorting the warriors to be ready to set out at the time appointed, that no delay should be made, lest the Five Nations, who were sharp sighted, might discern their intentions, and prepare themselves accordingly to frustrate the enterprise.

The spies on this discovery, hastened to their village, and gave the necessary information to the chiefs, who immediately dispatched runners to the Cayugwas, requesting them to assemble their warriors and hasten to their assistance. They forwarded the same intelligence to the Onontagues [Onondagas], and from those the warlike summons passed to the bands of Onniyout [Oneida] and Kanyenke [Mohawk].

On receiving the message, the warriors of the different bands, immediately seized their arms, and sang the song of war. They proceeded to the frontier without delay. When they arrived at the village of the Ondowaga, they met the scouts with intelligence of the approach of the enemy. They told that they left them making a bridge across the Geneseo River, about half a days journey from where they awaited them. The chiefs then sent a party of active warriors to pass in the rear of the enemy, after he had crossed the bridge, and there to cut the posts which supported it, almost through, so that with the additional weight of many people, they might break, and the whole fall into the water.

On the summit of a hill, the warriors of the five [Iroquois] bands were ranged in expectation of the fight. The invading enemy approached, when within the arrows flight, the war shout was given, the arrows flew, and the warriors rushed forward with the club and spear. The battle raged with equal fury on both sides, and many a valiant warrior fell. At last, those who had been dispatched to weaken the supporters of the bridge, shewed themselves in the rear of the enemy, and attacked those a little eloigned from the main body. This turned the fortune of the day, till then dubious, in favor of the Five Nations. The warriors of Caghkwague were thrown into confusion, and routed with great slaughter. They retreated, and when crowded on the bridge, the posts broke through, and all that were on it were thrown into the water. This accident redoubled the confusion, many were killed by the arrows of the victorious bands and others were overtaken in the river.

The vanquished, on undertaking the expedition, had felt so assured of obtaining an easy conquest, that they brought with them moccasins of different sizes to put on the children, whom they expected to lead back captives. Shortly after this misfortune, the Five Nations attacked them in their turn, and entirely overcame them. (Klinck and Talman 1970, 219–21)

About half of this account discusses the two Seneca spies and their perambulation through three "Kaghkwague villages." The first is Tegotchirheon, which could be the Wildcat's village, Teyotchirheo, "on the eastern bank of Niagara River, at the commencement of the Carrying Place." If so, the Wildcat herself is not mentioned. Proceeding south, they visit "Teyoghseroro, or Buffalo Creek," then Kaghkwague itself on present Eighteen Mile Creek.

When the Kahkwas and Iroquois come to blows, details important to the struggle include the river setting and the secret weakening of a bridge. The tide of battle only swings in favor of the Iroquois when a new force, "a party of active warriors," appears. The Norton account seems to provide considerable information about specific events and places. It includes a curious note about the invaders bringing moccasins for anticipated captives. Its last sentence baldly summarizes the rest of the war: After this battle, the Iroquois destroyed the Kahkwa nation.

The Canoe Trick

Norton did not identify the enemy people mentioned in the following story as Kahkwas or Eries. Because others did later, the account is properly presented in this context.

> There is a great bend in the river here [Ohio River], which corresponds with a tradition of the Five Nations, relative to a war with the people of the Ohio, whom they style the people *with wooden fortification* [Yakadaghkaraton]. The Onondagas, Cayugwas and Ondowagas undertook it without the Kaniyenkehaga or Mohawk; and after they arrived before the town, they summoned those within to surrender, threatening, that unless they complied, they would assault the town, and take it as soon as the Kaniyenkehaga should arrive. Therefore to deceive the inhabitants, and make them believe that they had really arrived, a party carried their canoes across the narrow isthmus formed by the bend; and descending the river, repassed the town, talking and singing in the Mohawk dialect; so that the inhabitants really believed the number of the assailants to be increased by the force of the Mohawks, and their courage being thereby enfeebled, the town was taken by assault. Some, it is said, escaped, and fled down the river, and at last found an asylum in the country of the Muscogui. Many were killed and taken. The latter have been adopted and there are several now remaining there, who are said to be of that descent. (Klinck and Talman 1970, 14, 109)

The canoe trick—the idea of endlessly parading in front of the foe to convey greater numbers—has a strong folkloric quality about it and shows up in the oral traditions of others (for example, Jack 1895, 203). Yet, just as with the story of the Wildcat's village, there is a credible argument to be made for an actual historical tie-in. In its stress on wooden fortifications, on the prominence of Mohawks, and on the importance of canoes to the outcome, the Norton account could refer to the Erie fortification assaulted by the Iroquois in 1654.

Current in Norton's time, then, were three separate stories relevant to war traditions of the Niagara region. One was about the Iroquois's treacherous but bloodless conquest of a foreign village on the east bank of the Niagara River. The villagers, including their female chieftain named the Wildcat, became adopted Iroquois. A second concerned war with the Kahkwas whose settlement, Kaghkwague, enjoyed a close relationship with two other villages seemingly to the north. Because of their "evil designs," the Kahkwas attacked the Senecas to the east. The resulting battle, won by Seneca reinforcements, turned into a bloody rout because the Kawkwa escape route, a bridge, was sabotaged. In the third, Iroquois warriors besieged a distant palisaded place. There they staged a circular parade of canoe-carrying warriors to demoralize the defenders.

Overall, Norton's stories have a strong historical feel to them. Partly, that is because major portions of his anecdotes sound similar to incidents documented more than a century and a half earlier. Partly it is because Norton provides more details about events and places than oral tradition usually deems necessary. And partly it is because Norton's stories do not claim—as many folktales do—to explain anything more than who some peoples' ancestors happened to be. The anecdotes filtered through Norton in 1816 are less concerned with presenting a moral or justification than are some of the stories examined next.

Seneca Traditions of the Nineteenth Century

River Battle

Norton's version of the Kahkwa War features an invading army defeated in a battle that takes place near a river. A similar story was documented from

Seneca sources twice in later years. In 1838, Henry Dearborn recorded an account taken from a Seneca he called Mr. Cone who, in turn, said it was the childhood reminiscence of his grandfather dating back more than a century. According to Mr. Cone, the Senecas were invaded by a coalition of Midwestern and Ontario Indians who were so confident of victory that they brought their wives and children with them. The enemy advanced to the vicinity of present Mount Morris where they built a bridge to cross over the Genesee River. Working their way along the eastern shore, they were ambushed from the side by a Seneca party hidden under the far river bank. The Senecas had guns; the invaders did not. Nevertheless, there followed a ferocious and hotly contested battle. As the invaders fell back, they discovered the Senecas had destroyed their bridge. "There the slaughter was renewed and the whole of the hostile army was killed, except a very few who escaped by swimming." The women and children of the enemy were taken prisoner and adopted. A similar invasion had taken place about fifty years before this one (Severance 1904, 74–76).

This account differs from Norton's in several respects. The invaders are not identified as Kahkwas. Nothing is said about the activities of the two Seneca spies. The self-assured attitude of the enemy is indicated by having them bring their families rather than moccasins for the anticipated captives. Nevertheless, Mr. Cone's account is recognizably the same story as given in the second half of the Norton account: The Iroquois turn back an invading army at a river. A bridge and some detached segment of warriors are importantly connected with the victory.

A second version of this tale, attributed to an elderly Seneca named Squire Johnson, dates to about 1880. Two hundred years earlier, it is stated, two Seneca spies had gone to the eastern shore of Lake Erie to investigate what their distrusted neighbors, the Kahkwas, were up to. When the scouts hurried home to warn of invasion, the Seneca chief announced they would meet the enemy some distance away so as to keep the "bad odor"—meaning the stench of Kahkwa corpses—away from their village. The Kahkwas, in contrast, carried with them many moccasins for their anticipated captives to wear (Caswell 1892, 241–42).

The invading Kahkwas (who comprised or included twenty-eight tribes from the west and south) encountered the Senecas at the Genesee River.

An extensive passage then describes a parley involving four persons from each side whose sentiments are expressed three times. This segment ends abruptly when the Senecas murder three of the interlocutors and send the last one off with dire warnings. The infuriated Kahkwas attack and, initially, drive the Senecas back.

> The Senecas then called upon the Brunt Knives (young men), of whom there was a large number hidden in the bushes, to engage in the fight. They came down the hill with great speed, armed with heavy clubs, and fought with such desperation that the enemy soon fled to the river, and many attempting to cross were drowned, while others were knocked on the head in the water. (Caswell 1892, 243)

Although Squire Johnson's version attenuates the spy sequence and fails to mention a bridge, it is still similar to the story Norton knew sixty years earlier: A Kahkwa invasion is decisively defeated with a force held in reserve, and a slaughter ensues at a river crossing. The Johnson version, however, sounds more folkloric than the earlier accounts by Norton and Dearborn. The confidence of each side is signaled by formal announcements about moccasins and stench. The parley, taking up much of Johnson's account, is unabashedly formulaic.

Wrestling War

Sometime around 1800, the traveler Benjamin Barton made reference to another variant of the Kahkwa War. Barton learned that the *causus belli* was a wrestling match in which the loser, a Kahkwa, was beheaded by the winner, a Seneca. Being sore losers, the emulous Kahkwas retaliated by invading Seneca country (Snyderman 1948, 34). This version is known in greater detail from similar Seneca accounts furnished by Jacob Blacksmith in 1845 (Schoolcraft 1975, 176–79) and by William Patterson in 1850 (Draper n.d., 85–93).

As the story opens, the Kahkwas of present Eighteen Mile Creek challenge the Senecas, living near the Genesee River, to a series of athletic competitions: ball games (lacrosse), foot races, and wrestling—death by beheading being the penalty of losing the latter event. Senecas prevail in all. Shortly thereafter, two Senecas out hunting give warning of a Kahkwa army entering Seneca territory.

Both accounts provide "two characteristic traits of boasting" (Schoolcraft 1975, 179). The Kahkwas come equipped with moccasins for the captives they will take; the Senecas declare, "Let us not fight them too near for fear of the stench." The two armies engage in battle, long in doubt until a contingent of young Seneca warriors appears suddenly, bringing decisive results.

According to the Schoolcraft version, a Seneca counterattack forced the abandonment of Kahkwa settlements "on the Deoseowa (Buffalo creek)"—Norton's Teyoghseroro—as well as on Eighteen Mile Creek. In both accounts, some of the Kahkwas fled down "the Oheeo, the Seneca name of the Alleghany." Pursuing Senecas caught up to them somewhere near present Pittsburgh, where they pulled the "canoe trick"—that is, carrying their canoes as though newly arrived, they paraded continuously by the Kahkwas to make their numbers seem greater. The discouraged Kahkwas fled again and have never been seen since.

In effect, this Seneca narrative connects two tales told separately by Norton: that of a Kahkwa invasion of Seneca country and that of an Iroquois attack (with canoe trick) on the people of wooden fortifications. In the accidental discovery made by two Seneca hunters, the Draper and Schoolcraft accounts echo Norton's pair of Seneca spies. Although those accounts say nothing about a bridge or a riverside place of conflict, they agree with Norton and the River Battle tales that the battle turned back a Kahkwa invasion and was decided by reinforcements who appeared suddenly.

Emphasizing such stock narrative devices as the moccasin and stench details and the canoe trick, the Wrestling War narrative is strongly folkloric in character. Its most conventionalized feature is the sequence of athletic events opening the story. It is a purely formulaic pattern of challenge and competition typical of Iroquois folklore generally. A Seneca story of war in Cherokee country, for example, begins in the same fashion (Hewitt 1918, 428–32).[2] Indeed, the same sequence (often with the penalty of death for

2. More generally, a formulaic challenge repetitively given by one chief to a reluctant counterpart that their people should fight or compete in a dangerous manner probably is an

the loser) is a fixture of many hero tales and wizards' duels (see, for example, Curtin 2001, 22, 351; Hewitt 1918, 184–85, 233–35, 428–32).

Perhaps the most folkloric feature of all is that the story in this form points a moral—in fact, two morals—more clearly than in any other version. "It is a very nice story—for the Iroquois," as one nonnative chronicler observed (Johnson 1876, 27). "It shows that their opponents were the aggressors throughout . . . and that nothing but self-preservation induced them to destroy their enemies." Although both the River Battle and the Wrestling War stress foreign invasion, it is only the latter that speaks of counterattack and dispersion of the Kahkwa enemy. The Wrestling War asserts that the Senecas possess Kahkwa territory by right of conquest in a just war. Far from initiating the conflict, the Senecas merely reacted to a perfidious sneak attack. In addition to justifying the conquest of western New York, the Wrestling War also proclaims the Senecas to be athletically and militarily superior to their neighbors.

The Wildcat

The lady called the Wildcat received no mention in Seneca accounts of the Kahkwa War during the nineteenth century. Schoolcraft (1975, 61), who was asking Senecas about their war tradition, was aware of the Wildcat only from having read Cusick's book (see below). Yet, the Senecas of the time did know something about Norton's Kakonghsaksea—the female leader named Wildcat living east of the Niagara—as indicated by Lewis Henry Morgan in 1851. His information probably derived from the Seneca Parker family of the Tonawanda Reservation:

> It is a singular fact that the Neuter Nation [the Neutrals], who dwelt on the banks of the Niagara river . . . was known among them as the Je-go'-sä.-sa, or Cat Nation. The word signifies a wild-cat; and from being the

---

old device in Iroquois oral tradition (Pendergast 1994, 108n. 8). Lafitau mentioned such a story among the Senecas similar to the one William Patterson told 150 years later (Fenton and Moore 1977, 105–6).

name of a woman of great influence among them, it came to be the name of the nation. (Morgan 1962, 337n. 1)[3]

As in Norton thirty-five years earlier, this wildcat is unconnected with the topic of war with the Kahkwas.

The Seneca Traditions Considered

Neither of the two Seneca stories about war with the Kahkwas alluded to a woman called the Wildcat. Both were regarded as history, and both stated the Kahkwas invaded the Seneca homeland. That attack was repulsed in a monumental battle decided by the appearance of some body of Seneca reinforcements.

The River Battle variant described a great clash with the Kahkwa attackers near a river and a bridge. This story, originally documented by Norton in 1816, broke off with the end of the battle. Possibly it was becoming more formulaic in its telling over time to judge by the larger number of stock elements present in the later version.

The Wrestling War version featured a series of athletic challenges and competitions preceding the Kahkwa invasion. The narrative continued on, after the great battle, to describe a Seneca counterattack directed toward the Kahkwa village as well as another in the vicinity of present Buffalo.[4] Then, the Wrestling War related the Kahkwa War to what Norton knew as a story about the people of wooden fortifications. Stressing conventions and stock phrases characteristic of the spoken word, this version

3. French writers of the seventeenth century consistently identified the Eries as the Cat Nation. According to Morgan (1962, 41n. 1, 337n. 1), the eighteenth-century chronicler Charlevoix assigned the Wildcat's name ("Je-go'-sä-sa") to the group of people called Neutrals. The creation of a second cat nation has caused confusion ever since.

4. During the nineteenth century, Senecas identified several locations of the Kahkwa War, especially one in Buffalo corresponding to the Buffam Street site (Turner 1849, 39, 68; Schoolcraft 1975, 155; White 1961, 60). James Pendergast (1994) argued that this tradition confirmed an Erie identity for the Kahkwas and, therefore, dated an archaeological site on Eighteen Mile Creek to the historically attested Eries around 1655.

has a strongly oral quality to it and, indeed, it may be the classic Seneca war story of folklore—the way, that is, they remembered and customarily spoke about war. Further, unlike Norton and unlike the River Battle, the Wrestling War firmly takes up the task of teaching lessons. It avers that the Seneca war of conquest was just and that Senecas are wonderfully mighty people.

Why Senecas told two stories about, ostensibly, the same thing seems odd. Could having more than one storyline be evidence of a subject's significance? The more important question posed in regard to both versions, however, is: Why was the Kahkwa War such an apparently important and interesting topic?

Part of the answer may have been to affirm Seneca ownership of western New York. This was the place they lived, of course, but it was also a place they knew was not their land of origin. They were well posted on the fact that their homeland, up to at least the mid-1600s, was east of the Genesee. For one thing, their particular myth of autochthony (where they came out of the earth) placed them there (see chapter 7). In the mid-1700s and with reference to the Niagara locale, the Senecas could recall that they had reduced the Cat Nation "to just a few persons who were adopted by the Sonnontoins [Senecas]" (Pouchot 1994, 469).

Rightful ownership may have been a point worth highlighting inasmuch as other people were living in the same place—recently the British at Fort Niagara and, during the Revolutionary War, the majority of the other Iroquois. The most salient fact of ownership, however, was that the Senecas had lost possession to nonnative American settlers moving in all around them. A claim to possession that is historic and right is surely important to a dominated people and may be the best they can do.

More generally, stories about the Kahkwa War come out of a context in which the Senecas were divided and demoralized, their sense of self-worth at its lowest ebb. Having emerged from the Revolutionary War halved in number from combat, disease, and pestilence, they were immediately subjected to mounting pressure from land loss and missionary penetration. They were surrounded by legions of foreigners challenging and devaluing their culture at every turn. In these times of despair and humiliation, the

Seneca prophet Handsome Lake began to experience visions that would revitalize Seneca beliefs and adapt them to radically changed circumstances. Hardship and spiritual malaise, in other words, inspired cultural reformulation and a new religion (Wallace 1972). In asserting that Senecas were people of consequence, stories of the Kahkwa War were of a piece with these developments. They helped people think well of themselves and get through bad times.

Tuscarora Chronicles of the Nineteenth Century

Embroiled in war with the English in their native North Carolina, the Iroquoian-speaking Tuscaroras fled north and were adopted by the Iroquois in New York as the sixth nation of their confederacy in the early 1700s. The refugees took up residence in designated areas of Oneida country but soon had to move again. During the Revolutionary War, a number of Tuscaroras ended up around British-held Fort Niagara.

> About the close of the war there were two families of the Tuscaroras hunting and fishing along the shores of Lake Ontario, and then up the east shore of Niagara River and as far as Lewiston, and there left their canoe; then traveled east and up the mountain as far as a place which they now call the Old Saw Mill (now on the Tuscarora Reservation). . . . They concluded to make their winter quarters at that place, which they did. (Johnson 1881, 72–73)

The Old Saw Mill—also known as "the citadel of Kienuka," an ancient "Indian fort," and, today, the Kienuka archaeological site—was regarded as the emotional capital of what became the new Tuscarora homeland (Carrington 1892, 31; Johnson 1881, 173; Rayner-Herter 2001, 82–83; Whipple et al. 1889, 13). And, even though the Old Saw Mill/Kienuka itself ended up just beyond their fence line, the Tuscaroras succeeded in maintaining themselves at this location and enlarging their holdings through subsequent purchase. The result was today's reservation in Niagara County just north of Niagara Falls and south of Lewiston (Landy 1978).

We have two Tuscarora sources on the Kahkwa War: David Cusick's 1827 work, *Sketches of Ancient History of the Six Nations* (Beauchamp 1892), and Elias Johnson's 1881 book, *Legends, Traditions and Laws of the Iroquois or Six Nations, and History of the Tuscarora Indians*. Both are in English and both are literary, that is, words committed to paper in contrast to Seneca word-of-mouth sources.

Cusick's Account

Long ago, according to Cusick, the country between the Genesee and the Niagara belonged to the "Kanneastokaroneah or Erians." These people had "sprung from the Senecas" and their "national sovereignty was confirmed by the Senate of the Five Nations."

Among the Kanneastokaroneahs was a queen called the mother of the nations and named Yagowanea, a name given without translation or explanation.[5] Her town was "the fort Kauhanauke, (said Tuscarora)," which is to say, Kienuka next to today's Tuscarora Reservation. Yagowanea lived outside the settlement in a "Peace House," a place of asylum for belligerents passing through on their way to fight with one another.

However, during a war between the Senecas and the Mississaugas (Algonquian-speakers on Lake Ontario's northern shore), Yagowanea delivered up two Seneca visitors to the Mississaugas to be killed. After her betrayal, she took council with the "chieftain of the band" at Kanhai-tauneekay, a place apparently in the vicinity of Buffalo Creek, and with the Erie commander at Kauquatkay, that is, Koghquauga or Kaghkwague— the place of the Kahkwas on Eighteen Mile Creek. The leaders decided to assemble their fighters there for an attack on the Senecas.

The Senecas got wind of trouble and sent two spies to Kauhanauke to ferret out the Eries' intentions. After dividing their combatants into two groups, the Senecas hunkered down east of the Genesee River to await the

5. Later in time, Yagowanea is called the Great Woman and the Mother of Nations. Whether these phrases are supposed to be translations of that name or word is unclear to me because the same epithets are applied to Jigansahse (A. Parker 1919, 44–46), the latter said to be the lady's name as opposed to her title, Yagowanea.

attack. "After a severe contest the first division was compelled to retreat, but the assistance of the second company came up" and seemingly turned the tide. The Eries lost the battle and withdrew to their home villages.

A combined military force of all the Iroquois nations then attacked the Kauquatkey. "The queen sued for peace—the army immediately ceased from hostilities, and left the Erians entire possession of the country" (Beauchamp 1892, 31–34). Many years after that, "the Erians declared a war against the Five Nations; a long bloody war ensued; at last the Erians were driven from the country, and supposed were incorporated with some of the southern nations" (38).

Like Norton, Cusick makes reference to a trio of enemy settlements, very possibly the same three villages visualized as situated east of Lake Erie and the Niagara River. Also like Norton but in contrast to the Seneca sources, Cusick emphasizes the existence of a female leader in charge of a neutral location. He provides additional details about the lady and seems to move her from the carry location on the Niagara River east to Kienuka or Tuscarora.

Cusick's story broadly agrees with all other versions of the war in its allusion to two Seneca spies and the Kahkwa invasion of Seneca territory. It most closely resembles the Seneca Wrestling War variant in its stress on the arrival of a new Seneca force as decisive to the battle's outcome. However, Cusick makes no reference to a bridge, to a sequence of athletic competitions, or to such stock elements of the Seneca tale as moccasins or stench.

The conspicuous feature of Cusick's version is that it places Norton's female leader within the Kahkwa War and asserts a causal relationship between them: The queen's actions were the reason for the Kahkwa War.

Cusick's plot seems to me a logical way to tie together the folkloric strands Norton understood to be unconnected. If Kakonghsaksea's settlement (Teyotchirheo in Norton's Wildcat story) was regarded as the same as, or very similar in name to, a village involved in the Kahkwa War (Norton's Tegotchirheon), why not place a female chieftain in the conflict in such a way as to provide motive for the otherwise senseless attack on the Senecas?

In any event, the story of a queen in the Kahkwa War was a plot long unique to Cusick. Norton knew nothing of this earlier and Senecas said nothing of it later. At midcentury, it remained unfamiliar to such nonnative investigators as Morgan and Schoolcraft.

Johnson's Account

According to Elias Johnson (1881, 173–85), the Iroquois created the office of peace queen at the time they formed their confederacy and vested it with veto authority over declarations of war. The peace queen was to maintain a place in which no blood could be shed and hospitality was due to all visitors. The precinct designated for this function was Kienuka (also called Gau-strau-yea), the Old Saw Mill that Johnson understood to be in the Tuscarora Reservation. At the time of the story, Kienuka was in Squakihaw territory, and the Squakihaws were of "one language and of one nation" with the Kahkwas around North Evans (vicinity of Eighteen Mile Creek) and the Eries to the southwest (vicinity of Erie, Pennsylvania). The queen appointed by the Iroquois to superintend Kienuka likewise was a Squakihaw, a virgin whose formal name was Ge-keah-sau-sa. Johnson offered no translation for this word, which looks like a variation on Norton's Kakonghaksea and the later Jigonsahse. Nor did he mention Cusick's name for this individual, Yagonwanea.

Johnson's story begins with the Kahkwas challenging the Senecas to a series of athletic contests: a ball game, a foot race, then a wrestling match in which the loser would be killed. The Senecas won all. The victory was bitterly resented by the peace queen, who secretly allowed several of her Seneca guests to be murdered by their Mississauga enemies.

Fearing Seneca retribution for the betrayal, the queen's people decided to launch a preemptive strike on the Senecas. The Senecas received warning and, accordingly, dispatched four spies to Squakihaw country. The scouts visited three places in turn: Kienuka, "Gill Creek, above Niagara Falls," and Kahkwa. At the latter location, they found the assembled inhabitants of all the towns preparing for war. The scouts conveyed this information, as well as the progress of the enemy advance, to their people.

The action pauses at this point as the Seneca chief, Onea-gah-re-tah-wa, delivers a lengthy motivational speech emphasizing that war has been forced on the Senecas by the actions of the queen. The Senecas are urged to meet the enemy at a distance to avoid having their bodies strewn around the settlement.

The furious engagement that ensues is interrupted several times for mutually agreed-on rest periods. During one of their breaks, the two sides engage in wrestling matches in which the losers' heads are bashed in. The battle is long in doubt until the appearance of the Senecas' reserve of warriors.

The losers retreat west. Finding all the enemy villages deserted, the pursuing Senecas infer that their foes have fled in canoes down the Allegheny River. "That is the way the Senecas came in possession of so large a dominion," Johnson concludes.

The Iroquois did not revive the appointment of a peace queen because, according to Johnson, Ge-keah-sau-sa's egregious behavior confirmed their suspicion that women were unsuited to exercising the authority of political office. And so the situation long remained

> until about twenty-five years ago, from the year 1878, there was a virgin selected from among the Tonawanda band of the Seneca nation by the name of Caroline Parker . . . who was ordained to the high office of queen, or Ge-keah-sau-sa. She is now the wife of a noted sachem of the Tuscarora nation, Mr. John Mount Pleasant, of no common wealth. She is located about two miles southwest of the antique fort Gah-Strau-yea, or Kienuka, on the Tuscarora reservation, where she ever held open her hospitable house, not only to the Iroquois, but of every nation, including the pale faces. Allegorical [sic] speaking, she has ever had a kettle of hominy hanging over her fire-place, ready to appease the hunger of those who trod her threshold. (Johnson 1881, 184–85)

Johnson's account retains Cusick's Kienuka location for the peace queen, continues to integrate the queen closely into the cause and course of the subsequent war, and agrees with the broad outline of a Kahkwa invasion culminating in battle decided by Seneca reinforcements. This is hardly surprising because Johnson, a "notable copyist" (Fenton 2002, 43), followed Cusick closely. Most of Johnson's section on oral tradition was lifted, almost verbatim, from Cusick's work.

What is more notable is how much his version differs from Cusick's earlier text. Two Seneca spies become four. Reference to three enemy settlements remains important, but one of them (Gill Creek) is situated at a new location. Johnson reintroduces the sequence of athletic games characteristic of the Senecas' Wrestling War and emphasizes, more explicitly than Cusick, that the war explains and justifies Seneca possession of western New York. The harangue of his Seneca chief is new. In Johnson, Squakihaws abandon their towns and slip away without offering further battle.

The most original features of Johnson, however, are details about the peace queen. First, this was an Iroquois office created at the time the League of the Iroquois came into being. Second, the title of peace queen had recently been revived in the person of a Seneca woman who married a prominent Tuscarora man. Thus, Johnson's peace queen was not only associated with the locale; she had returned to it and was now one with the Tuscarora people.

Earlier in his book, Johnson had linked the peace queen to the beginning of the Iroquois Confederacy by picturing Hiawat-ha, one of the founding chiefs, ordaining that fact. In context, it is a passage in which all of the nations are being assigned their identities and roles in the same oratorical fashion. This is how it reads (Hiawat-ha speaking):

> "Mohawk, and you, the people who live in the open country, and possess much wisdom, shall be the fifth nation, because you understand better the art of raising corn and beans and making cabins.
>
> "You five great and powerful nations, with your tribes, must unite and have one common interest, and no foes shall disturb or subdue you.
>
> "And you of the different nations of the south, and you of the west, may place yourselves under our protection, and we will protect you. We earnestly desire the alliance and friendship of you all.
>
> "And from you, Squaw-ki-haws (being a remote branch of the Seneca Nation), being the people who are as the Feeble Bushes, shall be chosen a Virgin, who shall be the peace-maker for all the nations of the earth, and more particularly the favored Ako-no-shu-ne, which name this confederacy shall ever sustain. If we unite in one band the Great Spirit will smile upon us, and we shall be free, prosperous and happy." (Johnson 1881, 51)

The inveterate plagiarist Johnson drew this passage from a history of Onondaga County (to the east) published thirty years earlier. In that source, Hiawat-ha has this to say:

And you—Senecas, a people who live in the "Open Country" and possess much wisdom, shall be the fifth nation; because you understand better the art of raising corn and beans, and making cabins.

You, five great and powerful nations, must unite and have but one common interest, and no foe shall be able to disturb or subdue you.

And you—Manhattoes, Nyacks, Montauks and others, who are as the feeble "Bushes" . . . may place yourselves under our protection. . . . We earnestly desire your alliance and friendship.

Brothers—if we unite in this bond, the Great Spirit will smile upon us, and we shall be free, prosperous and happy. (Clark 1849, 1:28–29)

Johnson's innovation, therefore, was to insert Jigansahse into an earlier account of the founding of the league, probably doing so with the book open in front of him. Descriptions of the league's founding prior to Johnson—such as the one quoted above—make no mention of a peace queen (Fenton 1998, 51–65).

Considered together, the written narratives of the Tuscarora authors share two distinctive features. First, their topic was a synthetic one. Both Cusick and Johnson combined what Norton and the Senecas treated as separate topics: the Kahkwa War and the female leader called the Wildcat.

Second, the Kahkwa War looms large in both Tuscarora accounts. Cusick devoted three pages to it in a work totaling thirty-six pages and in which the creation of the world receives no more than four pages. In Johnson, the Kahkwa War was even more prominent. Although its twelve pages comprise relatively less of the total book (234 pages), it is treated at greater length than any other historical tradition (including the creation of the world and formation of the Iroquois Confederacy) and is accorded its own chapter. To both Tuscarora authors, therefore, a tale of the Kahkwa War that included a Niagara queen was of signal importance.

The Tuscarora Chronicles Considered

That the narrative should be so significant to Tuscaroras appears, at first glance, puzzling because the Kahkwa War was *not* a Tuscarora affair. There was nothing authentically Tuscarora on the subject of past wars in the Niagara region because the Tuscaroras were not there then. The answer to the seeming paradox is that this topic, properly handled, answered the mythic needs of people in search of historic traditions of their own pertaining to the new land. It could also be applied, like salve, to soothe two emotional dilemmas specific to the Tuscaroras.

While the Tuscaroras experienced the same hardships detailed for the Senecas, they carried, in addition, a psychological burden of insecurity peculiarly their own. Not only were they newcomers, they were, in Cusick's time, refugees whose very capacity to reside in the Niagara region was called into question. As recently as the War of 1812, they had been burned out by the British and forced to flee, yet again, back to Oneida country.

Further and in the Iroquois scheme of things, the Tuscaroras were regarded not as peers but as perpetual guests and transients. Adopted as younger kinsmen of the five original nations of the Iroquois League, they were "never admitted to a full equality" and "never allowed to have a sachem, who could sit as an equal in the council of sachems" (Morgan 1962, 44, 98). By all accounts, they were never permitted to forget their secondary status (Graymont 1973, xix). Well into the twentieth century, the Tuscaroras were characterized as "haunted with the self-image of themselves as junior partners in the Iroquois alliance, a mendicant cousin who shuffles with self-consciousness and embarrassment into the peripheral shadows of the Council fire" (Landy 1958, 251).

Suffering from rootlessness and inferiority, these were people who longed to feel worthwhile in the general scheme of things and worthy in the eyes of their Iroquois hosts. Thoroughly deracinated, the Tuscaroras also needed local roots reconnecting them to a meaningful past. Establishing ties with the landscape and making the present feel comfortable as the fitting outcome of the past are, of course, tasks undertaken by myth. What I see in the Tuscarora texts, therefore, is a kind of mythological construction zone in which fundamental issues of identity were being hammered out.

In Cusick's writing, the Tuscaroras were connected to the tradition of a female leader spatially—the queen lived in what was considered to be Tuscarora ground adjacent to the reservation. The queen, in turn, was made the focus of the Kahkwa War with the result that, at least geographically, the basic Iroquois account of regional ownership now attached to the Tuscaroras. Johnson's work elaborated each of these points but, in addition, affirmed that the now Tuscarora-ized account lay at the very heart of Iroquois identity, the great oral narrative about confederacy origins known today as the League Tradition.

The chain of association came to life in Johnson's time. It was literally embodied in the marriage of the queen's descendant to a Tuscarora chief and demonstrated by their residence on Tuscarora land next to the legendary queen's home at Kienuka. In effect, the Tuscaroras were now related to the local landscape and equipped with a past worthy of their elder Iroquois brothers' respect. The story of the queen and the Kahkwa War figured importantly in the work of the Tuscarora chroniclers, therefore, because, by them or through them, mythological work essential to their people's history and pride was being performed.

Conclusion

I have reviewed an unusually well-documented set of Native American stories about war(s) in the Niagara region. In folkloric terms, they are legends: tales locally based, historically rooted, and claiming credibility by making reference to what is regarded as historically true. The Iroquois who told and wrote them down regarded them as factual statements about their past. There is no reason to doubt that they reflect events documented by Europeans in the mid–seventeenth century about Iroquoian peoples they called Eries and Neutrals.

The question I pose is, why these stories and not others? And, assuming Norton provides us with a reasonable overview of traditions extant at the opening of the nineteenth century, why do Seneca and Tuscarora sources differ in narrative emphasis?

The most reasonable answer is that these stories were performing mythic functions. When a people's history becomes fragmented or irrelevant, "they are moved to 'restory' the past so as to make it all seem at least continuous again"—through myth (Ramsey 1983, 154). When people come to occupy a new place, they "construe some 'primordial tie'" to the topography they will call home—through myth (Nabokov 2002, 132).

During the nineteenth century, this subject happened to be a salient medium for constructing a mythic past tied to the Niagara region, one that contributed positively to a sense of identity. For both Senecas and Tuscaroras, though in different ways, the topic was performing Malinowski's "hard-working, extremely important" cultural work (1984, 196). It told people who they are and how, and "through what origins and transformations, they have come to possess their particular world" (Ramsey 1983, 4).

3

Killer Lizards, Eldritch Fish, and Horned Serpents

ANYONE PERUSING THE LITERATURE of Native American oral narrative "soon learns to recognize many recurrent patterns or types, which transcend geographical and linguistic boundaries" (Thompson 1929, vii). Here, I discuss three old friends of this sort—story types repeatedly documented either as self-contained tales or as episodes within longer narratives.

These tales of marvel are of the Northeast, of course, but they also occur more widely. All, in fact, were distributed over enormous distances. Additionally, they possess rather complex plots unlikely to have been independently invented. Hence, they indicate that communication involving storytelling took place across great reaches of geographic space.

This chapter muses on the phenomenon of widespread story distribution—what it implies about interaction between regions, how it might have come about, and what might be indicated about behavior or belief of long ago. When something is known of historical circumstances, as is the case with the first plot considered here, one follows the facts trying to make sense of the story's dissemination. When nothing is known of history, as is the case with the second and third examples, extensive geographical scale testifies to deep time depth.

Killer Lizards

Popular among the Iroquois around 1900 was a tale about a beneficent lion-being who fights a murderous lizard to the death. Here is the story as first documented by David Cusick in 1827 (Beauchamp 1892, 23).

[Centuries ago] a small party went out to make incursion upon the enemy that may be found within the boundaries of the kingdom. They penetrated the Ohio River and encamped on the bank. As they were out of provision, the warriors were anxious to kill a game. A certain warrior discovered a hollow tree, supposing a bear in the tree, he immediately reported. The warriors were in hopes to obtain the bear—went to the tree. One of them climbed and put a fire in it in order to drive out the creature. The warriors made ready to shoot, but were mistaken.

There instantly came out a furious Lizard, and quickly grasped [a warrior] and leaped into the hollow of the tree and the young ones devoured it. A grumbling noise ensued, the warriors were terrified at the monstrous creature and were soon compelled to retire, except one stayed at the tree while others fled. He remained until the party was destroyed and the last warrior was chased. The warrior immediately left the tree and ran on the way fortunately met the Holder of the Heavens who advised him to stop and offers the aid of material resistance which was accepted. The warrior was instructed to make fire without delay and to get some sticks to use with which to prevent the Lizard's flesh from uniting the body or being efficacious.

The protector changed into a lion and laid in wait. In a meanwhile the monster came up, a severe engagement took place. The warrior hastened with a stick and began to hook the Lizard's flesh, when bit off by his defendant and throws it into the fire, by means the monster was quelled. The warrior thanked for the personal preservation. The protector vanished out of his sight. The warrior returned to the fort and related the occurrence.

Later versions describe the lizard's home as a "bear tree," a high, hollow tree stump covered with claw marks. The story often details a specific number of warriors (or hunters) who will be run down, one by one, by the angry saurian. The party's only survivor is the man who climbed the tree to toss down burning material to flush out the supposed bear. When it comes time for him to flee, he encounters a mysterious man who, when identified, is none other than the great Iroquois god, Sky Holder.

The supernatural protector transforms himself into a lion (or, in two versions, a bear) and engages the lizard in a titanic struggle. The supernatural guardian insists on the necessity of the mortal's help in the upcoming fight. The man must be equipped with sticks to prevent pieces of the lizard from magically reconnecting with the monster.

Five Iroquois versions were recorded between 1827 and 1918 (Johnson 1881, 56–57; Rudes and Crouse 1987, 530–32; Waugh n.d., E. Cook 202 f24).[1] In one, the lizard runs down a hunter's dogs rather than people (Waugh n.d., Mrs. P. John 201 f27). The action of the chase sequence, however, remains the same. All accounts agree in essential details, and all are consistent with a fundamental theme in Iroquois oral narrative: a supernatural needs human help to overcome its mortal enemy. In two cases, the account specifies that the branches employed by the human must be of red osier dogwood—the quintessential magical substance of Iroquois oral narrative (Wonderley 2004, 145–56).

I assumed the "Killer Lizard" was an Iroquois story because it is documented among those folk early and often. With the possible exception of the tropical-looking lizard, the story seems comfortable in an Iroquois setting. Elsewhere in the general region, the story is reported only from the Wyandots (Barbeau 1915, 137–41) and from one Ojibwa source in eastern Michigan (Smith 1897)—limited occurrences, that is to say, historically or geographically close to a presumed Iroquois hearth.

However, the lizard tale also was known far to the south. In three versions attributed to the Alabamas, Hitchitis, and Caddos, a group of hunters flushes out, from a bear tree, a monster lizard (a "Cannibal," in one instance) who pursues and slays all but one of the hunters (Dorsey 1997b, 57–58; Swanton 1929, 96–97, 153). A closely related Creek/Muskogee variant (two accounts) has the lizard running down the hunter's dogs (Swanton 1929, 27–29). In any event, the protagonist is saved (in four of five examples) by a large feline who kills the lizard.

---

1. The reference is to the unpublished Iroquois folklore papers of Frederick Waugh at the Canadian Museum of Civilization in Hull, Quebec. The format of the citation specifies informant, box number, and then folder. As preparator in Ethnology for the National Museum of Canada, Waugh (born 1872) collected over 150 Iroquois texts between 1912 and 1918. The vast majority were recorded in English from informants of the Six Nations Reserve at Grand River, Ontario. Waugh disappeared in 1924 and was never able to publish these materials.

These versions from the Southeast do not mention a deity in human form who speaks to the man, requests the man's aid, and finally transforms himself into the lion. The southeastern lion does not even speak to the human protagonist. In comparison with the northern plot, the Southeast's version of "Killer Lizard" is undeveloped.

Nevertheless, it is much the same story, and it testifies to some form of interaction between the Iroquois and southeastern regions. Two clues as to the nature of that connection are embedded in the northern accounts. The first is the giant lizard, something for which a northern clime offers few precedents. Iroquois versions identify this villain as the Great Blue Lizard (rendered Djai 'nosgō wa or Djino-sano-sgowa), a saurian that "seems to be a beast looking something like an alligator" (Parker 1989, 17). The second is the setting of the story. According to a pair of Tuscarora versions, the story took place in the Tuscarora homeland of North Carolina (Johnson 1881, 56–57; Rudes and Crouse 1987, 530–52).

Such evidence suggests the "Killer Lizard" could have been a story of the Southeast brought north to Iroquois country by Tuscarora storytellers fleeing their homeland during the 1700s. If so, the story was cordially received and quickly integrated into the Iroquois repertoire. What remained of the narrative in its hypothesized southeastern homeland was, by about 1900, greatly attenuated.

Eldritch Fish

This widespread story is called the "Man-who-became-a-snake" or the "Snake-man." As it opens, two men are out hunting. Late one day, the weary travelers come across one or more fish swimming around in water contained within the bowl of a tree stump or somehow existing in a hollow tree. When one of the hunters announces his intention of eating the unusual creatures, he is sternly warned not to do so. "These fish are not right," the second hunter typically asserts, "and should not be eaten."

But, of course, the first hunter makes a meal of his find. A little later, the fish-eater becomes consumed with thirst and spends the night writhing in pain. With the morning light, it is clear that he has become a snake. He disappears into a spring or pond or river, enjoining the companion to tell his relatives what has happened to him. "Tell them," the snake-man often says, "I have eaten forbidden fish and become, in consequence, a water-snake." Many versions conclude with the family visiting the snake to bid him a tearful farewell.

"Snake-man" was known in the East among the Iroquois (Curtin 2001, 416–18; Hewitt 1918, 111–12, 169–72). It also occurred sporadically in the Midwest among the Menomini and Sauk (Skinner 1928, 160; Skinner and Satterlee 1915, 475–76). It was popular in the Plains where it is reported from the Arapaho, Arikara, Assiniboine, Blackfeet, Gros Ventre, Hidatsa, Kiowa, Mandan, Pawnee, and probably others as well (Dorsey and Kroeber 1997, 145–46, 150–51; Lankford 1987, 102–3; Momaday 1969, 38; Parks 1996, 207–9).

The "Snake-man" story occurred with at least equal frequency in the Southeast where versions are attributed to the Alabama, Caddo, Cherokee, Cherokee, Hitchiti, and Yuchi (Dorsey 1997b, 65–66; Grantham 2002, 199–200, 202–3; Lankford 1987, 92–93; Mooney 1995, 304–5; Swanton 1929, 97–98, 154). The southeastern distribution centered on the Creek/Muskogee region (Alabama, Georgia, Northern Florida) in which at least eight versions were collected (Grantham 2002, 204–8, 217–20; Swanton 1929, 30–34).

Certainly there are internal differences occurring over this wide region. Although the group discovering the unusual food usually consists of two men, for example, it does vary in composition. Fish heavily predominates as the forbidden food although eggs or meat are sometimes named. Occasionally, the transgressor eating the discovery against the advice of the other becomes a form of water monster other than a snake (Lankford 1987, 83–86).

However, the range of variation seems comparatively minor, and the versions are strikingly similar in their emphasis on (1) encountering a strange food; (2) containing a warning to the effect that eating the food is wrong; and (3) describing the transformation of man to snake as a result of disregarding the warning. Randle (1953, 625) illustrates this tendency in a summary of Iroquois variants from the Six Nations Reserve in Ontario:

Dire consequences follow the eating of fish. Two stories . . . tell how humans, in one story a woman, in the other a man, are transformed into water snakes . . . as a consequence of eating fish and developing an unappeasable thirst thereby. These tales reinforce the taboo against the eating of fish, and they reflect the fear and suspicion attached to water creatures, snakes especially.

Randle touches on two psychological explanations here. The first is an aversion to snakes, but if such a phenomenon exists, it fails to explain the existence of this specific plot or why it exists in certain places but not in others. Randle's second explanation is that the tale embodies a cultural injunction against the consumption of fish. This is interesting because it is counter to fact. The Iroquois loved to eat fish and many of them ate a lot of it (Kuhn and Funk 2000; Recht 1995; Wonderley 2006a, 11). The Iroquois had no taboo against eating fish nor, I suspect, did other tellers of the story elsewhere.

Lankford (2007a, 134–35) offers the historical hypothesis of common heritage to explain the distributional pattern of the Snake-man. Not only are Snake-man accounts particularly frequent in the Southeast and the Plains, tellings in those regions hint at mythological significance. In the Southeast, the story often concludes with the expansion of the Snake-man's habitat—that is, the pool becomes a lake or the river violently floods, sometimes destroying a nearby town (Lankford 1987, 92–93).

Among the Hidatsa of the Upper Plains, "Snake-man" is incorporated into a major myth about two brothers who free the game, then visit the agricultural land of the Old-Woman-Who-Never-Dies. Subsequently, the siblings "visit the great snake, the owner of buffaloes, whom the heroes deceive. In both [Hidatsa] cases, the foolish brother commits the error of eating the snake's flesh and turns into a large reptile at the bottom of the Missouri river" (Lévi-Strauss 1990b, 442). In the Mandan version, the heroes encounter a giant serpent lying across their path and build a fire under it. "One of them eats the flesh, despite warnings, and is transformed into a large water serpent, which henceforward lives in the Missouri River and acts as protector and spirit of the river" (Lankford 1987, 103).

One further oddity of the "Snake-man" is its presence thousands of miles to the south among the Sumu on the Caribbean Coast of Nicaragua. There can be no doubt, Robert Rands (1954, 81) asserted, that this and the southeastern story are historically related. Lankford (1987, 100–102) suggests the Sumu story more generally relates to a narrative cycle concerned with a pair of brothers, a great tree, and a flood discernible in the mythology of the Caribbean and Amazonian regions. "The Sumu connection raises the possibility that the key to understanding this myth-complex may lie south of the United States" (105).

A more evenly distributed "Snake-man" would suggest a common primordial past. In this context, I am struck by a set of mythic fragments recorded in the Central Highlands of Mexico during the sixteenth century. In all cases, cooking fish seems to be offensive to the gods, a sin resulting either in the formation of the present world or the destruction (sometimes flood-related) of a previous one (López Austin 1996, xiii, 77–78). "The fact that this myth . . . is still widespread among peoples as diverse as the Tepehuas, the Popolocas, the sierra Totonacs, and the Chontal of Oaxaca," Michel Graulich (1983, 579) observes, "indicates how fundamental it is."

Crossing-Water-on-a-Snake

This plot opens with a person being stranded on an island, that is, lured and left there to die by some villain, often a father-in-law (Thompson's [1929, 326] motif K1616, "Marooned egg-gatherer"). When a horned water serpent offers to ferry the deserted individual to the mainland, the person climbs on to the beast's head for the journey across the water.

Sometimes the rider is instructed on how to make the steed go or keep it going or make it go faster. The Iroquois do this by supplying the rider with red willow whips with which to lash the snake. The more common method is to tap the beast's head or horns with a stone.

The snake generally asks his passenger to warn him about the appearance of a cloud, for this heralds the arrival of the steed's mortal enemy, a Thunder armed with lethal lightning bolts. Wishing to reach the shore, the rider withholds this warning. The human makes it across just as the snake comes under violent attack.

This tale, with some variation, was widely distributed throughout the greater East, being recorded among the Arapaho and Caddo (Dorsey 1997b, 26–27; Dorsey and Kroeber 1997, 28); the Ojibwa, Saulteaux, and Eastern Cree (Michelson 1919, 185, 383–85; Skinner 1911, 82, 171; Smith 1995, 106–7); the Iroquois, Wyandot, and Delaware (Barbeau 1915, 102–3; Bierhorst 1995, 63–64, 98–99; Cornplanter 1986, 58–65; Parker 1989, 223–27); and the Passamaquoddy and Penobscot (Fewkes 1890, 260–70; Prince 1921, 22–23; Speck 1935a, 17).

In a second narrative pattern, the protagonist arrives at the bank of some body of water that he must cross. The person often summons a series of potential steeds, rejecting each in turn until settling on the biggest snake or water monster available. Here, also, the rider may be asked to warn the beast of a cloud or to indicate when the water is becoming dangerously shallow. In the Southeast where this pattern probably occurs most frequently, the rider makes the serpent go by throwing food in front of it and/or shooting arrows ahead (Grantham 2002, 183–84; Lankford 1987, 203–4; Swanton 1929, 127–28, 174–75, 238–39).

This pattern, far more than the first, occurs as one incident within a longer story. Sometimes the hero is running away from a pursuer (Bloomfield 1928, 147; Skinner 1911, 89). As a rule, however, the protagonist is simply wandering around from place to place. Getting across a body of water happens to be a problem to solve in order to continue the journey across the landscape. In addition to the Southeast, this form of the tale was recorded in the Plains (Lévi-Strauss 1990b, 435–38) and in the Midwest (Bourgeois 1994, 52–54; Smith 1995, 106–7).

In several New England versions, the animal conveyance is not a water serpent but a whale (Leland 1992, 33–34; Prince 1921, 29; Rand 1894, 228–29; Wallis and Wallis 1955, 322–23). This serves to remind us of larger context. "Crossing-water" probably is a form of the Whale-boat motif (R245) in which "a man is carried across the water on a whale (or fish). In most cases he deceives the whale as to the nearness to the shore or as to hearing thunder" (Thompson 1929, 327). The name of the motif derives from Franz Boas's discovery of the whale as the mythical steed of choice on the northwest coast (Lankford 2007a, 125). Linking "Crossing-water" to Whale-boat expands the distribution of the motif to at least the circumpolar zone of both the Old and New worlds (Lankford 1987, 208, 255n. 21).

Perhaps even more than the Snake-man story, this one seems to keep important mythological company. Often the wandering protagonist who needs to cross water is a culture hero, such as Gluskap in the Northeast or Manibozho in the Midwest. In the Mandan telling, it is another incident in a cosmogonic saga accounting for both crops and game (Lévi-Strauss 1990b, 435–38). "Crossing-water" is said to be, among some Ojibwas, the myth chartering women's participation in the great Midewiwin medicine society and ritual cycle (Bourgeois 1994, 34, 52; Vecsey 1984, 454). Lankford and others have wondered whether the crossing of water on a snake might describe the journey of the dead to the afterlife (Lankford 2007b, 178, 182; Smith 1995, 107; Vecsey 1983, 64).

Discussion

These stories elude practical reason. When the occasion arises to suggest a logical basis for a story—as it does in the case of the Snake-man instructing his listeners about a fish-eating taboo—the apparent explanation flies in the face of reality. We came up against the inadequacy of functional explanation in the question of observational knowledge encoded in star stories. We will encounter it again in dietary conditions hypothesized to explain windigo-ism and in the device of nonexplanatory morals tacked on to many Native American narratives. Attempts to make functional sense of oral narrative often end in nonsense.

All three tales are linked with characters and themes one would suppose to be culturally significant. The murderous lizard runs up against the great god of the Iroquois. The Snake-man hints at the ending or beginning of an epoch or, in at least one instance, is built into a culture's fundamental chartering account. Crossing-water occurs as an incident of a culture hero's cosmogonic adventures and possibly as allusion to the great journey awaiting us all. Do the apparently thematic contexts and trappings account for these stories? Do they explain anything about origin, spread, preservation, or retention? The very diversity of individual answers and contexts cautions against pursuing such analysis very far.

While all three stories range across enormous areas, the distribution of the Killer Lizard story differs from the other two. It is discontinuous, confined to two widely separated centers that must have been connected by interaction of some sort. The obvious possibility, historically, is that the Northeast and Southeast were linked by the emigration of Tuscarora people north to Iroquois country during the eighteenth century. That would explain why Tuscarora storytellers a century later claimed the adventure was theirs in North Carolina. It would also clarify why an alligator-like being strides through the mythic imagination of northern people.

The other two story types are more widely and continuously distributed. Contemplating these and other narratives, Lankford (2007a) proposes they are the surviving evidence for a once-widespread belief in a deity he calls the "Great Serpent," lord of the watery Beneath-world. The Great Serpent took various composite forms, including Mishebishu, the underwater pantherlike being of northern Algonquians, but was chiefly known as a horned water serpent. Lankford (134–35) characterizes this cosmological notion as "a widespread religious pattern more powerful than the tendency toward cultural diversity." Beliefs about this being are "enshrined in a permanent way in the stories that are told about it" (124). The old cultural verities are identifiable in several story types that preserve ancient knowledge about the Great Serpent and about human dealings with it.

Important among the myths that reflect a worldview once universally understood throughout the Eastern Woodlands are the "Man-who-became-a-snake" and "Crossing-water-on-a-snake" (Lankford 2007a, 109–16, 125, 128, 134–35). A third is found in versions of "Crossing-water" that feature cloud warnings and Thunder attacks. This may be one of the most fundamental myths of all—conflict between Thunders or Thunderbirds in the air above and horned creatures, especially snakes, in the water below (124). These themes, therefore, seem deeply rooted in regional cosmology of a former time. In all likelihood, some of the Northeast's recurrent tales of the marvelous preserve vestiges of ancient, autochthonous thinking.

4

Old Good Twin

*Sky Holder During the Seventeenth
and Eighteenth Centuries*

FRENCH JESUITS in the seventeenth century gave his name, variously spelled, as Teharonhiaouagon, "he who holds up the sky," or Sky Holder.[1] Sometimes said to be one of two brothers, he was described by the missionaries as the great god of the Iroquois, their mightiest spirit, and the principal being "they acknowledge as a Divinity, and obey as the great Master of their lives." Midwinter, an important religious ceremony held in February, was dedicated to learning Sky Holder's will as interpreted from dreams (Thwaites 1896–1901, 42:197, 53:253, 55:61, 54:65). Mohawk chief John Norton wrote that this deity was the "Great Patron" of the Iroquois, and to him "they offered up their supplications, when they set out on an expedition; and in times of their greatest barbarism, it was to him, they offered the devoted victims taken in war" (Klinck and Talman 1970, 97). In 1827, Tuscarora writer David Cusick remembered Sky Holder as the deity who led the Iroquois in their tribal wanderings, protected his people from monsters, and instructed them in the arts of war (Beauchamp 1892, 11–18).

This older Sky Holder has little in common with the beneficent demiurge described around 1900 in various accounts of the creation. That being,

---

1. "He who holds up the sky" was offered by French missionary Claude Dablon in 1656. In about 1815, James Dean rendered the Iroquois name for Sky Holder as "the holder or supporter of the heavens" (Lounsbury and Gick 2000, 162).

under a variety of names including Sky Holder,[2] brought plants, animals, and features of the landscape into being for the benefit of humans, then fashioned the first people out of clay. At every step of the way, his wicked twin brother countered each good deed with a negative or destructive act. Although the kindly sibling prevailed, both brothers still compete to influence human behavior now and in the afterlife (see Fenton 1998, 34–50; Hewitt 1974, 470–791).

Nor does the older Sky Holder sound precisely the same as the high god described by Lewis Henry Morgan about the year 1850. That deity, usually known as the Great Spirit, benevolently administers this world in competition with his evil twin brother and governs the next—a heavenly abode for mortals abiding by his ethical precepts (Morgan 1962, 154–56).

All the sources named above almost certainly refer to the same deity or to different aspects of the same being. Yet, the widely differing characterizations pose a dilemma. Do they indicate that we do not understand Sky Holder's whole nature (a function of inadequate information), or do they reflect how ideas about Sky Holder may have evolved through the ages (Wonderley 2001)? Hale (1885, 13), Beauchamp (1897, 169), and Parker (1913, 11) thought major changes had occurred in the Iroquois pantheon during the historical epoch. Hewitt (1910) and, after him, Fenton (1962; 1998, 110), took a more timeless view of the matter, implying that the character of the most important deity was little altered with the passage of time. Tooker (1970, 3) and Wallace (1972, 252–53; 1978, 447) believed Handsome Lake's reforms in the early nineteenth century involved only minor revision of the good twin and his wicked brother.

To express such opinions implies that one controls the terms of a comparison. Yet, the most rudimentary exercise of historical research on this topic has never been performed. The evidence bearing on the earlier nature

2. Sky Holder is called Sapling (Odendonniha) in creation accounts from the Six Nations Reserve, Ontario, given by John and Joshua Buck (in 1889 and 1897) and by Seth Newhouse (in 1896–97; Hewitt 1974, 188, 301–2). In John Arthur Gibson's magisterial narrative of beginnings (1900, also Six Nations Reserve), Sapling is the first human created by Sky Holder (Hewitt 1974, 531). Later, during the early days of the human race as Gibson describes it, the Creator returns to the earth four times "in the guise of the fatherless boy named Sapling" (Fenton 1998, 46).

of Sky Holder—before Handsome Lake and prior to the great outpouring of written documentation after 1875—is marshaled in this chapter.[3]

Hoping to arrive at a better understanding of the Iroquois's great god, I survey what was said about Sky Holder by those who apparently knew something of the matter prior to the early nineteenth century. The evidence suggests that the acts, qualities, responsibilities, and powers most frequently attributed to the deity in the early sources differ from those described later. Sky Holder changed over time.

Brother Cain, Patron of Crops

Most extant descriptions come from mythological accounts in which Sky Holder plays an important role in Iroquois cosmogony—the great Haudenosaunee story of world beginnings. Such evidence is most complete in the early 1600s for the Hurons and around 1800 for the Iroquois.

The earliest documentation of the mythic twins is a Huron account recorded, in 1636, by Jean de Brébeuf (Thwaites 1896–1901, 10:129–31). According to him, the pregnant daughter of The Woman who fell from the Sky (motif A21.1 in Thompson 1929, 278) or Sky Woman delivered twin boys named Iouskeha—later said to mean "the good one" (Barbeau 1914, 292; Hale 1888, 181)—and Tawiskaron, or Flint. Turtle, the being supporting the earth on her back, taught Iouskeha the art of making fire. Having "some quarrel with each other," the brothers came to blows—Flint ineffectually armed with "some fruits of the wild rosebush"; Iouskeha equipped with the properly lethal "horns of a stag." Iouskeha killed Flint, whose blood was transformed into flint stones. Brébeuf, in company with most writers who would later describe this plot, was struck by its similarity to the biblical tale of Cain murdering his brother Abel.

Flint's role in the narrative remains enigmatic because there seems to be no other reference to him in the Huron literature. There was, however, a fair amount written on the subject of the good twin, Iouskeha:

3. Anthropological study of Iroquoians has not lacked a strong historical bent as witnessed, for example, by Tooker's study (1970) of the Midwinter rite or Fenton's investigation (1998) into confederacy sachem titles. However, the focus of such ethnohistoric research accorded with the goals of ethnographic work: to understand ceremony and rite.

They esteem themselves greatly obliged to [Iouskeha]. . . . without him we would not have so many fine rivers and so many beautiful lakes. In the beginning of the world, they say, the earth was dry and arid; all the waters were collected under the armpit of a large frog, so that Iouskeha could not have a drop except through its agency. One day, he resolved to deliver himself and all his posterity from this servitude; and, in order to attain this, he made an incision under the armpit, whence the waters came forth in such abundance that they spread throughout the whole earth, and hence the origin of rivers, lakes, and seas. . . . They hold also that without Iouskeha their kettles would not boil. . . . Were it not for him, they would not have such good hunting, and would not have so much ease in capturing animals in the chase, as they now have. For they believe that animals were not at liberty from the beginning of the world, but that they were shut up in a great cavern, where Iouskeha guarded them. . . . However, one day he determined to give them liberty in order that they might multiply and fill the forests,—in such a way, nevertheless, that he might easily dispose of them when it should seem good to him. This is what he did to accomplish his end. In the order in which they came from the cave, he wounded them all in the foot with an arrow. . . . [I]t is Iouskeha who gives them the wheat [maize] they eat, it is he who makes it grow and brings it to maturity. If they see their fields verdant in the spring, if they reap good and abundant harvests, and if their cabins are crammed with ears of corn, they owe it to Iouskeha. (Thwaites 1896–1901, 10:135–39)

Evidently, then, the Huron world began with Iouskeha performing a series of acts disposing the environment to yield fish, meat, and domesticated crops. Regarded as a keeper of the game and a patron of agricultural produce, the Huron good twin was thanked for providing food.

In the Iroquois region, a number of references to the male twins and to the good brother exist from the seventeenth and eighteenth centuries. Most, unfortunately, are brief and incomplete.[4]

4. For example, Dablon claimed the Onondaga Iroquois in 1656 regarded the twins as brother and sister but said nothing about a fight or a murder (Thwaites 1896–1901, 42:149).

Dutch cleric Johannes Megapolensis first identified the good twin by his Iroquois (Mohawk) name in about 1644: "Tharonhij–Jagon, that is, God, once went out walking with his brother, and a dispute arose between them, and God killed his brother" (Jameson 1909, 178).

A probable Iroquois (Seneca) account of the 1670s attributed to "un ami de l'abbé de Gallinée" states that Sky Woman became pregnant after a spirit (also from the sky) passed two arrows over her (Margry 1876, 360–62). The lady bore two sons, one unlucky in the chase and the other, his mother's favorite, a successful hunter. The father intervened to help the less favored son, giving the lad maize and revealing how the other brother had penned up the game for his exclusive use. Unfortunately, the narrative breaks off abruptly at this point. It is stated, however, that the brother who benefitted from paternal help later killed a huge serpent. His sibling was changed into a beaver.

Another apparent Iroquois version from the same time was authored by Recollect friar Louis Hennepin. Here again, Sky Woman and a spirit from the sky were parents of twin boys who

could never agree together after they were grown up. One was a better hunter than t'other, and every day there was some scuffling between 'em. At length their animosities grew to that extremity, that they could not endure one another. One of them especially was of a very violent humour, and had a mortal hatred for his brother, who was better temper'd, the last unable any longer to submit to the rude behaviour, and ill treatment which the other bestow'd upon him perpetually, resolved to separate himself from him; so he flew up into heaven. (Thwaites 1903, 452)

Jesuit chronicler Lafitau referred to a story he heard about 1720, probably from the predominantly Mohawk Iroquois of Kahnawake, a Jesuit-supervised reserve near Montreal. Sky Woman "had two children who fought one another. They had unequal arms whose force they did not know. Those of the one were dangerous and the other's could harm no one so that the [latter] was killed without difficulty" (Fenton and Moore 1974, 82). The one who killed the other was named Tharonhiaougen. Comparing the pair to Cain and Abel, Lafitau clearly understood them to be brothers (Fenton and Moore 1974, 83, 168).

About 1740, Pierre Charlevoix, another Jesuit historian, made reference to Sky Woman as the mother of twins, one of whom (Flint) killed the other (Barbeau 1994, 255).

More detailed knowledge of the subject emerges from a trio of Iroquois accounts at the turn of the nineteenth century. John Norton is the source of two (Klinck and Talman 1970, 88–97). The third was provided by James Dean, a fluent speaker of the Oneida tongue (Lounsbury and Gick 2000, 155–62; Tiro 1999).

In all three, Sky Woman's daughter marries a being who visits her only once. On that occasion, the groom places two arrows on or above her, which cause the conception of twin boys named Flint (Thanwiskalaw/Tawiskaron) and Sky Holder (Taulonghyauwangoon/Teharonghyawagon). The arrows, one tipped with flint, the other with bark, determined or prefigured the characters of the brothers: Flint being cruel and malignant, Sky Holder said to be of unbounded goodness and infinite benevolence. The latter is further identified as "the being who in Indian speeches, by a corrupt translation, is called 'the Great Spirit' or 'Good Spirit'" (Lounsbury and Gick 2000, 162; see Boyce 1973, 293).

After debating their means of egress while in the womb, Flint kills his mother by bursting out of her side. Being the more successful hunter, Flint establishes himself as his grandmother's (Sky Woman's) favorite. Sky Holder meets his father (Turtle in two versions; two accounts place the meeting under the sea) and receives the gift of corn from him. The father also warns this son about Flint's hostile intentions, or advises him how to overcome Flint. In two versions, Sky Holder frees game animals Flint had impounded in a cave. When the brothers exchange information about the substances they fear, Sky Holder falsely claims to be vulnerable to some plant material. Flint truthfully admits his banes to be flint stone and horn (or antler) and, in the ensuing struggle, Sky Holder employs those materials to slay him.

These narratives of the twins' rivalry focus on food as both leitmotif and subject. Flint, armed with his father's flint-tipped arrow lethal to forest game, was the successful food provider for a household comprising himself and his grandmother. Much of the twins' story details how Sky Holder achieves food-getting parity after he receives maize from Turtle and frees the game animals imprisoned by Flint. In the final struggle, Flint flails away helplessly with vegetal materials as Sky Holder prevails by applying the substance of the hunt against the hunter (arrowheads were fashioned from antlers and flint).

With Flint the archetypal hunter and Sky Hunter personifying horticulture, the brothers seem to symbolize food-getting pursuits competing for dominance in human life (Long 1963, 192). And, even though both protagonists are male, this allegory of subsistence established the dominance of horticulture over hunting in terms compatible with the Iroquois's gender-based division of labor. Flint practices acts of violence probably considered quintessentially male. Sky Holder, his bark-tipped arrow suggestive of domesticity, is identified with female responsibilities, including planting, tending, weeding, and cooking corn, and with maintaining the brothers' shelter. Bruce Trigger (1969, 92–93) discerns comparable gender associations at work in the Huron creation story. Similarly, Claude Lévi-Strauss (1987, 82) surmises that women, agriculture, and cooked food stand opposed to men, hunting, and raw food in Iroquois mythic thought. In any event and in both the early Huron and later Iroquois accounts, the good twin is responsible for a major portion of the human diet.

Does this finding differ from earlier interpretations? The most inclusive reading of Sky Holder as mythological subject surely would be that of J. N. B. Hewitt (1910, 719), who regarded the good twin as "the symbolic embodiment or personification of all earthly life, floral and faunal. The wise men of the elder time attributed to him the formation or creation and conservation of life and the living things in normal and beneficent bodies and things in terrestrial nature" (1974, 467–68). This notion of Sky Holder as a creative force out of whom fertility, growth, and life emanated was echoed in anthropological writing later in the twentieth century (Fenton 1998, 44).

No one can say that a poetic vision is wholly mistaken. Nevertheless, the Sky Holder described in early accounts was not chiefly a creator figure and not so clearly the font of nature's life energy. Hewitt's view derived partly from later material (the passage quoted is taken from commentary on Gibson's turn-of-the-twentieth-century creation account) and partly from his assumption, common in the late 1800s, that mythology was best understood as "primitive man's" metaphorical description of the natural world.

When we look at all Iroquois-related accounts of twins from 1644 to 1800, general agreement can be discerned on the following points: A fight occurred between twin brothers (according to eight of nine accounts, the only exception being the incomplete Gallinée narrative). One brother killed the other (in seven of nine accounts; the exceptions being the Hennepin version and, again, the incomplete Gallinée). From the earliest Huron version to the latest Iroquois account, one sibling is called Flint and (in six of seven accounts) that name designates the slain brother (only a brief notice by Charlevoix says otherwise). Iroquois accounts that identify the other brother invariably name him as Sky Holder. When the brothers fight, one usually is armed with an ineffective substance, the other with an antler that proves to be lethal. Several Iroquois versions insist that Flint, the malignant brother, impounds the game and enjoys hunting success pleasing to his mother or grandmother. The good brother, Sky Holder, receives assistance from his father that helps him to kill his sibling.

The death of one sibling raises several questions, most obviously—who is left? If an important character drops out, what major gods remain?

Ancient Dualities

Over the course of the seventeenth and eighteenth centuries, Iroquois gods are characterized in two ways. In the first instance, a set of Anglo-Dutch observers make reference to a pair of gods—one good, one evil, both apparently male.

JOHANNES MEGAPOLENSIS, 1644: "They have a *Tharonhijouaagon* . . . that is, a Genius, whom they esteem in the place of God; but they do not serve him or make offerings to him. They worship and present offerings to the Devil, whom they call *Otstkon*, or *Aireskuoni*" (Jameson 1909, 177).

ROBERT LIVINGSTON, 1700: "They own there is a God and a Devil. God is a good man they say, and lives above. Him they love because He never does them any harm. The Devil they fear and are forced to bribe by offerings &c. that he do them no harm" (O'Callaghan 1853–87, 4:652).

GUY JOHNSON, 1775: "They have an idea of a deity who rules, and is the author of all things, as well as of an evil spirit, who is at variance with him and the world, into which he introduced confusion, and that he flew over the face of the earth, rendering it uneven, and forming mountains and vallies, cataracts, rocks, &c., concerning all which they have a variety of stories, which renders it extremely difficult to reduce their mythology to any regular system" (Hamilton 1953, 323).

All three descriptions emphasize an opposition of two gods strongly reminiscent of both a European Christian outlook and of the Iroquois duality holding sway in the nineteenth century: the Great and Evil Spirits, the Creator and the Tormentor (Morgan 1962, 152–64; Parker 1913, 48; Seaver 1990, 146–48). These passages, therefore, may indicate that two brothers were thought, during the 1600–1700s, to rule the world as moralistic high gods. If that is the case, the concept had respectable time depth in Iroquois belief as Tooker and Wallace believed.

However, testimony to that effect is problematic. One difficulty arises out of uncertainty about the identity of the reigning pair. Presumably they are the mythological twins but, if so, one evidently did not die. Only the earliest passage, that of Megapolensis, speaks to this identification by equating the good god with Sky Holder. There is confusion or error woven into this statement, however, because in the next breath, Magapolensis states that the evil being is not Flint as one would expect but rather Otstkon or Aireskuoni. The first of these is surely *otkon,* a word probably meaning "power"—either good or evil (Rudes and Crouse 1987, 199–200n. 20; Wonderley 2004, 122n. 1). The second, a Latin-Huron form of *Agreskwe,* is a word Magapolensis learned not from the Iroquois but from a French guest he entertained (Goddard 1984, 229, 234). I think *Agreskwe* designates a deity or power indistinguishable from Sky Holder. The passages by Livingston and Johnson resist further analysis because they are given baldly without reference to a larger discussion.[5]

---

5. These passages present other analytic difficulties. Since all derive from the same region (vicinity of Albany, New York), for example, it is logically possible that they convey some regionally distinct belief, presumably an otherwise unknown Mohawk viewpoint. For

A second set of descriptions speaks of a different pair of deities—the good twin and his grandmother or mother. This view is expounded in five passages listed below. The first three describe gods of the Hurons, the next two those of the Iroquois.

JOSEPH leCARON, 1615–16: "They commonly believe a kind of creation of the world, saying that heaven, earth, and men were made by a woman, who with her son governs the world; that this son is the principle of all good things, and that this woman is the principle of all evil" (Shea 1881, 216).

GABRIEL SAGARD, 1623–24: "The general belief of our Hurons (although they understand it themselves very imperfectly and speak of it in very different ways) is that the Creator who made the whole world is called Yoscaha . . . and he has also a grandmother named Ataensiq. . . . They say that they live far away. . . . By nature he is very kind, and makes everything grow, and all he does is done well, and he gives us fine weather and everything else good and advantageous. But on the contrary his grandmother is spiteful, and she often spoils all the good her grandson has done" (Wrong 1939, 169–70).

JEAN DE BRÉBEUF, 1636: "They hold that Iouskeha is the Sun and Aataentsic the Moon, and yet that their home is situated at the ends of the earth. . . . Now, although their cabin is so very distant, they are nevertheless both present at the feasts and dances which take place in the villages" (Thwaites 1896–1901, 10:133–35).

JOSEPH FRANÇOIS LAFITAU, CA. 1720: "[The woman the Hurons called Ata-entsic] is the grandmother of Tharonhiaougon, their God . . . but she was quite different from her other grandson, who seeks to do only good; she was of a very evil nature; she subsisted only on the flesh of serpents and vipers; she presided at death; she likewise sucked the blood of men, causing them to die of illness and weakness. She is the Queen of the Shades to whom they must pay the tribute of everything that has been

---

the same reason, it is also theoretically possible that the three reflect the same authorial tradition in which writers after Megapolensis drew on an earlier description.

buried with their bodies; and she forces them to divert her by dancing before her" (Fenton and Moore 1974, 168).

JAMES DEAN, 1815: "[The grandmother] has ever since been employed in gratifying her malignant disposition by inflicting upon mankind all those evils which are suffered in the present world. Taulonghyauwangoon, on the other hand displays the infinite benevolence of his nature by bestowing on the human race the blessings they enjoy, all of which flow from his bountiful providence" (Lounsbury and Gick 2000, 162).

In all of these passages, a malicious older woman (Sky Woman, almost always named as grandmother) is contrasted to a kindly disposed younger man (Iouskeha/Sky Holder, the good twin and, almost always, Sky Woman's grandson). Dean's account identifies precisely the same pair who reigned supreme among Lafitau's Iroquois a century earlier and among the Hurons a hundred years before that. It is a pattern that must predate European presence because LaCaron and Sagard documented its existence before Christianity could have influenced Huron thinking.

Apparently independent sources, then, attest to a dyad of gods comprising a malicious grandmother and a compassionate grandson—a widespread mythic tradition of considerable antiquity. It would be foolish to assume (as Megapolensis, Livingston, and Johnson remind us) that the same two gods dominated Iroquoian theology everywhere. Yet, so far as it goes, the documentary evidence on this point is unequivocal. The evil grandmother and her good grandson were powerful beings of opposite disposition who intervened in mortal affairs. They, after all, were the ones who lived on after Flint's death.

This finding differs from that of researchers who hold that Handsome Lake's reforms of the nineteenth century gave new purpose to Haudenosaunee religion but did not fundamentally transform ancient beliefs about the twin brothers. Both Tooker (1970, 3) and Wallace (1972) saw in the duality of Sky Holder and Flint the traditional core features of the old retained in the new. Handsome Lake, Wallace argued, did not introduce a radically new religion. He merely endorsed the old.

He fully supported the ancient calendar of ceremonies, and his pantheon was isomorphic with the old, for the Creator of Handsome Lake's revelation was simply the ancient culture-hero Tarachiawagon . . . the Punisher was but Tawiskaran, the culture-hero's Evil Twin. . . . . These deities were, of course, now revealed to have unsuspected powers and sentiments, but the revelation of these qualities and desires and the propriety of using new names in reference to old divinities was not upsetting to a people who were prepared for such progressive revelation by the customary usages of name change and by their theory of dreams. The idea of a cosmic struggle between the Good Twin and the Evil Twin had in the old mythology been relegated to the origin myth. Now it was made a salient issue in contemporary life, with the two beings contesting for power over the minds of men on earth and ruling the dead in heaven and hell. The principal cosmological innovation was, in fact, the notion of heaven and hell itself. This had not hitherto been a general belief. (Wallace 1972, 251–52)

The evidence of the 1600s–1700s suggests the nineteenth-century change in the concept of Sky Holder was a far more comprehensive overhaul than believed. In the early 1800s, cosmogonic ideas were reconfigured to emphasize the importance of Sky Holder and Flint rather than Sky Holder and the grandmother. The more ancient polarity of good-versus-evil, in other words, now comprised twin brothers and, as the new central duality, their competition was redefined as a struggle over creation. Once rivals over food and food-getting, the twins of the 1800s competed to fashion an earthly setting customized for people. Further, what took place between these two came to be seen as explaining the world, offering moral guidance, and warning of postmortal consequence (Wonderley 2001; 2004, 71–72).

God of War

Next in importance to being patron of crops, Sky Holder was consistently invoked as a war god, the divinity who championed his people in conflict and who dispensed good fortune in battle. In 1799, Thauloonghyauwangoo or "Upholder of the Skies or Heavens," was implored by an Oneida to continue his guardianship, to grant a plentiful harvest, and to inspire Iroquois warriors "to drive the enemy from our country with shame and loss" (Pilkington 1980, 367). It was Sky Holder who spoke these words through the dream of a young Onondaga in 1656: "I preserve men, and give victories to warriors. I have made you masters of the earth and victors over so many nations" (Thwaites 1896–1901, 42:197). Sky Holder's voice, issuing from an Oneida kettle in 1670, prophesied victory over the Susquehannocks (53:253). In 1801, an Iroquois god of war whose name meant "holding the heavens" was also said to preside over the affairs of men (Boyce 1973, 293).

However, the sun, the Huron-Iroquois deity Agreskwe, and the Huron divinity Ondoutaeté also were identified as gods of war (Goddard 1984; Hewitt 1974, 468; Richter 1992, 115, 303–4n. 12; Tooker 1970, 87). How could there have been so many gods doing the same thing?

The Huron word *Ondoutaeté,* meaning "one who bears the reed mat of war" or war bundle, was used in reference "to a leader who threw a feast of war and then led a raiding party" (Steckley 1992, 486). However, Jesuit priests (that is, the people who documented this as the name of the war god) used that same word to characterize Jesus as a holy warrior in their sermons to the Hurons (Steckley 1992, 485). *Ondoutaeté,* therefore, does not constitute strong evidence for the existence of a distinct and specialized god. It might, however, illustrate an Iroquoian propensity to apply multiple euphemistic titles to the same referent.

More frequently mentioned than Ondoutaeté was Agreskwe, a deity cited in both Huron and Iroquois contexts. While the derivation of this name remains uncertain, almost all usages of it derive from a small circle of Jesuit writers who seem to say much the same things about Agreskwe and Sky Holder—but never at the same time.[6] Thus, the Onondaga leader Garakontié rejects dream feasts that are said to be identified with Sky Holder in 1671. The next year, dream feasts are still being held for Garakontié

6. Hewitt (1910, 719) translated Agreskwe as "the reason or cause for absence." Tooker (1970, 86–87) thought the word might mean "spirits." According to linguist Ives Goddard (1984, 234), the morphology of the name is unclear. The names Sky Holder and Agreskwe do not appear together in Jesuit writings of the 1600s although they do show up in the account by Dutch pastor Megapolensis quoted in this article. Megapolensis's knowledge about Agreskwe derived from Isaac Jogues, a French Jesuit whom Megapolensis assisted in escaping from Mohawk captivity in 1643 (Goddard 1984, 234). The Dutch text, therefore, is the exception that proves the rule.

although now they are associated with Agreskwe (Thwaites 1896–1901, 55:61–63, 57:157).

Further, Agreskwe is not solely a god of war. He is also Master of Life and god of dreams (Thwaites 1896–1901, 53:225, 58:205). He is an all-purpose deity properly invoked in a variety of contexts, a god for whom different kinds of offering are appropriate (53:265–67, 281, 295; 57:97, 147). All are exactly and more clearly the characteristics of Sky Holder.

Mutually exclusive appearance of the two names defined in the same fashion is not the pattern one would expect of two distinct supernaturals. On the contrary, it suggests the two terms designate the same being and are better regarded as different attributes or forms of address. Just as the Hurons applied different names to the soul "depending on the function which was being alluded to at the moment" (Wallace 1958, 237), so different epithets and titles have been "mistaken for names of distinct divinities" (Hale 1891, 293). That is how Lafitau understood the matter in the early 1700s: Agreskwe and Sky Holder were one and the same (Fenton and Moore 1974, 106).

Lafitau also said the god of war was the sun and the sun was Agreskwe (Fenton and Moore 1974, 148; 1977, 111).[7] Here again, the names of all these beings were applied to what might be the same deity (Abler and Logan 1988, 9). Thus, a Frenchman among the Oneidas in the early 1660s

---

7. The fact that Lafitau identified the sun with Agreskwe and Sky Holder is taken by Goddard to mean that Agreskwe was *not* the sun or Sky Holder. The Jesuit, according to Goddard (1984, 232–33), was so heavily biased by a desire to find sun worship ("universal heliolatry") everywhere that his first-hand, ethnographic testimony is untrustworthy. By the terms of this view, we would have to dismiss much—probably most—documentary evidence about native peoples in the Northeast. Goddard also argues for the distinct status of Agreskwe on the basis of passages that mention a war god *and* other deities. In one instance (1636), Hurons were exhorted to torture a prisoner because the act would be viewed "by the Sun and by the God of war" (Thwaites 1896–1901, 13:61). In another (1648), Hurons are said to invoke the deity Agreskwe called, in war, Ondoutaeté. Further, "they address themselves to the Sky" and "call upon the Sun to be witness of their courage, of their misery, or of their innocence" (Thwaites 1896–1901, 33:225). For Goddard (1984, 231–32), these statements attest to a "clear distinction" between or among the named entities. I would say the passages are susceptible to other interpretations.

claimed that his hosts did "not recognize any other God than the Sun, and it is to that they address themselves in all their needs, as much for war as for the hunt" (Brandão 2003, 57). Yet, among the same Oneidas in 1670, the great god was named Sky Holder. Three years later, the Oneida divinity was Agreskwe (Thwaites 1896–1901, 53:253, 58:205). The sun, in other words, was contextually synonymous with both Agreskwe and Sky Holder. The most parsimonious explanation is that the terms made reference to the same entity.

Whatever the status of Agreskwe and the sun may prove to be, Sky Holder's associations with war were clear and durable. By the end of the eighteenth century and when Agreskwe was no longer being mentioned, Sky Holder was still invoked as the major patron of war:

"Do you, our Great Captain [Sky Holder], march in front of our warriors, that . . . they may always conquer their enemies." (Pilkington 1980:367)

They say Teharonghyawago always assisted them in their wars, when they were undertaken with just cause; and many anecdotes are related of his being present in the battles they fought, spreading dismay through the ranks of the enemy, by his gigantic appearance, and by the havoc he made; also in attracting their notice, by his lofty stature, to cause them to aim their arrows at him, whom they could not wound, and thereby to overshoot the warriors of his favorite host. (Klinck and Talman 1970, 91)

Sky Holder, therefore, was not merely or only a deity with war associations (Tooker 1970, 87). He was *the* "national god of war" (Blau 1964, 110).

Summary and Discussion

Sky Holder was the great god of the Iroquois during the seventeenth and eighteenth centuries. Apparently, he was the principal deity of all the confederated nations (Mohawk, Oneida, Onondaga, Cayuga, Seneca). Although he appears to have been a protean divinity and all-purpose culture-hero, the early sources emphasize certain of his functions or characteristics.

As a key mythological figure in Iroquoian cosmogony, Sky Holder was one of a pair of brothers of opposite disposition. Several accounts indicate that his evil-natured sibling, Flint, penned up the game animals and enjoyed hunting success appreciated by the boys' mother or grandmother. Sky Holder, the good twin, received help from his father prior to a showdown with his brother. The fraternal rivalry culminated in mortal combat in which Flint was equipped only with a useless weapon while Sky Holder went at it armed with an antler. Sky Holder prevailed and Flint was killed.

The competition between these brothers referenced or symbolized food in several ways. The elimination of one sibling by the other elegantly explains—in mythological terms—the dominance of agriculture over hunting in Iroquois life. The early sources do not describe the rivalry as a creative struggle resulting in a human-friendly environment or in the appearance of human beings.

Sky Holder continued to preside over mortal affairs in opposition to a counterpart exerting a baneful influence on human life. The wicked half of this duality could have been Flint as was asserted later in the nineteenth century. More clearly from the evidence and more logically in view of Flint's death, it was the grandmother—the woman who fell from the sky.

The early sources often associate Sky Holder with victory in battle. His name seems to have been synonymous with warlike deities the European chroniclers, especially French Jesuits, called Agreskwe, and the sun. Certainly Sky Holder himself was a god of war.

5

The Story of Windigo

AS AN ANTHROPOLOGY STUDENT during the 1960s, I was taught that windigos were mythical cannibal giants known to Algonquian speakers (Cree, Ojibwa-Chippewa, various Algonquin bands, Montagnais-Naskapi) from Saskatchewan to Quebec. Embodying cold and the far north, these beings were said to be reflections of their boreal forest setting. Algonquian people who believed in windigos, I also learned, were subject to a mental disorder called "windigo psychosis" in which the sufferer craved human flesh as food and believed he or she was becoming a windigo giant. This was caused partly by the prospect of starvation, an ever-present possibility for people living in small groups and dependent on hunting success over the course of long winters. That only these people suffered from the illness—and not their neighbors living in similar subarctic conditions—was because Algonquians held distinctive beliefs and values disposing them to think that way.

While undergraduates were taking in this sort of thing, their teachers were beginning to wonder about it to judge by an upsurge in windigo research at that time. From the 1970s through early 1980s, the topic became something of an academic boom industry devoted to reexamining the windigo disorder from a variety of perspectives.

Those favoring psychological explanation included Raymond Fogelson (1965), who offered a typology of supposedly distinct forms of windigo illness—each a behavioral syndrome diagrammed with boxes and arrows characteristic of systems analysis. Thomas Hay (1971) proposed that the psychosis existed in the absence of cultural institutions that, elsewhere, channel or displace cannibalistic urges. Anthony Paredes (1972) argued the disorder was best understood through study of an individual's dreams and life history.

Others pursued a more materialist tack. A nutritional cause—seasonal vitamin deficiency—was debated (Rohrl 1970; Brown 1971). An environmental cause—increasing frequency of starvation due to post-European game depletion—was examined (Bishop 1975; Waisberg 1975; J. Smith 1976).

The comparative framework was enlarged when Robin Ridington (1976) documented the existence of erratic behavior linked to belief in a cannibalistic monster among non-Algonquian people. Fogelson (1980) demonstrated that belief in a cannibal monster was far more widespread than the distribution of Algonquian speakers.

And, there seemed to be increasing interest in oral narratives about windigos (McGee 1972). Assuming that cannibalism was a metaphor for a group's recruitment policies, D. H. Turner (1977) interpreted a western Cree story to be a parable of social structure. Two researchers argued that a story about a cannibal giant defined what was culturally and ethically human (McGee 1975; Morrison 1979). Curiously, both interpreted the same story, a narrative from the Miqmaq of New Brunswick—far beyond the land of windigo psychosis as traditionally charted and in a place cannibal giants were not called *windigos*.

Then, seemingly discouraged, the inquiry turned negative. According to Richard Preston (1978, 1980), meager data on the subject had been overwhelmed by interpretive schemes more indicative of anthropological than Algonquian thinking. Lou Marano (1982) claimed the subject itself was nonexistent. Windigo psychosis was simply the Algonquians' rationalization for killing marginal people under stressful conditions. Credulous anthropologists had bought the lie and, from it, spun their own fabrication, placing the onus on the victim, not the executioner.

There it seemed to end although, several years later, Jennifer Brown and Robert Brightman (1988) made available important new historical evidence. Further, Brightman (1988) demonstrated that windigo illness did indeed exist as a culturally specific disorder. Regina Flannery, who had spanned the anthropology of windigoism from its inception in the 1930s through the interpretive malaise of the 1980s, said much the same thing. At the turn of the twentieth century, native people certainly had a well-developed sense of the "windigo complex"—that is, belief in windigo beings of both human and nonhuman form coupled with ideas and stories about people "going windigo" (Flannery et al. 1981). Even with the reality of a windigo disorder apparently reaffirmed (and rehabilitated?), however, the subject was played out. It ceased to be a frontline intellectual pursuit featured in peer-reviewed publications.[1]

Elegiac in tone, much of this literature conveys regret that windigo is a thing of the past. Acts of windigo cannibalism and execution, most agreed, had ceased by the early twentieth century. Such behavior was strongly discouraged by increasing Christian presence and the imposition of state-administered court and police. Then too, this aspect of windigoism faded with the cessation of the itinerant round of winter subsistence in which isolated groups routinely experienced hunger (Brightman 1988, 374; Flannery et al. 1981, 59; Guinard 1930, 70; Marano 1982, 392–93; Teicher 1960, 107).

Anthropologists also reported that the windigo cannibal giant had receded from consciousness. Fieldwork of the 1970s among both Cree and Ojibwa groups uncovered only vague notions about the mythic creature who was "always far away and long ago" (Smith, in Marano 1982, 404; Preston 1978, 1980). In 1943, Horace Beck (1947, 261) was told that the windigo was seldom seen, having withdrawn to the north. Some three decades later, James Smith (1976, 25–27) learned that the last windigo had been run over by a train in 1962. The windigo of these fieldworkers was a historical subject accessible through older documentation preserved chiefly in folklore and myth.

Indeed, windigos were supposed to have been a major topic of Algonquian folklore, and virtually everyone agreed that knowledge about windigos expressed in tales and myths would be crucial to understanding the windigo complex.

I was surprised to learn, therefore, that the scholarly literature (with the limited exceptions noted above) all but ignored oral narrative about windigos.

1. The only subsequent publication I found pertaining to windigos is Carolyn Podruchny's study (2004) of folktales told by French Canadian voyageurs. Her argument is that the voyageurs, in the course of close association with native people, took up windigo stories because they found them consistent with their own notions of werewolves and witchcraft. Podruchny apparently documents one of the few instances of Native American folklore influencing European-derived folklore.

Like the weather, everybody talked about windigo stories but no one ever did anything about them. This chapter is my attempt to answer the seemingly simple question: What do the older stories actually *say* about windigo?[2]

A History of Windigo Giants and Psychosis Through 1960

Algonquians sought to acquire information from supernatural beings and believed that what one learned from them (through dreams and visions) inevitably would come to pass. Strong faith in this form of predestination lay at the heart of the Algonquian world view, according to Brightman's interpretation (1988), and it resulted in a fundamentally fatalistic attitude toward life. Since fatalism and predestination seem a heavy burden to lay on others, I will pause for a moment to illustrate why Brightman (and others) would offer such a characterization.

In one of the few "native" descriptions of windigo disorder dating to the early twentieth century, Cree author Edward Ahenakew, quoting a Cree informant, stated that a person goes windigo by offending a spirit power or by having had the bad luck to be sponsored (possessed) by an evil guardian spirit. Most of all, however, the condition arose from having been bewitched by an enemy, an action that counteracted success in hunting. To an isolated family in the winter bush, the result was starvation:

> As days of fasting go by, hope dies and despair takes its place. A time comes when one of the party begins to look longingly though slyly at another. This person is being tempted to kill, so as to eat. It becomes an obsession with him or her. At last—chance offering, it happens. The person kills and soon he (or she) is eating. He has passed from being a human being to beastliness.
>
> The rest of the family realizes that they have a Wetikoo to cope with. All that they have heard about such monsters comes into their minds. A

2. My topic is not, therefore, windigo stories of the present or recent past (for example, Norman 1982). Nor does it address the degree to which windigo stories documented in, say, 1900 and 2000 resemble one another. Useful reviews of the historical evidence pertaining to the windigo complex can be found in Bishop 1975, Brightman 1988, Fogelson 1965, J. Smith 1976, and Wallis and Wallis 1955. For the anthropological history of windigos, see Bishop 1975, Fogelson 1965, Marano 1982, and Preston 1980.

great dread overwhelms them, the marrow inside the bones seems to melt and they have no power to move or fight. While they might have met ordinary dangers bravely, they were as frightened children in the presence of a powerful inhuman monster. They give in and very soon share the fate of the first victim. (Ahenakew, in Preston 1980, 123)

This does sound fatalistic, and Brightman argues that convictions about predestination and windigos were inculcated from earliest childhood, then reinforced through social acts and activities during a person's lifetime. Beliefs held in common comprised the common lens through which Algonquian people interpreted the reality of the windigo disorder. Since the windigo complex was a cultural phenomenon (he does not use the word *culture* to describe the socially transmitted beliefs and practices characteristic of a human group), it is explicable only in cultural terms. Brightman's view, it seems to me, has much in common with anthropological perspectives on the subject as they existed up to the 1960s.

The earliest and most informative account of windigos and windigo psychosis was penned in 1823 by a knowledgeable fur trader named George Nelson. Most of his observations concerned the Lac la Ronge Cree of Saskatchewan, but he also related experiences with Northern Ojibwa (Saulteaux) people in Manitoba. Nelson described windigo sickness as "a sort of mania, or fever, a distemper of the brain" specific to the people he knew. Those who suffered from it became wild and glassy-eyed in appearance and began to crave human flesh. Over time, their hearts turned to ice as they became transformed into ghoulish giants. Such people "are generally rational except at short, sudden intervals when the paroxysms [seize] them: their motions then are various and diametrically contrary at one time to what they are the next—Sullen, thoughtful, wild look and perfectly mute: staring, in sudden convulsions, wild incoherent and extravagant language" (Brown and Brightman 1988, 91). When these windigos were killed, their bodies were burned to put an end to the windigos' icy hearts.

Nelson also emphasized that people suffering from windigo sickness were treated kindly and assisted through their illnesses with substances such as alcohol, which supplied warmth to counteract the coldness of a windigo's heart. Normally, windigo people would regain their senses when warm weather came. Nelson was personally familiar with the case of a young woman who "was this winter seized with the frenzy. The consequence was that the men durst not leave the tent for any length of time, being obliged to assist the women in holding and preventing her from biting or eating any of the children, and perhaps herself. . . . She recovered and is now well." Her memory of the affair was that a giant windigo had taken possession of her, and she could recall being of giant size and form (Brown and Brightman 1988, 93–94).

Windigo sickness could be induced by famine. It might result from dreaming about the spirits of ice and the north—being stuck, that is, with the wrong guardian spirits. It could be inflicted on a person by outside spiritual forces as punishment for having ridiculed ceremonies. Perhaps most importantly, it resulted from having one's spirit taken over (as happened to the woman mentioned above) by a fierce cannibal giant of the north (Brown and Brightman 1988, 85–86, 88, 90–91, 94).

This kind of giant went by the name *windigo,* which Nelson understood to be "the proper signification" of that word. These nonhuman ghouls inspired both "unaccountable horror" and "extravagant and fantastic" stories. Tales about this windigo were "as devoutly believed by these poor creatures as the Gospel is by the most orthodox among us" (Brown and Brightman 1988, 85–86). Nelson recounted only one of them.

The oldest recorded tale occurred "in the days of Noah" when people were preyed upon by giant windigos. Hoping to deal with their enemies, the humans built an enormous deadfall capable of trapping a windigo, its bait an elderly woman volunteer. When a windigo arrived, the woman said, "Ah! My Grand Child!" When the windigo reached in for her, she triggered the weight of the trap that then fell on the brute. Pinned to the ground, the windigo was dispatched by men armed with axes and chisels. The people then "enjoyed themselves as usual without further apprehensions" (Brown and Brightman 1988, 86–87).

Nelson apparently was the first to define human and nonhuman forms of windigo. Those who have researched earlier records left by fur traders of the Hudson's Bay firm have found that the word *windigo* may have designated a single malevolent deity, apparently similar to the Christian devil, during the eighteenth century (Fogelson 1965, 76–78). It is possible, therefore, that a belief in windigos as giant monsters is a recent development (Brown and Brightman 1988, 160–61).

Nelson's dichotomy of human and nonhuman windigos was confirmed by others including the traveler Johann Georg Kohl in 1855. Kohl reported that the word *windigo* among the Chippewa of Wisconsin was "nearly synonymous" with cannibal. Under harsh conditions and suffering from starvation, people occasionally ate human flesh. And, because of strong cultural predispositions expressed in stories, these unfortunate souls were regarded (and regarded themselves) as windigos. "It is very natural," Kohl concluded, "that in a country which really produces isolated instances of such horrors, and which a nation so devoted to fancies and dreams, superstition should be mixed up in the matter, and that at last, through this superstition, wonderful stories of windigos should be produced, as among us, in the middle ages, the belief in witches produced witches" (Kohl 1985, 356–57).

Like Nelson, however, Kohl emphasized that the word *windigo* was "much more frequently used with reference to the giant race of cannibals known by the name, than to the monsters now having their being among us. Stories are told of these old fabulous windigos which are quite as amusing to listen to as our 'Hop-o'-my-thumb'" (Kohl 1985, 365).

Windigo giants became familiar to a large reading public in the early twentieth century through a celebrated short story called "The Wendigo," published in 1910 by Algernon Blackwood. Blackwood's interest was in literary effect, in trying to convey a feeling of horror through the written word. Nevertheless, his subject was based on first-hand acquaintance with native lore in Minnesota and Ontario, and the resulting story remains true to that tradition. Blackwood's Wendigo is a giant supernatural being who takes physical and spiritual possession of a person. "When an Indian goes crazy," one of the nonnative characters is made to say, "it's always put that he's 'seen the Wendigo'" (Blackwood 1964, 291).

Windigo stories (about both the human and giant sorts) also became part of the anthropological literature in the form of ethnographically collected folklore (for example, Davidson 1928b; Guinard 1930; Michelson 1917, 1919; Skinner 1911; Speck 1925). In 1933, an issue of Catholic University's ethnological journal, *Primitive Man,* contained two articles introducing the topic of windigo as a psychological disorder into the anthropological arena.

In the first, J. E. Saindon (1933, 11) mentioned a case of "windigo sickness" in which a woman visualized people around her as animals she wanted to kill. In the second, John M. Cooper (1933, 20) coined the term *Witiko psychosis,* defining it as a craving for human flesh accompanied by the "delusion of transformation into a Witiko who has a heart of ice or who vomits ice." The cannibalistic tendencies resulted from famine conditions during the winter that, in turn, found expression in the windigo concept. Epitomizing hunger and winter, the cannibal giant was the subject of numerous stories. The idea of becoming a windigo giant "seems to be derived indirectly, through the Witiko folk-lore concept, from the same [environmental and social] conditions" (1933, 24).

Well posted on the larger ethnological picture, Cooper (1933, 25) observed that the Cree windigo was "obviously identical" with the mythological figure called Chenoo by the Miqmaq in Labrador. Thus, he perceived a common and continuously distributed windigo concept among Algonquian speakers stretching from Saskatchewan to the Atlantic.

A. Irving Hallowell (1934, 1967) discussed windigo sickness as the result of commonly held assumptions and fears (about windigos and witches) channeling everyone's perception of reality toward the same conclusion. Hallowell was not interested in oral narrative. However, since he, like Cooper, linked windigo illness to belief in a windigo monster, one would suppose that stories about windigo monsters could play an important role in understanding the windigo complex of beliefs.

For Ruth Landes (1938), human windigos comprised a category of deviant personality in which certain people, tormented by a desire to eat human flesh, go insane (become windigo) during the winter. A person goes windigo because of or through starvation, as a victim of witchcraft, or "from visitation of a windigo spirit" as occurs when one dreams of the monster or accepts it as one's guardian spirit. Yet again, it is emphasized that *windigo* refers chiefly to the giant cannibal being of myths.

Landes argued that the Ojibwas project their fear of starvation onto this concept and, possibly as a consequence of such projection, personify the windigo as starvation and winter. Further, windigos frequently were killed in fantasy, that is, in the palliative action of storytelling. Hence, the term *windigo* reflected several mental operations (projection, symbolism, displacement), all of which, presumably, would privilege myths and stories as important sources of information.

By the 1950s, windigo psychosis was firmly established in the anthropological literature as a mental sickness peculiar to Cree and Ojibwa peoples across a wide swath of Canada and the adjacent United States. A sufferer felt compelled to eat human flesh and, having done so, turned into or became possessed by a windigo—a ferocious ogre about which many stories were told (Honigman 1953, 329–30; Teicher 1960, 1, 5–6).

In 1960, Seymour Parker introduced a culture-and-personality reading of windigo psychosis that assumed the illness mostly afflicted Algonquian men troubled by the conditioning pressures of childhood. Algonquian boys supposedly experienced the abrupt withdrawal of food and love when they were encouraged to seek visions that would provide them with spiritual power and supernatural protection. This traumatic loss of affection resulted in a society of paranoid men feeling defensive, helpless, and dependent on supernatural powers. Given this litany of personality defects, a lack of success in hunting was likely to provoke

> anxiety, not only because it threatens starvation, but also because it is loaded with the dangers of a drastic loss of self-esteem. Failure in hunting not only means that "I have no food," but also that "I have lost my power," "I am empty and worthless." To the objective fear of starvation is added the powerful anxiety of ego obliteration. It has been mentioned that a failure of supernatural power indicates that "someone is practicing evil magic against me." This belief illustrates that supernatural rejection is the psychological equivalent of being rejected by significant others in the social environment. It is a dramatic and ultimate frustration of dependency needs. (S. Parker 1960, 618)

An Algonquian man went crazy under such stress because of unsatisfied cravings caused by his mother, for it was she who had curtailed food and nurturing early on. In the mind of the resentful sufferer, the maternal figure became identified with the wicked windigo of oral narrative.

Evidence for this assertion was to be found in Algonquian folklore. Arguing that myths (I would say oral narrative generally or folklore) were useful as a projective device for understanding attitudes and emotions, Parker studied several stories about rolling heads, mistreated orphans, and a boy who demands his father obtain summer for him. From such material, he concluded that an Algonquian male viewed his mother "as both the main nurturent [sic] and the outstanding persecutory figure. It is toward her that the child directs his eating and his sexual phantasies. At the same time, it is she (or older women) who wants to kill and eat the child" (Parker 1960, 615).

Having emphasized the importance of oral narrative as a data source for analyzing windigo psychosis, Parker failed to consider a single story about windigos. It remained for Morton Teicher (1960) to compile those stories as well as testimony on the subject of windigo sickness. For the latter, he pulled together seventy accounts of the malady from the reminiscences of Euro-American traders and travelers, from ethnological reportage, and from miscellaneous historical and legal sources. As for the folktales, Teicher reprinted thirty-one texts from predominantly ethnological works of the early twentieth century,[3] a selection comprising "only those stories which add to our understanding of the windigo concept" (1960, 17). Almost all derived from Ontario and Manitoba sources employing some form of the word *windigo*. Teicher acknowledged, however, that the Cree-Ojibwa windigo, found further east, was known by other names (1960, 2).

It was important to include both the fictional and the factual because the former, as folktales, occupied "a dominant position in the folklore of the northeast" and comprised a rich source of information about the culture.

3. Teicher presented thirty-one texts in his section of Algonquian oral narrative. Two, however, are not folktales (1960, 39, 42–43). In one, anthropologist Horace Beck refers to a conversation with an Algonquian informant who told him windigos can assume the appearance of logs. The informant is quoted as remembering that he once shot at a log that then ran away. Offered as personal experience, the anecdote is what used to be called a *memorate* (Dundes 1965, 220). In any event, it is not, strictly speaking, folklore. Nor is the other in which a European traveler reports a meeting with an Indian who muttered darkly about windigo. Discounting these two texts, my sample from Teicher consists of twenty-nine stories.

The stories reflected the tellers' reality and values, and especially their concern with getting food in a harsh environment (Teicher 1960, 12, 107).

The conclusion to Teicher's study is that Algonquians were interpreting erratic behavior and starvation cannibalism through oral narrative. The windigo belief

> was embellished by fearsome stories until the belief became a fact of life. It entered the mainstream of the belief system to the point where it was traditional and dominant. It stood as the unquestioned and widely held concept, occupying a foremost position in the belief system of every individual who shared the culture. As a fundamental cultural generalization, the Windigo belief provided a basis for ready deductions leading to action. Thus, it may truly be said that the Windigo concept determined behavior. (Teicher 1960, 110)

Having begun with the idea that stories reflect culture, Teicher arrived at the position that stories determine and shape culture. From whatever direction one approaches the causality of the matter, the stories and myths mentioning the subject are essential cultural data. What, therefore, are the stories about? The astonishing fact is that Teicher says nothing about their contents.

Sample and Method

Any survey of windigo stories must take into account the twenty-nine folktales assembled by Teicher as the canon, the work common to all researchers after 1960. To this core sample, I added six stories from Barnouw (1977) and fifteen from Flannery et al. (1981) to arrive at a total of fifty, all of nineteenth- or early-twentieth-century date. The two newer sources greatly expand Teicher's geographical coverage to include Wisconsin and the region east of James Bay in Quebec. Further, they provide some comments about the contexts and meanings of the narratives.

The stories under consideration are not historical accounts describing what people said they personally experienced or saw. They do not explain the assumptions once held in common by tellers and listeners alike. They convey virtually nothing about linguistic complexity, verbal performance, or social setting. Further, Barnouw (1997) and Flannery et al. (1981) notwithstanding, the majority come without "emic" classification. That is, we do not know what narrative genres or distinctions were recognized by the storytellers (for example, tales set in primeval times as opposed to those occurring in the recent past).

The data are brief written texts in English, each presenting a sequence of incidents. Accordingly, the plot or story line is the appropriate unit of study. After outlining each tale, I characterized its apparent point or theme.[4] This exercise resulted in fourteen kinds of stories, most of which seem regionally clustered. The content of each story type, lettered A–N, is summarized in the following discussion.

I then went pattern-hunting at a higher level, seeking commonalities among groups of story types. I arrived, inductively, at three larger orders into which 90 percent of the stories can be grouped: those visualizing windigos as powerful supernaturals in a world lacking referents to familiar space and time (Category One), those emphasizing a human's personal power and the ability it confers to assume the form of a windigo (Category Two), and those ascribing humanlike behavior to windigos operating in the familiar world (Category Three). Transcending regional preferences for certain plots, these broadly distributed ideas about windgo storytelling illuminate what is common to nearly all the Algonquian sources. The story types are discussed within the framework of these higher-order, more-inclusive categories.

The stories of all three groups are constructed out of the same fundamental premises: windigos are evil, windigos must be killed. They are related, in other words, by strong, underlying opinions as to what constitutes a proper windigo story. I conclude that all three categories are best visualized not as distinctly bounded entities but as emphases of storytelling situated on the same continuum. A logic of bodily transformation links them together.

Four stories, discussed as story types M and N, convey ideas about windigos incompatible with those of the other forty-six. A good definition tells not only what a thing is but what is not. I regard these four tales as

4. I will provide synopses of the fifty stories at the request of anyone interested.

anomalies that, through contrast, throw light on the character of the other windigo stories.

I mentioned above that most of this sample lacks emic or insider context. There is, however, one aspect of native interpretation inherent in many of the narratives: the moral ("therefore, people don't eat each other anymore") or etiological point ("that's why weasels look as they do") that closes about a third of these tales.

These do not figure importantly in my treatment because most are poor characterizations of the preceding plot. Some endings seem irrelevant to the narrative. A windigo story having nothing to do with relations between humans and buffaloes, for example, concludes with the sentiment: So instead of eating people, buffaloes will now be eaten by people (Barnouw 1977, 124–25). Other conclusions are contradictory. That's why there are no windigos now, says one (Teicher 1960, 24). That's why there are so many windigos now, says another (Flannery et al. 1981, 60). The essentially arbitrary character of such concluding statements has long been remarked (Ramsey 1983, 92–93; Thompson 1929, xvii; Waterman 1914). Some students of Native American folklore regard the "faux moral" as nothing more than a terminal marker, a literary coda, or a stylistic embellishment (Boas 1914, 401, 405–6; Dundes 1967, 65).

The Stories

Category One: Windigos in Narrative Space

A. Windigo Killed by Supernatural (n=2)

Both stories in this group derive from Wisconsin Chippewa informants. In one, the baby of human parents reveals himself to be a supernatural capable of speech. Whether he is a human transformed into a windigo or a windigo who takes over the baby's being (or manages to become born as a human)—we are not told. In any event, he turns into a giant windigo who attacks a nearby manito (also commonly written as *manido* and *manitou*—a spiritually powerful presence) for no apparent reason. The windigo is killed by the manito's praetorian guard of fifty dwarfs. When his icy body is burned, the figure of a tiny infant is revealed (Barnouw 1977, 123).

The other is a hero tale set in the timeless world of myth. The protagonist is a person with extraordinary power who can kill a giant windigo with impunity and cause a mountain to exist over his home.[5] Windigos in this story are beings separate from and apparently unrelated to humans (Barnouw 1977, 124–25).

B. People Protected from Windigo by Supernatural Guardian (n=4)

What appears to be the same story was documented three times among different bands of Ontario Ojibwa (Michelson 1919, 171–75; Teicher 1960, 18–19, 25). One or more persons arrive at a distant land after a journey across a body of water. Two giants live in that country, one of them a kindhearted soul unnamed or called "Me Sah ba," the other a windigo. After protecting the human visitor(s) from the evil-minded neighbor, the kindly giant and his dog (two versions) get the visitor(s) home safely.

In a fourth story of Ontario Ojibwa origin (Teicher 1960, 33), Misabe watches over Indians in this world, notably by slaying a windigo determined to "kill and eat Indians." The name given in two of the tales is variously identified as the younger brother of Manibozho/Wesakaychak (the principal creator/culture hero of Algonquian mythology), a word said to mean "giant," "great man," or "spirit guardian" (Brown and Brightman 1988, 113, 126, 155; Davidson 1928a, 275; Marano 1982, 392).

C. Windigo Placeholder

This theme comprises well-known and widely distributed narratives in which a windigo's presence seems arbitrary, little more than a guest appearance in a slot that could as easily be filled by another character or device. In most, windigo is the villain doing something that any other stock monster (a rolling head, say) could perform as well. In all, windigo is a fierce giant, and the action occurs in purely narrative space or mythic setting. Generally, the windigo's nonhuman nature is clear.

Manibozho and the Windigo (n=3). Three examples derive from Ojibwas in Minnesota and Crees in Manitoba and Saskatchewan. All recount

---

5. A similar story was documented among the Menominis and the Tête-de-Boule Algonquins (Davidson 1928b, 273–74; Skinner and Satterlee 1915, 311–12).

the same incident in the Manibozho (Ojibwa)/Wesakaychak (Cree) sequence of trickster adventures (Brown and Brightman 1988, 124–36; Vecsey 1983, 84–98). Manibozho has the bad fortune to meet a windigo who, both parties seem to understand, is the more powerful being. Preparing to eat Manibozho, the windigo has him gather firewood and/or a spit for his own broiling. Manibozho prevails upon an ermine or weasel to leap inside the windigo (entry via anus or mouth) and kill it by eating or disabling its heart. In gratitude, Manibozho paints the small animal with white stripes and black trim—the weasel's winter look today (Ahenakew 1929, 352–53; Michelson 1917, 197–203; Teicher 1960, 25–26, 34–35). This theme ("hero is rescued from cannibal") was discussed by Fisher (1946, 247; see also Barnouw 1977, 72–73 and Bloomfield 1934, 293–95).

Lodge-Boy and Thrown-Away (n=2). Two windigo accounts (Chippewa from the Lower and Upper Peninsulas of Michigan) are Algonquian versions of this, one of the classic plots of native North America (Thompson 1955–58, 5:564, motif Z210.1). Taken from the body of a slain mother, one boy is raised by the father while a brother grows up wild. After the father and first brother catch the second, the brothers triumph over a series of supernatural enemies (Voegelin 1984). In one of these stories, a windigo who killed the mother is dispatched by the boys (Teicher 1960, 31–32). In the other, a windigo is the source of arrows used by the brothers to avenge their mother (Teicher 1960, 42).

Obstacle Flight (n=1). This is a sequence of events in which a fugitive throws several objects backward that magically turn into impediments slowing a pursuer's progress. One of the most widely distributed motifs in world folklore (Thompson 1929, 333, motif D672), the obstacle flight has been reported from a considerable part of the globe, including a band stretching across Eurasia from Siberia to France (Aarne 1930; Swanton 1929, 270–71). In this example from the James Bay Cree of Ontario, a windigo-like cannibal chases two boys he has been fattening up to eat (Skinner 1911, 114–15; Teicher 1960, 35–36).

Discussion: Windigos in Narrative Space
Stories of this category do not pretend to be realistic and do not take place in a world of normal human experience. They feature mythical windigos—a

race of nonhuman giants inhabiting settings that seem abstract, fictional, timeless, and unanchored to specific place. These windigos are powerful beings who pose serious threats to god- and herolike characters, and it takes greater-than-ordinary heroes and manidos to kill them. Since windigos are inimitable to human life, human beings need to be protected from them. Not surprisingly, some stories express longing for supernatural guardians against such unearthly dangers. These windigos are the subjects of standardized plots widely distributed among Algonquian speakers (Manibozho), found throughout North America (Lodge-Boy and Thrown-Away), or even occurring across several continents (Obstacle Flight).

Category Two: Windigos in a World of Spiritual Power

D. People Protected from Windigo: Spiritually Powerful Man Overcomes Windigo (n=2)

The windigo in these stories is a fierce, cannibalistic giant who strides into the human setting from elsewhere. His appearance in our world is unambiguously bad: Human life is threatened. The people are saved by a human champion who possesses spiritual power superior to that of the invader.

In one story (Ojibwa of Lake Timagami, Ontario), an Ojibwa shaman conjures up the threatening windigo in the shaking tent—a characteristically Algonquian divinatory practice in which a shaman communes with spiritual entities called manitos "to discover or manipulate information and events in the future or at a distance" (Brown and Brightman 1988, 146; Vecsey 1983, 104). Overmastering his enemy, the conjurer sends the windigo back to the place he came from (Teicher 1960, 32–33). In the second (Montagnais-Naskapi from the Labrador Peninsula), a windigo drops dead when confronted by a Catholic priest holding aloft a crucifix (Speck 1925, 21; Teicher 1960, 21).

E. People Protected from Windigo: Spiritually Powerful Person Becomes a Windigo to Fight Windigo (n=4)

These tales (Chippewa-Ojibwa of Minnesota, Wisconsin, and Ontario) seem to take place in the familiar world although one text insists that the story happens "at a time when they did miracles through the manitou"

(Michelson 1919, 175). In all four, a windigo invades human space to destroy people (Barnouw 1977, 120, 122; Michelson 1919, 175–79; Teicher 1960, 18, 26–27).

With the possible exception of one tale ending with a human figure revealed inside the melting ice of the brute's body, the windigos are not human and seem nonhuman in origin. When a windigo approaches, the earth rumbles or kettles shake (three cases). Most (three cases) windigos are males, and most come accompanied by dogs (three cases). A windigo's cry is terrible to hear and can cause paralysis (one case). One giant comes armed with a metal staff.

As in the preceding story type, a spiritually powerful individual capable of confronting the invader exists in the community. The power is a given; its nature and source receive little explication (one man dreams he has the power whereas a humpback and a girl are simply introduced as powerful). The gifted person apparently is recognized as such—in one case, a boy demonstrates his suitability by lighting a pipe without a match.

Equipped with sumac twigs that become copper weapons, the powerful one then assumes the form of a giant windigo and meets the enemy in mortal combat. The windigo is killed and the point is conveyed that the champion saved the community.

The spiritually powerful person then returns to normal size and condition, the transformation having been purely a temporary condition. No rapprochement was established between the human and nonhuman races.

In both examples from Wisconsin (Barnouw 1977, 120, 122), the windigo-slayer, a child prior to the combat, must drink hot tallow to return to the earlier human state. Inclined to Freudian imagery and to the assumption that the tales reflect a child's viewpoint, Barnouw (1977, 130–31) thought the stories exemplified the emotional distance between Chippewa mothers and their children. The mother's milk, so frustratingly withheld, was represented by the tallow. Further (and, like Parker 1960), Barnouw speculated the mythical windigo symbolized the mother.

F. Wizards' Duel (n=2)

Two stories feature a fight to the death motivated by envy over hunting success or anger from trespassing on another's hunting territory. The human male rivals are powerful wizards able to assume the form of giant windigos for the showdown. Both tales derive from the same Wisconsin Chippewa provenience (Barnouw 1977, 121, 127), and, like others from that source, the protagonist must drink something (tallow or dog broth) to return to normal size. Impressed by the strong feelings of resentment and male jealousy expressed in these narratives, Barnouw (121–22) found in them evidence of a highly competitive society.

This plot is one example of a contest between wizards, a theme widely known throughout native North America. Typically the wizards match powers in a footrace or an ordeal of endurance, or a contest of hiding, dream-guessing, or shape-changing (Wonderley 2004, 94, 179–80). Typically, the loser's life is forfeit.

Discussion: Windigos in a World of Spiritual Power

In most stories of this category, the giant windigo charges into our world to kill people. It is emphasized (as it is in story type B above) that people must be protected from the ferocious brute. In real life, Algonquian speakers were often reported to be terrified of windigos. These stories come closest to evoking that emotion.

The guardian is not a god but a spiritually powerful human champion who usually turns into a windigo to combat the invader (it takes a windigo to beat a windigo). The tales do not dwell on the sources of spiritual power beyond noting, in a single instance, that it was revealed in a dream. The power simply exists in a given individual at the hour of need and its possessor is recognized as such by the community.

If one could become a windigo at will, what would prevent such a person from assuming windigo shape for some other purpose? In two stories, men who are wizards settle grudges by fighting each other in windigo form. As examples of a general plot enjoyed throughout much of native America, these tales are standardized and formulaic. Yet, they are also the most realistic in that they describe individuals operating in what sounds like a familiar realm of human experience. In this sense, they provide a transition from the narrative/mythical setting (above) to a normally functioning world (below) characteristic of the next set of stories.

Category Three: Windigos in a Human World

G. Person Goes Windigo (n=3)

All three Cree tales (Battleford, Saskatchewan, and James Bay, Quebec) occur in the familiar world and, although details of setting are sparse, they seem to reference daily life among small groups of people in the bush, probably during the winter (Bloomfield 1934, 153–55; Flannery et al. 1981, 68; Teicher 1960, 37–38). The windigo may be male or female, but nothing about giantism is mentioned, and nothing indicates an appearance outside the human range. In all cases, the windigo is killed, apparently in self-defense, in ways and with weapons that would kill any human being. The windigo's body is always burned. The conflagration leaves, in one instance, a residue consisting of an icy heart; in another, a stone that later becomes a bear. All accounts touch on an interesting feature of windigo recognition: Windigos carry around human hands or fingers.

Since the theme of these stories is that windigos are transformed human beings, we might expect they would indicate how a person goes windigo. What we learn is that the change arises through a combination of circumstances, including a state of starvation (n=2). In one case, the transformation is related to the possession of strong spiritual power and, possibly, the rejection of an invitation. In the other two, there is a refusal to obey the dictates or logic of a dream and, possibly, the refusal to accept an elder's advice. At any rate, the subject of how or why one goes windigo does not call forth elaborate explanation. Although this topic has been the focus of anthropological interest, its infrequency here (three stories) suggests it was of relatively little concern to native storytellers.

H. Windigo Killed by Person (n=6)

Six Quebec Cree stories (James Bay and Lake Waswanipi) take place in the familiar world. All concern a nuclear family or a small social unit in the bush, apparently during the winter. The windigos are almost always male as are the majority of their human slayers. The men kill the windigos with arrows, axes, knives, ice chisels, or by drowning. Nothing is said of giantism or nonhuman appearance. The windigo's body, in five of six instances, must be burned although no mention is made of icy hearts or any other unusual residue.

In four cases, something about the relationship between the windigo and children seems to be important (Flannery et al. 1981, 66–67; Teicher 1960, 34–35). Often the windigo cross-examines youngsters whose parents are absent. The windigo has the magical power to induce amnesia about these conversations. The plot of these four tales is substantially the same as one told by Athapaskan Beaver Indians (British Columbia) about their windigo-like being, the wechuge (Ridington 1976, 110–11). In another story, a windigo on the roof stares down through the smoke hole at the human family he is about to attack (Flannery et al. 1981, 67). Seeing the monster reflected in her cooking pot, the wife warns the husband. He pretends to tell a story requiring gestures with his bow and arrow, then abruptly turns the weapon on the windigo. This plot, without the windigo, is told elsewhere (Skinner and Satterlee 1915, 441–42). The incident of the image reflected in the cooking pot is widely distributed and occurs, for example, in the founding tradition of the Iroquois Confederacy (Deganiwida motif).

In the most elaborate of these narratives, a windigo and his two sons are killed by a man and his two sons. As soon as the males are slain, the female members of the windigo family make an appearance and are dispatched also. Three human captives held by the windigos to provide food are then freed (Flannery et al. 1981, 68–69). Frank Speck (1925, 19–20) documented a version of this Cree story (James Bay, Quebec) among the Montagnais-Naskapi to the east.

All these tales take it for granted that windigos exist; they eat people; they should be killed. There is little obvious instruction unless it be that windigos can be killed in normal fashion and their bodies should be burned. There is little concern with definition or explanation. Nothing is said of windigo origins or volunteered about etiological results.

I. Hansel and Gretel (n=5)

Windigos in these Ontario Ojibwa stories fatten people up in anticipation of eating them (Teicher 1960, 20–24). The intended meal may be a captive (n=3) boy (n=2). Often the windigo seems to monitor the weight-gaining program by cutting his victim in the arm or hand. Human victims react by ceasing to eat or going on a diet. Humans, it is implied, can outwit the windigo as when a captive boy hangs a bag of rubbish around his neck, apparently to hide the fact that he is not eating. In another instance, Indians trick the windigo into going to a location where they can kill him. In all, a single male windigo lurks near human camps or settlements, although details about social units are not given. The only allusion to time of year is the occurrence of snow in one story.

As in the preceding story type, all end in the brute's death at human hands. Here also, windigos are dispatched with pedestrian tools and weapons in the same fashion as other mortal beings. Disposal of the windigo's body is a variable affair. In one case, the windigo is burned and melts away but, more frequently, windigo corpses seem normally physical: One is cut into pieces; another is given to the dogs; a third is buried.

The windigo is said to be a giant in all cases and, in one, a moral is tacked on to the effect that "that's why there are no giants now." However, nothing is said about how windigos come about, and there is no hint of other-worldly origin. On the contrary and as in the stories of story type H (Windigo Killed by Person), the action occurs in the familiar, apparently real world. Putative giantness aside, the windigos behave much like humans: They move in a human world and routinely engage in human-like interaction with people. These windigos must resemble human beings as when, for example, one goes into a human settlement for supplies and another tries to convince people he is a human like them.

J. Nimble Jack (n=5)

These Quebec Cree and Ontario Ojibwa stories describe how a human outsmarts a dim-witted windigo, usually in the course of an extended chase sequence. One, occurring in a narrative world strongly reminiscent of a European fairy tale, is the only one of this group to describe the windigo as a giant (Teicher 1960, 20). The other four take place in a familiar setting peopled by Cree of the James Bay region (Flannery et al. 1981, 59–62). These tales share the same scatological humor as well as an incident in which a human, chased by a windigo, climbs a tree. Even as a shower of feces and urine rains on him from above, the windigo does not understand what has become of the person.

Three seem to be variants of a story also reported among the western Cree (Ahenakew 1929, 339–43). All supply additional Rabelasian detail, including an incident in which the windigo misinterprets the bare buttocks of his quarry after close examination. All three end with the windigo, wounded by the human, returning to his own windigo community. There he dies as result of bad medical treatment administered by his own kind.

Then the narratives take an etiological turn. The other windigos eat the deceased corpse, thus becoming cannibals and implying that windigos result from eating windigos. They disperse with the announcement that, henceforth, when any two of them meet, they will fight to the death and the loser will be eaten. An alternative ending is—and that is why there are so many windigos.

K. Old Woman Bait (n=2)

As told by James Bay Cree (Quebec), a sleeping elderly woman is unaware that she is being used to attract a windigo. Men are able to stab the windigo to death then burn his body (Flannery et al. 1981, 67). In an Algonquin version from the St. Maurice River (Quebec), the old woman is placed inside a deadfall to trigger the collapse of weight on the windigo. Although she successfully accomplishes her task, the windigo is only stunned and wanders off (Davidson 1928b, 267; Teicher 1960, 42). These stories resemble the giant windigo story documented by Nelson. Especially close to Nelson's account, the second tale demonstrates respectable narrative stability from about 1820 to 1928.

L. Deceitful Philanthropist (n=5)

Windigos pretend to help humans, often their relatives, but only to ensure a future meal for themselves. In four tales (Ontario Ojibwa and Quebec Cree of James Bay), a pair of windigos—father and son—wander around slaughtering and eating people. When they encounter a human family starving to death, however, they behave solicitously, supplying the people with deer meat and other food. Of course, they merely wish to fatten the humans up. The recipients of their aid become suspicious and flee to a hiding place covered over by snow. At some point, the younger windigo marries a human girl of this or another family and, during the summer, the windigos coexist peacefully with their affines although the windigo husband may bite his wife in the neck or cut her arm with a knife. In the end, two young men (possibly the wife's brothers) kill the windigos (Flannery et al. 1981, 62–65; Skinner 1911, 114–15; Teicher 1960, 23, 36–37).

In the fifth story (Quebec Cree), an elderly windigo man eats people during the winter but lives with them during the summer. When staying with his daughter's family, he murders his grandchild while pretending to feed it in a tender fashion. When the people flee from him, the windigo eats the baby's body, remarking on its savory taste. "He wasn't killed because he would always get ahead of the others somehow" (Flannery et al. 1981, 69–70).

These stories take place in the familiar human world. In one case, it is stated that the two villains become windigos (for unknown reasons) so perhaps a human origin is assumed for all. In any event, the windigos are humanlike. Indistinguishable from people, they seem to interact in a reasonably civil fashion with people at least on a seasonal basis. The idea of routine relations taking place between humans and windigos is new to stories of this type, but its motivation is not. The arrangement is inspired by the windigos' desire to fatten people up, just as it was in the Hansel and Gretel stories (story type I) and in other tales as well.

What is truly innovative is the idea that windigos normally establish kinship bonds with people, especially through marriage. Even in this most intimate of connections, however, the arrangement is a normally selfish one from the windigo standpoint. Married windigos eat their relatives or test them to see if they are fat enough to eat.

Parts of these relatively long narratives seem familiar. The endings of several, for example, repeat an elaborate set of events concluding a Quebec Cree tale included in story type H (Windigo Killed by Person; Flannery et al. 1981, 68–69) as well as a tale documented by Speck (1925, 19–20). The stories describe two young men who kill a younger and then an older windigo (son and father) in much the same ways. The beginning of the same set of stories, however, features the father-son windigo pair whose adventures can also be found in a Cree myth analyzed by Turner (1977) as an expression of social structure. Assuming cannibalism is a metaphor for social recruitment and incorporation, the story (Turner argues) tells how society creates its units of production through alliance and marriage. If so, the same sequence of episodes turns out to be embedded in longer plots with seemingly different themes.

Discussion: Windigos in a Human World

These stories are about windigos who inhabit or mostly seem to operate in a realm of humans and normal human experience. A few windigos are said to be giants, but most behave in a recognizably humanlike fashion and move comfortably around in human settings. Their interactions with people are frequent and often imply that they resemble people.

The windigos seem to be of human origin although that concept is made explicit in only three instances. In those cases, starvation, in combination with spiritual potency and something being out of kilter, contribute to one's becoming a windigo. For the most part, however, causation and origin are not addressed.

Windigos are sometimes dim-witted (story type J, Nimble Jack), a source of narrative humor. Sometimes they are credited with certain extraordinary powers such as the ability to make children forget a conversation. They like to carry around parts of human bodies, a habit which often alerts humans to their windigo natures. They are killed in the same way humans are slain—with such weapons as ice chisels and axes. Very often their bodies are burned and, very occasionally, some unusual feature such as an icy heart is revealed in the ashes.

Preying on human families in the bush, these windigos go about their business with a certain low cunning and seem to understand deferred gratification. Often they will hold off until a human becomes fat enough to make the meal seem worthwhile. They maintain captives for future meals and seem incessantly to test people by cutting a hand or arm to check the quotient of fatness.

They routinely interact with humans. They help the occasional starving family by supplying proper human provender. They even become members of human families through marriage, at least during the summer when their windigo-ism goes into remission. Such behavior is never altruistic, however. Friendliness is a sham, a means to obtain human flesh.

Anomalous Stories

M. Windigo Island (n=1)
Indians who have built a sailboat get shipwrecked on an island inhabited by windigos. They survive by trading gold for deer meat. What begins as a strange story then takes a bizarre turn. The Indians are rescued by white sailors who refuse to allow the windigos on board their ship. Only in this Ontario Ojibwa tale do we learn that windigos might be motivated by economic gain (Teicher 1960, 19–20). But then, this is also the only windigo story that features a Native American shipbuilding industry and alludes to a triracial situation composed of Indians, windigos, and white people. An appended moral tries to steer back to more familiar windigo ground: If not for those gold rings and brooches, the windigos would have killed the Indians.

N. Friendly Visitor (n=3)
A giant windigo shows up at a nuclear family's camp in the bush in a trio of Chippewa-Ojibwa narratives from Michigan, Minnesota, and Ontario. The husband being absent, the wife rushes to meet the intruder, desperately addressing him as "Father." Though skeptical, the windigo seems to accept the woman's assertion that he is a relative. He stays with the human family, apparently through the winter, and helps by providing more game and firewood. In one version, he entertains the children who dance on his palm as he sings, "Rotten navel, rotten navel." All during his stay, the windigo continues to be a cannibal eating human flesh obtained elsewhere.

The windigo's departure is linked with the appearance of another windigo, but the connection is different in each version.

In one, the first windigo protects his human family from a second windigo bent on destroying the humans (Teicher 1960, 22–23). In another, the first windigo inexplicably fights a second (and female) windigo in a distant country (Michelson 1919, 655–69; Teicher 1960, 27–30). In the third, a new windigo slaughters the wife (Teicher 1960, 39–42), and the plot suddenly turns into a story about Lodge-Boy and Thrown-Away.

The windigo of these stories seems out of character in several respects. First, instead of being killed when he charges into the human world, he joins a human family and becomes domesticated. Second, the method of establishing family membership is distinct. Although humans and windigos occasionally marry (in story type L, Deceitful Philanthropist), the bond in Friendly Visitor stories is established through the device of fictive kinship. The relationship is desperately proffered by the human wife and reluctantly conceded by the windigo but, once established, it leads to real family intimacy.

Feeling himself to be a member of the human family, the windigo begins to behave kindly—the third anomalous feature of this group. Although they continue to enjoy their meals of human flesh, these windigos engage in genuinely peaceful concourse with members of their own family.

Conclusions

This study focuses on a neglected form of early-twentieth-century evidence pertaining to the Algonquian "windigo complex." The data comprise fifty English-language texts forever separated from the complexity of their own linguistic expression, from the matrix of living performance, and from the assumptions and knowledge once shared by teller and listener. All that we have as cultural testimony from long ago are the stories themselves.

Spare in delivery and indifferent to character development, the tales provide so little description that we do not even know what windigos looked like. Like folktales everywhere, these tend strongly toward the formulaic, the conventionalized, and the standardized. That means, in turn, that certain windigo plots and motifs are widely distributed. The "mythical windigo" is not limited to Cree/Chippewa/Ojibwa peoples who employ the word *windigo,* and, as Fogelson (1980) observed, a similar or cognate cannibal monster is not confined to the Algonquian-speaking world. Indeed, had anthropologists begun their windigo studies with an examination of oral narrative, it is difficult to imagine they would have been strongly committed to the idea of cultural exclusiveness.

The windigo stories of this study were not formulated in response to such anthropological interests as windigo illness, a topic about which these tales seem rather indifferent. These stories are neither ethnographic summaries of belief nor tightly reasoned manifestos of religious faith. They do not take an explanatory bent and seem unconcerned with exploring cause and origin. They propound no obviously pedagogical curriculum. Though people often recognize windigos by the human body parts they carry around, these stories are not users' manuals on the subject of identifying windigos. And, while these narratives may conclude with a lesson or parable, the etiological punch line seems, more often than not, arbitrary.

The old stories speak of about a dozen subjects, many of which may reflect regional preferences in storytelling. At a higher order of generalization, the story types are classifiable into three larger categories. In the first, mythical heroes or godlike protagonists oppose powerful mythical giants. Unfettered by the exigencies of reality, the tales of Category One (Windigos in Narrative Space) make no allusion to quotidian circumstance or specific place. In the second (Category Two, Windigos in a World of Spiritual Power), a human gifted with spiritual power usually assumes windigo form, most frequently to do battle with a malevolent windigo invader. In the third (Category Three, Windigos in a Human World), the cannibal monsters are humanlike predators inhabiting the human world. Whether or not they are giants, these windigos are capable of living among, being mistaken for, and even intermarrying with Algonquian folk. In their icy hearts, however, their sole interest is to secure human prey.

These three metathemes convey similar attitudes about windigos. While some windigo stories may contain a dollop of humor, the subject was not, on that account, a topic for risibility. Windigos are ferocious. They are terrifying, and people long for protection from them (Categories One and Two). Windigos are evil. "There was never any such thing as a good witiko," Guinard (1930, 69) observed, and these stories prove it. Windigos must be killed (all categories) and, once slain, their bodies should be burned (Category Three). Transcending regional variation, these basic ideas about windigos unify the stories. Cut from the same cultural cloth, they comprise a fundamental substratum common to Algonquian folktales about windigos.

My scheme posits two categories that could be opposites: those set in narrative (Category One) and in human space (Category Three). The apparent dichotomy corresponds very approximately to the widely recognized distinction between windigos of the nonhuman and human types. It is also reminiscent of a distinction Crees make between tales set in primeval and recent times (Flannery et al. 1981).

Category Two, in contrast, is not defined in terms comparable to those of the other two groups. It is about spiritual power and the ability to alter one's shape. Transformation is perhaps the most important concept of these stories as Ridington (1976) and others have suggested in other contexts. Overholt and Callicott (1982, 142–44) found metamorphosis to be one of the key themes in Algonquian folklore generally. Category Two cautions against interpreting the other two as mutually exclusive or unequivocally opposed because, through transformation, one can easily move back and forth between mythical and real time zones and between nonhuman and human states. I suggest Category Two bridges and mediates the other two. If so, Algonquian windigo stories are best visualized as situated in the same conceptual universe along one storytelling continuum. Further, if transformation between extremes is an acceptable concept, it helps to explain why storytellers might be indifferent to questions of origin. A windigo's proximate derivation and nature are not very important points if metamorphosis is fundamental to the whole.

Hardship and the threat of starvation were the lot of people who told stories about windigos, and it is undoubtedly true, as anthropologists have always thought, that windigos are symbolic expressions of danger, isolation, and the frozen north (Cooper 1933; Flannery et al. 1981, 59). This corpus of windigo stories lends credence to some of the psychological generalizations offered by researchers over the years. Many of these stories suggest what Parker (1960) argued was a strong feeling of dependency toward supernatural powers, an attitude surely consistent with what Brightman (1988) perceived as belief in predestination. Parker (1960) also argued that the tales are strongly male-oriented and, at least as regards the sex of the protagonists, these data confirm that.

Are stories about windigos very old? Since few narratives were recorded before 1900, little can be said of their contents. The windigo concept behind the stories, however, is surely old. Belief in cannibal giants (though not called windigos) is reported as early as 1603 (Bishop 1975, 241–42; Wallis and Wallis 1955, 417–18, 430–31). Then too, the enormous geographical range of the subject matter suggests the idea that windigos must have considerable time depth (Brightman 1988; Fogelson 1980).

If we know something of the basic Algonquian repertoire of windigo narratives, we can recognize it in other contexts. As I became familiar with the corpus of windigo oral narrative, I often discerned plots and motifs embedded in historic and ethnographic sources where they were not specifically identified as folklore. Back in about 1820, for example, George Nelson described "a young Indian a few years ago" who begged his companions to kill him when he realized he was becoming a windigo (Brown and Brightman 1988, 92). This anecdote is much the same as a folktale documented among the Miqmaq far to the east some years later (Leland 1992, 251–54; Rand 1894, 246–49). More recently, Ruth Landes (1938) provided several "accounts" and "stories" from informants that she treated as ethnographic data illustrating how windigos behave and how they come about. Much of her source material seems strongly folkloric, and two of her important examples resemble story types H (Windigo Killed by Person) and I (Hansel and Gretel; Landes 1938, 221–24). This suggests that Algonquian informants offered stories to their interlocutors in response to anthropological queries. Or, the phenomenon may demonstrate how the mythopoetic framework of oral narrative influenced the informants' construction of reality and interpretation of the past (see, for example, Bricker 1981; Erickson 2003; Ireland 1988; Ramsey 1983, 123–32). In any event, "fact" (in case studies and first-hand testimonies) and folklore may be more thoroughly intertwined in the windigo literature than has been recognized.

And, knowing the basic Algonquian windigo repertoire permits recognition of items that seem wildly out of line. Two story types (totaling four examples) are of this sort. One (story type M, Windigo Island) stands alone, an anomalous curiosity about which nothing can be said. The other three, however, share a plot that was rather widely distributed and documented over the course of about eighty years (story type N, Friendly Visitor). What the story type says about windigos contradicts the basic windigo premises in tales comprising Categories One to Three. Why would that be? The most likely explanation is that the Friendly Visitor happens to be of foreign origin. But that requires comparative information beyond this Algonquian context.

6

The Friendly Visitor

*An Iroquois Stone Giant Goes
Calling in Algonquian Country*

THE TALE MOST CLOSELY resembling a literary short story in all of
native North America may be one documented among eastern Algonquian
people of the Canadian Maritimes. It tells of a male cannibal giant who
suddenly emerges from the woods at the camp of a small, human family.
Welcomed as a person, the monster takes up residence with the humans and
even defends his adopted family against the onslaught of a second cannibal
giant. After the battle, the domesticated creature chooses to remain with
his human kin when they return to their village (Rand 1894, 190–99).

Unusually detailed, this tale is remarkable for its complexity and philosophical nuance (Fogelson 1980, 145). To a folklorist a century ago, it
spoke of "the gradual civilization of the savage by kindness" (Leland 1992,
244). More recently, it is characterized as a musing on human nature and
social solidarity (McGee 1975).

But the Canadian tale is only one example of a narrative known to
Algonquian speakers from the Midwest to the Atlantic Coast (Fisher 1946,
248). Wherever it is found, it seems to distill and express values common to
its tellers across a large area. "The consistency of imagery that runs through
the various versions of these tales," as Kenneth Morrison (1979, 62) puts it,
"indicates a universal agreement among the Algonkian peoples about the
nature of the cannibal giant and of the threat he posed to society."

I described this plot in the preceding chapter as windigo story type N,
the Friendly Visitor. Here, I widen the definition of the plot: A cannibal
giant (variously named; windigos are one example) comes to live with a

human family, then protects the family by fighting and killing another cannibal giant.

I became interested in the Friendly Visitor story type when I realized it was also present among the Iroquois. As they told it, however, the cannibal giant is a female fleeing her abusive husband. The second cannibal giant is her spouse, who comes after her and is slain. The same story type, in other words, looks like an altogether different tale in Iroquois country.

The recognition of Iroquois variants greatly expands the story's geographical distribution and increases its number of accounts. That makes possible the comparative study presented in this chapter. What follows is, in part, a geographical survey of the story's occurrence. The Friendly Visitor seems to have been centered in Iroquois country, where it was recorded more frequently and told with greater consistency than elsewhere. If the story was Iroquois in origin, when did it spread outward?

This chapter is also a comparative examination of the story's content, a mapping of similarities and differences among its regional variants. Because the Friendly Visitor story type comprises such a plentiful and rich body of material, one can discern how the same story was regionally handled. It turns out that storytellers in different places were supplying their own motivations to the actors and drawing different conclusions about what the story meant. Ultimately, patterns characteristic of different regions raise questions about cultural distinctions between Iroquois and Algonquian oral narrative.

Study of the Friendly Visitor story type properly begins among the Iroquois, who provided the greatest number of accounts. But first, let me introduce the distinctively Iroquois cannibal giant.

Iroquois Stone Giants

Iroquois folklore was peopled by a windigo-like creature usually rendered in English as stone coat or stone giant. Basically humanlike in appearance, it had a pointy head and wore, like a garment, an exterior covering made of stone (possibly of flint). According to a print done by an Iroquois artist in 1827, stone giants were about twice the size of humans (Bryden 1995, 62; Sturtevant 2006, 48). Like windigos, they were credited with extraordinary strength and with such magical powers as the ability to disable humans with a shout (Beauchamp 1892, 28–29; Goldenweiser 1914, 474). Stone giants did not have hearts made of ice although, like windigos, they were of the north.

The Iroquois giants were highly accomplished hunters capable of conveying luck in the chase to humans (Curtin 2001, 216, 511; Hewitt 1918, 437; A. Parker 1989, 336–39). Often, they were considered to have mystical ties with game. An association with forest animals and hunting magic implies the stone giants were at home in the deep woods of the east and may have been ancient in and autochthonous to that setting (Wonderley 2004, 87–107).

Great favorites of Iroquois folklore, stone giants probably are mentioned more frequently than any other mythic being. Many stories about these creatures feature plots that are formulaic, standardized, and apparently endlessly retold. There are three such recurrent patterns or story types.

In the first, stone giants swept out of the north to terrorize the Iroquois. Rendered impervious to human weapons by their lithic exteriors, the fierce cannibals had an easy time of it until Sky Holder, the great god of the Iroquois, came to the aid of his people. That deity assumed the aspect of a stone giant, lured them into a ravine near Onondaga, then buried all but one under a torrent of boulders (Beauchamp 1892, 15–16).[1]

The second stone giant story type is a chase sequence in which an Iroquois hunter is pursued by a stone giant. When the hunter climbs a tree, the giant standing beneath becomes perplexed because it is physically incapable of looking up. The stone giant pulls out a magic pointer or game-finder consisting of a human hand or finger. Pointing upward, the object's behavior puzzles the dim-witted brute, whose hesitation allows the hunter to seize the pointer and race away. The man may keep the charm or return it. In either event, the man benefits in some fashion, usually as the recipient of luck in hunting.

---

1. The story of stone giants being entombed at Onondaga can be consulted in Curtin 2001, 122–23; Hewitt 1918, 682–85; E. Johnson 1881, 55–56; A. Parker 1989, 340–41, 394–96, 425–26; and E. Smith 1983, 13.

This story often has the man crossing and recrossing a river while the stone giant lumbers slowly across on the river bottom. Emerging from the water, the monster encounters a stone ax left by the man. Spitting on it or rubbing the blade with his finger, the stone giant unwittingly imparts to the ax the power to split rock. When the man regains the tomahawk, its effectiveness becomes obvious to both parties. This story segment concludes with the giant fleeing or being dispatched with the ax.[2]

Clearly, stone giants were dangerous and wicked creatures as exemplified in the first kind of story. But they were also objects of humor enjoyed, as in the second kind, for their awkwardness and stupidity. The Iroquois probably had more fun with their cannibal giants than Algonquians had with their windigos. And, among the Iroquois, a stone giant who was friendly was not all that unusual.

The Iroquois Friendly Visitor

In the third type of stone giant tale (as discrete tale or sequence within a longer narrative), a human couple living with their baby in a forest wigwam is visited by a stone giant woman. The humans need not be frightened, the giant assures them, because "she had run away from her cruel husband, who wanted to kill her, and she wished to stay a while with the hunter's family" (E. Smith 1983, 16). In other versions, this explanation is rendered as: "My husband and I quarreled and I ran away" (Curtin 2001, 510); "I am fleeing from my husband who seeks to kill me. Only be my friends and I will give you something" (A. Parker 1989, 335).

The human family takes her in and, in so doing, provides asylum for a battered spouse. In return, the stone giant helps the family by supplying firewood and granting them hunting success (Beauchamp 1922, 147–48). However, the idyll ends when the guest announces, "My husband is coming; he's angry because I left him" (Hewitt 1918, 437–39). "After he has looked everywhere else for me, he will come here. I will help you till he

---

2. For examples of this second type of stone giant story, see Beauchamp 1892, 28–29; 1922, 41; Curtin 2001, 122–23; Hewitt 1918, 682–85; E. Johnson 1881, 55–56; A. Parker 1989, 337–41, 394–96, 425–26; and E. Smith 1983, 13, 17–18.

comes, then you must help me" (Curtin 2001, 510). The two stone giants will fight to the death. The one who is kindly disposed will lose unless the humans help her. Human assistance is essential: "You and your husband must help me to kill him" (E. Smith 1983, 17).

When the spouse arrives, the two giants go at one another in a titanic struggle. The friendly one emerges as the winner with the prearranged aid of the humans. Most frequently, people stab the attacker in the back or anus with fire-hardened, basswood spears.[3]

The Iroquois Friendly Visitor account, then, is about an abused wife seeking shelter from an angry mate determined to pursue her. Given the premise of marital difficulties, the story line developed out of it always explains why a monster suddenly appears, why she is kindly disposed toward people, and why the specific climax—the fight between stone giants—occurs. The Iroquois telling supplies clear motivation to its characters, who then follow out the logic of their circumstances. The Iroquois Friendly Visitor coheres.

All Iroquois tellings (eight examples and a summary of a ninth) emphasize the importance of human assistance. Humans take the good giant in, and human help is essential to overcoming the bad giant. There is general agreement, as well, about plot and most details.

Nevertheless, there are two variations on the story, each mentioned in two versions. In one variant, the human male had been seduced by the stone giant female the previous hunting season (Hewitt 1918, 555–64; Turner and Hickerson 1952, 11–12). The giant woman reappears to show the man the child they engendered together. This modification complicates the plot but does not alter the basic denouement. The fierce husband of the stone giant wife (presumably even angrier for having been cuckolded) is coming to exact revenge. And again, the stone giant wife requires human help to prevail against him. This variation simply develops and intensifies the idea of marital discord at the heart of the tale.

3. Accounts of the Iroquois Friendly Visitor are given in Curtin 2001, 510–11; Hewitt 1918, 437–39, 555–64; A. Parker 1989, 335–36; Rudes and Crouse 1987, 469–521; E. Smith 1983, 16–17; Turner and Hickerson 1952, 11–12; and Wonderley 2004, 95–96. Beauchamp (1922, 147–48) summarizes another version, the original apparently lost.

In the other variant, the sex of the stone giant guest is male—that is, the abused spouse is the husband rather than the wife (Rudes and Crouse 1987, 469–521; Wonderley 2004, 95–96). Regardless of the visitor's gender/sex, however, the good stone giant still faces the approach of its murderous mate and still requires human help to survive that onslaught. These variations, therefore, remain faithful to the overall pattern of the story.

The message or theme of this story (humans help monster) is typical of Iroquois folklore around 1900: a supernatural needs human help to overcome an enemy (Wonderley 2004, 224). The Iroquois Friendly Visitor also is of a piece with the spirit and subject matter characteristic of the vast corpus of folklore. Iroquois oral narrative rarely mentions communal living in longhouses, settled villages, matricentered residence units, or even corn and other domesticated foods. Rather, Iroquois folklore focuses on life in small family units far from the village, on incidents in the deep woods, on game, and on supernatural beings at home in the forest (222–23). Fenton (1978, 298) described the essence of Iroquois folklore as, "They went to the woods to hunt for meat." The Iroquois Friendly Visitor story fits comfortably within the domain of forest concerns in a woods setting.

However, the story is anomalous in one respect. In general, women are not well represented in Iroquois oral narrative. In the older creation story, for example, women's tasks and maize (the quintessential contribution of women to Iroquois life) are present in the plot but attributed to or embodied by a male (chapter 4).

Iroquois folklore contains few important female characters. My list consists of an occasional reference to a woman chief (Hewitt 1918, 537–38) as well as the Niagara queen discussed in chapter 2. Additionally, a female leader of tribal migrations sometimes is mentioned (Fenton and Moore 1974, 86–87; Klinck and Talman 1970, 98).

The female protagonists who do exist in Iroquois folklore tend to be fickle, unfaithful, in need of correction, or passive sufferers of unfair circumstances. Here again, the creation myth exemplifies such portrayal. The older versions describe three generations of women who suffer unpleasant fates for having been magically impregnated (Wonderley 2001; 2004, 60–68, 223).

And finally, such women who do make an appearance do not receive a very favorable or sympathetic hearing. Sky Holder's grandmother, in some ways the emblematic female of Iroquois oral narrative, was, after all, malicious (chapter 4).

The Iroquois Friendly Visitor runs against the grain of such misogyny in telling of a female who flees an abusive spouse and, in self-defense, kills the unregenerate husband. In effect, the story thinks through these circumstances and seems to find them acceptable. This female-centered message sets the Friendly Visitor apart as possibly the most radically feminist tale within Iroquois oral narrative at the turn of the twentieth century.

One account from a Tuscarora informant in 1889 presents two details not present in any other version of the Iroquois Friendly Visitor story (Rudes and Crouse 1987, 522–29). First, this narrative states that, when the stone giant man (one of two male instances mentioned above) shows up at the human habitation, the human wife addresses him as "Father," and he accepts the idea that he is related to the family. Second, after the fight sequence normally concluding the story, there follows an extensive passage in which the guest is transformed into a human by taking an emetic made from red osier dogwood. "After the Stone Giant had drunk about half of the medicine, he grew pale and nauseous and vomited once more. Mixed in with his vomit were all kinds of bugs and crawling things, for the medicine had knocked the evil out of him" (Rudes 1994, 474). It is precisely these details that loom large in accounts of the Friendly Visitor story type told elsewhere.

The Friendly Visitor in the Midwest

The sample from this region includes three Chippewa-Ojibwa accounts in which the visitor is a windigo (story type N in chapter 5) and a Menomini (also Algonquian speakers) version from Wisconsin, naming the cannibal giant as a *Mowaki* (Skinner and Satterlee 1915, 332–37). In all four, the friendly visitor is a male giant who appears at the camp of a nuclear family. In every instance, he is domesticated by the quick-thinking wife, who addresses him as a relative (father, grandfather, uncle). Accepting his status as kinsman, the giant takes up residence with the family although he himself (in three of four cases) continues to eat human flesh. All versions emphasize how the giant helps his human relatives by supplying them with game. At the end of the winter, he goes his own way.

The giant's departure is connected with the appearance of a second giant but in three different ways. First, a new male giant suddenly shows up and slaughters the wife, a brutal incident that redirects the narrative into the story of Lodge-Boy and Thrown-Away (Schoolcraft 1999, 183–90; Teicher 1960, 39–42). Second, the friendly guest goes to a distant country where he conquers a female giant (Michelson 1919, 655–69; Teicher 1960, 27–30). Third, the giant warns his family that a second (male) giant is coming (this variation given in two accounts). The good giant then fights and kills the ferocious newcomer in defense of his people (Teicher 1960, 22–23; Skinner and Satterlee 1915, 332–36). In the Menomini version, one of the humans helps the giant dispatch his adversary. In neither case, however, is human assistance in the combat required. After the fight, one of the tales again veers into a rendition of Lodge-Boy and Thrown-Away (336–37).

At the heart of all midwestern stories is the bonding incident of fictive kinship. Believing the humans to be his relatives, the normally murderous being has reason to refrain from slaughtering people, to live with them, and to aid them. Since all midwestern accounts emphasize the giant's assistance, their most obvious message is that monster helps humans. The other two accounts advance a second theme: The giant protects people.

In contrast to the Iroquois principle of quarreling giant spouses, however, the mere recognition of kinship does not require the appearance of a second giant or explain why they must fight. As premise, it provides no means to connect the first part of the story (giant meets family) to the second (giant fights giant). An absence of developmental logic may go far to explain considerable diversity in the second half of the midwestern Friendly Visitor.

Two midwestern accounts employ the Friendly Visitor sequence as prelude to a different narrative: Lodge-Boy and Thrown-Away. Why, in versions published as far apart as 1839 and 1915, was the story treated as a way to begin another mythic adventure? I visualize an Algonquian storyteller preparing to perform the tale on a winter night. He realizes, as he mentally rehearses the plot, he is a little uncertain about introducing that second cannibal, and this inclines him to turn the story back onto more familiar rails. He draws on Lodge-Boy and Thrown-Away because that narrative begins with what he needs: a stock scenario instantly introducing a bellicose monster to an isolated human family. And, having invoked that scene, he may as well continue to tell the other story, which he might know better anyway. Or so I imagine. At any rate, the link made between the two stories is a wonderfully strange regionalism.

Midwestern versions of the Friendly Visitor are, in comparison to Iroquois occurrences, diverse in plot and detail. All agree, however, that a human woman offers a kinship relationship that a male giant accepts. A common thematic emphasis motivated by this premise is that the giant helps his human hosts. Two versions add another message: The giant protects his humans. Two versions use the story as prologue to another.

A detail mentioned in only one of the midwestern accounts has the human family giving a child to the visitor. The reformed cannibal lays on hands; that is, he rubs the child and magically transforms the youngster into a Mowaki, a creature of his own kind (Skinner and Satterlee 1915, 335). This curious transformation anticipates a theme of the story characteristic of the Atlantic Northeast.

The Friendly Visitor in the Maritimes and New England

The best-known version of the Friendly Visitor is that penned by the Reverend Silas Tertius Rand (1894, 190–99), a missionary among the Miqmaqs of Nova Scotia for some forty years. Rand said he heard it in 1859 from a native informant who heard it, in turn, from *his* elderly grandfather in 1843.

The tale begins with a nuclear family camping in the bush. While the husband is away one day, a Chenoo, the Miqmaqs' dreaded windigo-like creature, suddenly confronts the wife and child. The woman "concluded he was one of that horrid tribe, a cannibal, and that he would surely kill and devour her. With great presence of mind, she determined to try the effects of a ruse, and treat him with unwonted attention and kindness; she would pretend to mistake him for her own father, and rejoice over him as though he were so in reality."

Addressed as "Father," the Chenoo acquiesces to the proposed familial relationship and proceeds to cut an enormous load of firewood for the household. The monster takes up residence with the people and, after a few days, begins "to yield to the power of kindness." Requesting a purgative of hot tallow, the Chenoo vomits up "a vast amount of offal, and all abominable things that were appalling to the senses" and becomes more or less human. Subsequently, he and the husband go hunting together and bag a pair of giant lizards, which will serve as the Chenoo's food.

One day, the guest announces they will be attacked by another Chenoo. Needing human help to overcome the attacker, the friendly Chenoo arms the husband with a dragon's horn in preparation for the coming showdown. When the other Chenoo (also a male) appears, the two combatants grow to the size of mountains as they fling themselves into furious struggle. "Rocks are hurled from their places, the ground is torn up, trees are broken and crashed down in all directions." The human rushes to his guest's aid at a timely moment, and the two of them overcome the enemy. A heart of solid ice is revealed when the body of the deceased Chenoo is burned.

When spring comes, the Chenoo decides to accompany his family back to their village. At one point in their journey, the Chenoo hides from another of his kind off in the distance. It is explained that concealment is necessary because, if the two see one another, they are compelled to fight to the death. The "tamed and humanized" Chenoo becomes progressively weaker as the party travels south. By the time the human village is reached, he is near death. In his last moments, the Chenoo is converted to Christianity by a Catholic priest.

Rand's narrative is the longest and most obviously metaphorical of the published tellings of the Friendly Visitor. Not surprisingly, perhaps, it provided the basis for introducing folklore, as an emic or authentically native voice, into investigation of the windigo complex. Focusing specifically on this version, Harold McGee (1975) argued that it was an Algonquian disquisition about what is human and social as opposed to monstrous and solitary. The cannibal giant of Rand's Miqmaq, Morrison (1979, 55) concurred, "was perhaps the central image of savagery and evil for the Algonkians, combining the most brutal possibilities inherent in man and in the natural order: deepest winter and cannibalism. These creatures revealed to the Algonkians what people were not, and must not be." Morrison also believed the narrative reflected the historical experiences of northeastern Algonquians with Jesuit missionaries over the course of centuries.

Rand's version is the most purely literary of the Friendly Visitor accounts because he, as author, seems to be the source of at least some of the commentary and explanation that keep the story flowing smoothly. One can form a rough impression of how much of this would have been told by native people by placing the Rand story in a larger regional context. For, in fact, the Friendly Visitor story type was popular among speakers of closely related Algonquian languages distributed continuously across northern Maine (Penobscot), New Brunswick (Passamaquoddy), and into Nova Scotia (Miqmaq). We have at least four other versions of the story from these sources (Leland 1992, 247–48; Parsons 1925, 59–60; Speck 1935a, 14; Wallis and Wallis 1955, 343–45).

Collectively, the story they tell is that a young couple with a youngster (four cases; in Parsons's version, a mother and child) is camping in the woods during the winter. When a male cannibal giant appears, the woman addresses him as "Father" or "Grandfather." The giant accepts this status and apparently moves in with the family. However, hardly anything is said about the giant's time spent among people and, with the exception of Rand's Chenoo providing firewood, little or nothing is said about the giant providing help to the household.

The guest announces that a second giant is coming and a fight is imminent but, with the exception of Rand's tale, no reason is given for these events. The sex of the second giant is variable (two male, two female, one unspecified). The friendly giant may evince some concern to protect his hosts from the invader (n=3).

All versions showcase the fight between giant guest and giant intruder. The kindly being always prevails in the showdown, and human help usually proves to be useful (four of five cases). However, the help may be indirect (preparing weapons for the giant's use, as in Parsons) or volunteered (as in Leland). Only two Miqmaq versions (those of Rand and Wallis) insist that the aid given by people is necessary for the victory of the good giant.

In the three northernmost tellings (Miqmaq), the enemy Chenoo's icy heart is revealed when its body is burned. This windigo-like detail is absent from the two more southerly accounts, both of which indicate that cannibal giants, like their Iroquois counterpart, wear a hard outer rind. The exterior covering of the Passamaquoddy-Penobscot monster (called a *Kewahqu'* or *Kiwakwe*) consists of a layer of leaves, sticks, and moss adhering with fir balsam to the creature's body.

Four of the Maritime–New England stories stress the transformation of the giant into a human state. This is done by taking an emetic. In all versions other than Rand's, this incident occurs after the fight and at the end of the story. The act of being cured and becoming human, in other words, is the conclusion.

One version proposes the logically opposite form of metamorphosis: person to giant. In Parsons, the guest transforms the human child into another cannibal being by magically stroking the youngster with his hands. Here again, however, the transformative incident closes the story.

These northeastern versions of Friendly Visitor all agree that the human woman offers the prospect of being related and the monstrous guest accepts. This is precisely the same incident seen in the Midwest: The monster recognizes a family relationship with the humans. In the Northeast, it presumably suffers from the same logical liabilities. Simply being related does not set the stage for a second giant nor explain why the giants must fight.

Yet, the northeastern versions are not hobbled by the logically weak premise, possibly because everyone knew that, when two cannibal giants encountered each other, "a dreadful fight took place in which the victor devoured the vanquished" (Guinard 1930, 69). They *had* to fight each other to the death. That, at any rate, is what Rand states. Other eastern Algonguians may have thought the same.[4]

After the fight, however, the northeastern versions diverge in detail. There is no agreement, for example, on the second giant's sex. Further, what little motivation the kinship premise does provide (an explanation for the monster's friendliness and help, readiness to take up residence with people) remains largely undeveloped here. Unlike his midwestern counterpart, the northeastern Friendly Visitor is not particularly helpful, and his tenure among humans is narratively truncated. Nor does it greatly matter in the Northeast whether the friendly giant fights on behalf of his family or even whether people help in that fight. All these points receive diverse treatment within the northeastern corpus.

4. The belief that if windigos met, they would have to have fight each other, is expressed among the Cree east of James Bay, Quebec (Flannery et al. 1981, 60–61). I have not seen it documented further west.

In addition to fictive kinship and the giants' fight, all versions of the northeastern Friendly Visitor insist on the idea of transformation from one species or state to another. Usually, the windigo-like guest becomes human through the action of expelling his nonhuman essence. Whatever the nature and means of transmogrification, however, the northeastern storytellers not only added metamorphosis to the plot, they made that act central to the narrative. Rand aside, physical alteration both concludes and becomes the point of the story. Transformation is the most obvious theme of the northeastern Friendly Visitor.

It is also, of course, a familiar topic in windigo stories, one that seems broadly consistent with the windigo-like character of the Northeast's Friendly Visitor (especially the Miqmaq Chenoo with its icy heart). Further, altering one's nature and state is a concept that may offer more narrative possibilities than fictive kinship. In the hands of the Miqmaqs and Silas Rand, it developed into a sophisticated allegory on the human condition.

There are about as many published versions of the Friendly Visitor story type in the Northeast (n=5) as there are in the Midwest (4), which is to say relatively few in comparison to the Iroquois region. In contrast to the Iroquois plot, every Algonquian version in the Midwest and the Northeast insists that a human woman offers kinship to a male giant. The northeastern accounts are more uniform than those of the Midwest in describing the appearance of a second giant who fights with the first. The northeastern versions, however, are otherwise inconsistent on many circumstances and details, including the idea of helping the humans (consistently emphasized in the Midwest) or of humans helping the guest (Iroquois emphasis). Overall, the internal diversity of the northeastern tale contrasts with the more nearly uniform treatment among the Iroquois of this story type.

A Delaware Friendly Visitor

The story type is not recorded from the great band of boreal forest between the Maritimes and southern Ontario. It was, however, documented among the Delaware/Lenape, Algonquian speakers whose traditional homelands in present eastern Pennsylvania, New Jersey, and southern New York bordered Iroquois country. The Delaware cannibal creature *(Mhú-we)*, was a winter giant of the north who "bears an obvious relationship to the ice-hearted cannibal, *chenoo,* of the New England and eastern Canadian Algonquians; the cannibal ice-giant, *windigo,* of the Ojibwa; and the stone coat" of the Iroquois (Bierhorst 1995, 12).

According to a Delaware account (part of a longer narrative) recorded in Oklahoma in 1939, a male Mhú-we shows up at the camp or residence of a human family consisting of a man, his wife, and their baby. The intruder smells the child and wants to eat it but becomes distracted by two bags of grease, which he wolfs down. Apparently gravid from the meal, the Mhú-we falls asleep and, when he awakens, a stream of insects pours out of his nose. With the ejection of the vermin, the Mhú-we's evil nature is expelled and he becomes human.

The former cannibal warns that a second Mhú-we is coming (its sex unspecified in Bierhorst's summary) and the humans will have to assist him by spearing it in the anus. Sure enough, the new monster arrives and is killed. However, the reformed Mhú-we now announces other cannibal giants are on their way and the people should flee to a further country (Bierhorst 1995, 59–60).

As in other Algonquian accounts, the Delaware Friendly Visitor is male although, in contrast to midwestern and northeastern versions, this guest is not joined to humans through the device of fictive kinship. Likewise, the Delaware telling does not employ the Iroquois rationale of feuding spouses to explain the bond between guest and hosts. Nothing is said in the Delaware account about the giant taking up residence with the humans (although that may be implied), nor is the giant described as helping the family in any way. Like cannibal giants in the Northeast, this one is transformed into a person. The metamorphosis, however, is not so clearly caused by taking an emetic and seems more accidental. The appearance of the second giant and the inevitability of combat with it are, as is generally the case with Algonquian versions elsewhere, unexplained. Human help is required in the showdown with the bellicose invader as it is with the Iroquois and in some accounts of the Northeast.

Discussion and Conclusions

A complex story was shared by speakers of Algonquian and Iroquoian languages from Wisconsin to New Brunswick and from Ontario south to, possibly, New Jersey. Its presence in these areas was not the result of chance, and it was not because the story was repeatedly invented. The same story was present in those places around 1900 because people in one place told it to people in another who liked it and, in turn, told it to others.

Whose story was it originally? The Friendly Visitor certainly is out of character as a windigo. Algonquian cannibal giants were disinclined to become sincerely cooperative members of human families. However, the story may occur most frequently among the Iroquois and seems to be present elsewhere in the form of an arc around Iroquois country. Such circumstances imply Iroquois origin.

If so, when did the story spread outward? Some native tales spread rapidly during the late nineteenth century when Indian youths were brought together in government boarding schools. This time is too late to account for the appearance of the Friendly Visitor in the Midwest by 1839 (Schoolcraft 1999, 83) and in the Northeast by 1859 (Rand 1894, 83). Another possibility is that the story dates to the late eighteenth–early nineteenth centuries because it describes a nuclear family that, as a residential unit, was not a common living arrangement until that time. This interpretation assumes that Iroquois lore directly, simply, and obviously reflects a specific aspect of social reality. It does not.

The Friendly Visitor more likely diffused toward the north, west, and south at a time the Iroquois are known to have been active in precisely those directions: the 1600s–early 1700s. Documented Iroquois interaction was mostly violent—they waged war. However, the spread of a complex and rather philosophical story implies that peaceful, intimate forms of interchange routinely took place also. Iroquois influence of this sort may be detectable chiefly from the evidence of oral narrative.

The Friendly Visitor was told in many places in strikingly different ways. A remarkable feature of Algonquian versions is consensus on the premise of the story: how it starts and what moves its characters to behave as they do. Storytellers in both the Northeast and Midwest insisted that the story of the Friendly Visitor can only be initiated by a woman offering a male cannibal giant the status of being her kinsman, and the story gets told because he accepts. How to account for this? Algonquian lifeways, in contrast to those of the Iroquois, often involved small, mobile groups of people precariously dependent on success in harvesting wild foods in harsh circumstances. Perhaps making a living in this fashion demanded a particular wariness of strangers that Seymour Parker (1960) and others of the culture-personality school interpreted as being defensive and paranoid. At any rate, the premise of fictive kinship so characteristic of these stories surely reflects, as Morrison (1979, 62) observes, an uneasiness and reticence toward outsiders.

In the Iroquois setting, human and female cannibal giant ally because the lady monster needs refuge from her abusive husband and the arrangement offers benefits to the hosts. In extending hospitality and in fighting the wicked giant, the Iroquois emphasized the importance of human assistance for the good giant. The idea that humans assist the giant was perfectly at home in Iroquois oral narrative, which often stressed that a supernatural needs human help.

But if the overall theme was culturally compatible, the proximate story and its moral implications were not. The Iroquois Friendly Visitor advances a strongly female-centered perspective unusual in Iroquois oral narrative.

Iroquois life was organized as a sexual division of labor in which men were responsible for what was public, of the forest, and at a distance. Women's activities, in contrast, were private and of the clearing and hearth. Women were responsible (among other things) for planting, tending, harvesting, storing, and cooking the domesticated plants corns, beans, and squash. Women's productive labor in agriculture probably made a greater contribution to the Iroquois diet than what men provided. Further, cores of related women were the basic building blocks of social reproduction and residential stability. The most important rights of descent, inheritance, and membership passed exclusively through the female line. For all these reasons, Iroquois women surely were honored. As an Oneida expressed in late 1700s, "Our ancestors said: Who bring us forth, who cultivate our lands, who kindle our fires and boil our pots, but the women?" (Hough 1861, 279). And, for the same reasons, Iroquois women are said to have enjoyed high political and social standing (Allen 1988, 42, 51; Brown 1970; and see Tooker 1984).

Why, then, are there not more women's stories recorded from a society in which women supposedly enjoyed high standing? Part of the answer may be, as it is with this tale, that one must learn to recognize the evidence for women's expression.

7

Mythic Imagery
in Iroquoian Archaeology

ANYONE VISITING AN archaeological dig in the Northeast sees that virtually every object removed from the earth—mostly chips of stone with an occasional fragment of bone or pottery—looks unremittingly plain. Most artifacts
bespeak little beyond simple technology and a nose-to-the-grindstone concern
with subsistence because decoration or elaboration of any sort rarely survives.
When an object of art shows up—say, something fashioned to represent an animal—it is a dramatic and haunting find. Its finder feels a sense of wonder and a
bond of common humanity extending across centuries to the object's creator.

This chapter was inspired by such wonder. Its subject is a remarkable series of humanlike faces and figures (effigies five hundred years old)
depicted on certain smoking pipes and pottery vessels, both of fired clay,
in present upstate New York and adjoining Canada. The pipe effigies are
among the most complex pictorial material in Northeast archaeology.
Those on pottery constitute the largest surviving database of material symbols significant to ancestors of Oneida and Onondaga people.

Obviously, these were deliberately created representations reflecting the
consciousness of their creators. The icons must be coming out of their makers' reservoir of metaphoric and symbolic codes that, among all human
beings, also find expression in mythopoetic language. Certainly they *look*
mythic—depictions of beings, one suspects, that figured importantly in oral
narrative and religious belief. These humanlike representations bring us
literally face-to-face with a past reality. They confront us with the question:
What did the images mean? The challenge to the living is to grant voice to
the dead, to "put tongues in inanimate objects" (Glassie 1988, 86).

That is done, in archaeology, by moving from the known to the unknown. It is an inferential strategy of working back in time from what is ethnographically and historically understood to elucidate the archaeological record. A common-sense form of interpretation called the direct historical approach, it yields the best results when the terms of the comparison relate to the same social group at two moments in time that are not far apart (Steward 1942; Strong 1942). Naturally, it is especially important to work within the same continuous tradition when investigating material symbols that carry culturally specific meaning (Flannery and Marcus 1996; Trigger 2001).

In the Iroquois area, continuity is strong and evidence is copious. Written materials documenting the Iroquois may be the most plentiful for any native people in North America during the seventeenth and eighteenth centuries. Substantial ethnographic reportage during the nineteenth and twentieth centuries supplements the historic record. The enormous corpus of Iroquois folklore and myth includes the earliest such material recorded on the continent. Among the Iroquois, therefore, a person journeying back in time can set out with sound information and multiple kinds of evidence. Here, prospects for understanding mythic imagery are uniquely favorable.

Effigy Pipes

Archaeology of Pipes

The dominant pipe form throughout the Northeast during the European 1400s and 1500s was a small (typically about six inches long), single-piece object of fired clay. Such implements were elbow shaped with a right angle at the stem-bowl juncture, their conical or trumpet-shaped bowls holding about the amount of tobacco found in a twentieth-century cigarette. A minority of them (less than 25 percent) carried effigies, that is, naturalistic images of apparent humans, birds, mammals, reptiles, and other subjects created on the bowl facing the smoker.

My interest is in three types of humanlike depiction, each featuring a distinctive and recurring visual pattern. Given similarities in subject matter and presentational format, all could be thematically related (Wonderley 2005a).

These pipes show up in the eastern Iroquois area of upstate New York in the regions historically belonging to the Mohawks, Oneidas, and Onondagas (map 3). However, they occur much more frequently among the St. Lawrence Iroquoians, people who formerly lived along the river of that name extending east from Lake Ontario to beyond the city of Quebec. Their material remains are viewed as an archaeological culture area with its own characteristics and developmental trajectory that set it apart from better-known Iroquoian societies in New York and Ontario. Researchers have proposed that it might be composed of anywhere from two to seven more or less distinct archaeological subregions (Jamieson 1990a; Pendergast 1991b). At least some St. Lawrence Iroquoians were speakers of Iroquoian languages (Lounsbury 1978).

Their disappearance, by 1600, is the subject of considerable speculation. The introduction of European diseases and climatic deterioration are frequently cited as possible factors in their dispersal (Jamieson 1990b). Because St. Lawrence Iroquoian villages were consistently fortified and manifest other indications of pervasive violence, warfare probably played

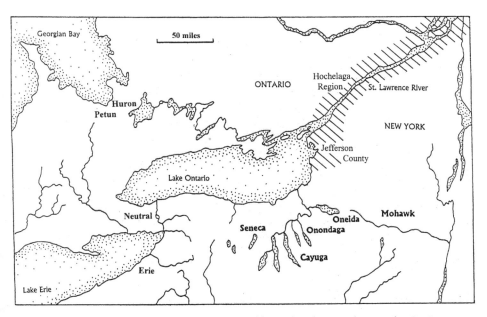

3. The Northeastern Iroquoian Region. Oblique hatching indicates the St. Lawrence Iroquoian area.

a role in the process (see Chapdelaine 2004, 67; Engelbrecht 1995, 49; Jamieson 1990b, 81–82; Pendergast 1990, 24).

Where did they go? In 1642, several Indians told the French

> that they belonged to the nation of those who had formerly dwelt on this [Montreal] Island. Then, stretching out their hands towards the hills that lie to the East and South of the mountain, "There," said they, "are the places where stood Villages filled with great numbers of Savages. The Hurons, who then were our enemies, drove our Forefathers from this country. Some went towards the country of the Abnaquiois [Abenakis], others toward the country of the Hiroquois [Iroquois], some to the Hurons themselves, and joined them. And that is how this Island became deserted." (Thwaites 1896–1901, 22:215)

Recent discoveries in Vermont dramatically confirm the presence of St. Lawrence Iroquoian pottery (and, presumably, the St. Lawrence Iroquoian makers of that pottery) in Abenaki country (Peterson et al. 2004). Other archaeological investigations have demonstrated a high incidence of stylistically St. Lawrence Iroquoian pottery (20 percent or more) on certain sites of the Hurons and their close neighbors, the Petuns (Engelbrecht 1995, 52; Kuhn et al. 1993, 78; Ramsden 1990a, 382–83; 1990b, 90; Robertson and Williamson 1998, 147–48). Aspects of this St. Lawrence Iroquoian ceramic tradition appear to have persisted in the Huron setting through several generations of pottery-makers (Pendergast 1999, 105, 111).

Some St. Lawrence Iroquoian pottery also occurs among the Iroquois although it is very meager in comparison to what is seen among the Hurons. For example, only about 2 percent of the relevant Mohawk assemblages, apparently locally made, display St. Lawrence Iroquoian attributes (Kuhn et al. 1993, 85; Funk and Kuhn 2003, 157). The pottery distributions suggest, therefore, that a fair number of St. Lawrence Iroquoians were assimilated among the Hurons while comparatively few ended up among the Iroquois.

Pipes discussed in this chapter are strongly associated with one of the St. Lawrence Iroquoian subregions, that of present-day Jefferson County in northern New York. This region contains the largest concentration of St. Lawrence Iroquoian sites and, indeed, one of the densest site concentrations anywhere in Iroquois country (Engelbrecht 1995, 37; Pendergast 1996, 44). It is also an area long recognized for the number and distinctiveness of its smoking pipes. Nowhere else in Iroquois country, Skinner (1921, 118) observed specifically of Jefferson County, did "effigy pipes attain such a high degree of development" (see also Ritchie 1980, 320).

Being relatively spectacular finds, these pipes were sought after by antiquarians and collectors. Most were gathered many years ago from unknown circumstances. Sitting in museums today, they typically come with little provenience information beyond the county in which they were found.

The first of the three pipe types discussed comprises a humanlike face or figure within an arch (figs. 1a–e). Usually one person is indicated although a group scene exists. We generally see two or three nested arches. Frequently two or more incised lines connect the top of the head to the interior apex of the arch. Such lines apparently radiate outward and upward from the head.

I identify nineteen examples of this, the Figure-in-Arch pipe, that have at least some provenience information. Eight derive from Jefferson County, four from the Mohawk Valley, three from the area of the Oneidas, and two from Onondaga territory as historically known (Wonderley 2005a).

This composition seems to be depicted on a carved-bone artifact from the Oneida Nichols Pond site (figs. 1f–g), and it also appears on a series of pipes fashioned from steatite/soapstone, polished limestone, or marble. From known provenience, I found eleven examples of a figure within an

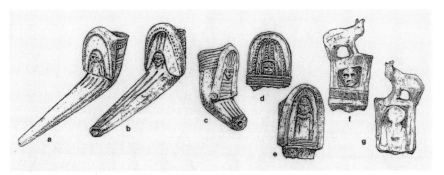

1. Figure-in-Arch ceramic pipes (a–e) and object of carved bone (f–g; front and back views) (after Wonderley 2005a, figs. 2, 4). The artifacts are from the Mohawk (a), Oneida (b–c, f–g), and Onondaga (d) areas, and from Jefferson County (e).

arch executed in stone, seven of which derive from Jefferson County and are likely to have been produced there (Ritchie 1980, 320).

The second type is the Figure-in-Crescent (figs. 2a–e). The crescent may be unembellished, notched with incised decoration, or equipped with distinctive horseshoe-like markings. The humanlike component is, most frequently, a face. Multiple faces are known; sometimes a complete human figure is depicted, and there is one instance of a quadruped. Usually the face or subject of the composition is shown not so much on the flat surface enclosed by the crescent but on the edge of the plane where the crescent is open.

Thirteen examples from known provenience include three from the Mohawk and Onondaga regions, nine from Jefferson County, and one from the Roebuck site in Grenville County, Ontario. At the Dawson site (present Montreal), there apparently is a stone version of the Figure-in-Crescent (Pendergast and Trigger 1972, 121–22). The design may have been rather common in the "Hochelaga Province," the St. Lawrence Iroquoian subregion between present Prescott and Montreal (Chapdelaine 1990; 2004, 68–70). Additionally, the composition is found in another medium: an antler pin or comb from the Mohawk Valley (fig. 2f).

The third type is the Dougherty pipe (figs. 3b–c), the name proposed from an Oneida archaeological site. Of nine ceramic examples with known provenience, four are from Jefferson County, two derive from Oneida sites (Madison County), and one each is known from Grenville County

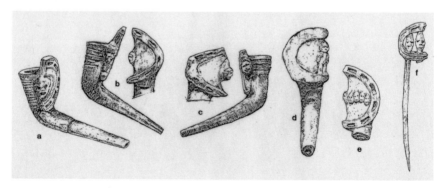

2. Figure-in-Crescent ceramic pipes (a–e) and carved antler comb (f) (after Wonderley 2005a, figs. 4, 6). These are from Jefferson County and the greater St. Lawrence Iroquoian area (a–e), and the Mohawk Valley (f).

(Ontario), the Onondaga area, and the Mohawk Valley. A stone version of the pipe is reported from northern Pennsylvania (fig. 3a). The Dougherty composition also occurs on a carved antler comb from the Mohawk Valley (figs. 3d–e).

The complete Dougherty composition comprises four registers:

1. At the top is a row of three or four humanlike faces with ray- or fan-like elements flaring up and outward.

2. The heads rest on a platform whose ends rise to frame the heads on each side. It looks like a bracket or a squarish letter *c* on its back.

3. Below that are two circular depressions, usually relatively large and separated by vertical lines or stripes.

4. Finally, a zone of geometric incision of simple lines or cross-hatching that, in the case of the comb, includes another row of heads lacking the ray-like elements noted above (fig. 3d).

Not all the registers need be present—a phenomenon reminiscent of the metaphorical process called *synecdoche,* a figure of speech in which a part

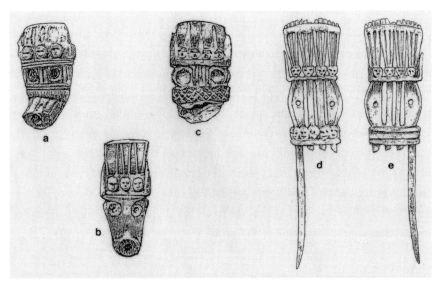

3. Dougherty pipes (a–c) and carved antler comb (d–e; front and back views) (after Wonderley 2004, fig. 20). Pictured are objects from northern Pennsylvania (a; an example carved from stone), the Mohawk Valley (d–e), and the Oneida (c) and Onondaga (b) areas.

makes reference to the whole. However, whatever registers are present must adhere to that relative order, implying that the overall sequence is essential to the meaning.

This pipe type is suggestive of an *imago mundi* or a mythic cosmogony, its ordered sequence of imagery calling to mind the developmental, linear syntax necessary to narrative. Since the incidents of a story are temporally related—one preceding and being the precondition of the next—a tale has to be presented in a certain sequence, not unlike this composition. It would not be surprising if this pipe imagery had a narrative referent, perhaps relating to a story performed, told, or contemplated.

Map 4 illustrates the composite distribution of these three visually distinctive pipe themes. Overwhelmingly concentrated in Jefferson County, they clearly are characteristic of that area. Smaller numbers are found elsewhere, and almost all of them fall within three clusters corresponding to the lands of the Mohawk, Oneida, and Onondaga nations as historically known. This seems to me strong evidence for a Jefferson County presence of some sort among the eastern Iroquois.

These pipes featured images of symbolic import, the meaning of which presumably was understood in each of their settings. Their distribution is the cumulative result of activity over a period of time, possibly a century. This is information exchange, communication effected through material symbols. A similar phenomenon typifies the interchange occurring among peer polities—autonomous, neighboring sociopolitical units (Renfrew 1986). However, an interpretive paradigm more at home in the generally egalitarian Eastern Woodlands is "interaction sphere" (Caldwell 1964), in which the sharing among several communities of distinctive material culture is thought to result from episodes of a particular kind of behavior (Hall 1997, 155). Here, it seems, we have a Jefferson County–centered interaction sphere involving effigy pipes.

Social Context of Pipes

Effigy pipes attract a wide range of speculation. Perhaps they commemorated historical incidents, for example, or comprised a genre of realistic portraiture, or reflected life-crisis events (Kapches 2003; Kearsley 1997,

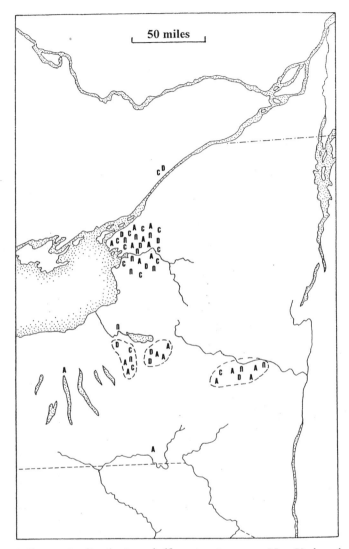

4. Composite distribution of effigy pipes in eastern New York and adjacent Canada. A = Figure-in-Arch (n = version in stone); C = Figure-in-Crescent; D = Dougherty.

115–25). Pipes bearing likenesses of human faces have been interpreted as depicting masks and, therefore, signal the appearance of the Iroquois False Face medicine society as a group-integrating sodality (Ritchie and Funk 1973, 367). Pipes with animal effigies may connote seasonality and the renewal of nature (Kinsey 1989), or they might represent totemic eponyms—emblems of clans named for animals (Noble 1979, 83).

Most researchers, however, connect effigy pipes, in some fashion, to supernatural power and shamanism. Imagery on bowls facing the smokers "related to the spiritual communication between men and their guardian spirits, cultivated by means of meditation while contemplating the representations of these spirits" (Brasser 1980, 100; and see Hamell 1998, 272). These or other pipes may also have been used by shamans in the act of curing or communing with the numinous (Mathews 1976). Possibly they represented transformation of a human into an alternate form (Mathews 1981, 14–17; Sempowski 2004), or provided the means to achieve some other (drug-induced?) state of consciousness (von Gernet 1992). Any or all of these interpretations are possible, but not one of them is clearly documented.

What the documentary evidence indicates is that men were the primary owners and users of smoking pipes (Kuhn 1985, 58–67).[1] Over and over again, men are described as smoking pipes as leisurely or political activities. The first, recreational use, is the kind of smoking more frequently mentioned. Typically, a man passed the time puffing away "through pleasure and habit" (Fenton and Moore 1977, 86), a form of relaxation so pervasive that reference to it served as a metaphor for the good life: "We should have nothing to do," as one Oneida said, "but sit in our doors and smoke our pipes in peace" (Cantine and DeWitt ca. 1793, 123–24).

Leaving aside pipe-smoking as leisure activity, what the written record consistently indicates is a close relationship between pipes and politics, the latter being (at least in the public eye) the domain of men. Sources of the seventeenth and eighteenth centuries frequently mention men smoking pipes in the context of formal, deliberative gatherings. To Lafitau around 1720, an Iroquois council comprised a group of men, "all of them, pipes in their mouths" (Fenton and Moore 1974, 296, Pl. XVII). "They never attend a council," Brébeuf observed of the Hurons in 1636, "without a pipe or calumet in their mouths. The smoke, they say, gives them intelligence, and enables them to see

---

1. Men may have been the makers as well as the users of the pipes, but that is unclear (Kuhn 1985, 57–77). Nor does the point seem to me as essential to interpreting the pipes as it does to understanding the pottery vessels.

clearly through the most intricate matters" (Thwaites 1896–1901, 10:219). In 1645, the Iroquois assured a potentially hostile audience of Algonquins and Hurons that "Iroquois chiefs only smoke (hold council) in their country, that their calumets (pipes) are always in their mouths" (Fenton 1985, 130). Iroquois men entering the council setting in 1669 would "seat themselves in the most convenient place that they find vacant, without any consideration of rank, and at once get some fire to light their pipes, which do not leave their mouths during the whole time of the council, and they say that 'Good thoughts come while smoking'" (quoted in Fenton 1998, 22). Such behavior, Fenton added, "is a persistent theme in Iroquois political life."

Smoking together was a figure of speech synonymous with peaceful, friendly negotiations (Jennings et al. 1985, 121), as when the Oneidas remarked at a 1785 treaty: "We have now brought our pipes together" to enter into conversation (Hough 1861, 106, 102). The ritual of diplomacy called the Greeting at the Woods Edge (part of the Condolence Ceremony to raise up a replacement for a deceased chief of the Iroquois Confederacy) was, in large measure, an act of pipe-smoking. The foreign embassy coming to negotiate peace was met by an elderly "word-bearer" who, "after lighting his pipe . . . tells them very eloquently that they are very welcome" (Fenton and Moore 1977, 174). When foreign diplomats neared an Iroquois village, according to an account of 1674, "a fire is lighted, as a sign of peace, at the spot where the elders of the village are going to wait for [the visitors]; and, after smoking for some time and receiving the savage compliments that they pay one another, they are led to the cabin set apart for them" (Thwaites 1896–1901, 58:187–89).

These were occasions of diplomatic ritual in which certain oral narratives—notably aspects of the mythic charter of the Iroquois Confederacy—were publicly recounted. And with the exchange of words came an exchange of objects—including pipes. In 1774, East Coast Indians requesting Oneida help presented the Oneidas with a pipe "so at your assemblings ye might look on it; and smoke out of it, and remember us" (McCallum 1932, 165). In 1784 negotiations with New York, the Oneidas state, "[as] testimony of our approbation of your rekindling this council fire, we present you with this pipe of peace, there to remain as a token of peace from us, agreeable to the custom of our ancestors" (Hough 1861, 53).

Some pipes, therefore, certainly are material correlates of a characteristically male pattern of ceremonialism signaling diplomatic protocol. The presence of such pipes from a distant place may indicate a state of peaceful relations with that locale. As Peter Ramsden (1990b, 94) puts it, certain pipes—presumably the most distinctive ones—probably functioned "in ritual contexts involving men, perhaps in the negotiation or mediation of power relationships."

The historic evidence for diplomatic pipe use must be what led William Finlayson (1998, 1:409–11) to interpret an increase in pipes during the Middleport phase (ca. 1420–1500) of southwestern Ontario as signaling intervillage alliance. The same facts help to explain the appearance of Mohawk pipes in conjunction with a tremendous increase in pipe use in the Seneca archaeological record around 1600. Both phenomena, according to Kuhn and Sempowski (2001), probably reflected the entry of the Seneca nation (traditionally the last to join) into the Iroquois league. The league, they reason, was essentially an alliance based on the performance of ceremonial acts that encouraged exchanging pipes as gifts and smoking together in councils of collective decision-making. "The formation of a confederacy with these protocols would likely lead to an increase in smoking paraphernalia and an increase in exotic pipes on the sites of its member nations" (Kuhn and Sempowski 2001, 312; see also Engelbrecht 2003, 133; Sempowski and Saunders 2001, 3:700).

Even today, Iroquois pipe smoking is linked with ceremonial and public speech making because it is "thought to settle the minds of speakers and other key participants who receive the pipe" (Foster 1985, 114). Since the connection between pipes and council clearly is of longstanding duration, it is reasonable to project it back to a time immediately preceding European testimony. Hence, Iroquois archaeological pipes, including effigy pipes, of the recent past should be assessed with political activity in mind.

Historical Identification

Can the pipes and their suggested behavioral correlates be linked to historically attested or traditionally remembered events? The obvious correlation to consider is with the League of the Iroquois. This, the most famous native government in North America, exercised profound influence on the course of American colonial history for nearly two centuries. Opinions vary widely about when the confederacy was formed. Scholars have tended to date its beginning to the late 1400s–mid 1500s (Bradley 1987, 43–45; Fenton 1998, 129; Funk and Kuhn 2003, 157; Snow 1994, 49, 60). However, a somewhat later date for the completion of the league now seems likely based on the fact that Seneca and Mohawk connections do not seem strong until about 1600 (Kuhn and Sempowski 2001; Sempowski and Saunders 2001, 3:700).

To speak of completion implies a process occurring over time. In all likelihood, the confederacy emerged gradually out of a series of widening alliances culminating in the admission of the Senecas (Engelbrecht 1985; Fenton 1998, 72–73). Contemplating the formation process from its eastern terminus, Funk and Kuhn (2003, 157) propose the confederacy originated as a three-nation alliance among the Mohawk, Oneida, and Onondaga nations. Their scenario is consistent with the earliest Iroquois testimony on the subject (1743–1815) describing an initial Mohawk-Oneida compact subsequently expanded to bring in the Onondagas (Boyce 1973, 288; Fenton 1998, 53, 435; Hale 1969, 131; Klinck and Talman 1970, 103–4).

The effigy pipes of the Jefferson County interaction sphere might relate to this hypothesized stage of league formation because of their relatively early dating (1450–early 1500s) and the absence of the pipes from western Iroquois (Cayuga, Seneca) regions. If so, it is troubling that traditions of league origin do not mention the Jefferson County locale or refer to earlier alliances.

Another possibility is that the pipes relate to a different confederation, one mentioned in an Iroquois history as preceding the League of the Iroquois. The first chronicle of the Iroquois written by an Iroquois person was published (in English) by Tuscarora David Cusick, probably in 1827 (Beauchamp 1892). Few have taken Cusick's *Sketches of Ancient History of the Six Nations* seriously as history because it is, in large measure and in contemporary terms, a compendium of oral narrative themes then current among the Iroquois (Judkins 1987). A further strike against its historical credibility is a chronology claiming specific dates for events occurring hundreds and even thousands of years in the past (Fenton 1998, 64; Tooker 1978, 420).

Nevertheless, *Sketches of Ancient History* demands careful study as one of the great works of autochthonous historiography in North America (Brotherston 1992). And, for purely Iroquois reasons, it deserves at least as much respect as any other account of mythic history/historic myth. The Iroquois, Fenton emphasizes (1962, 283; 1998, 34, 120–23), periodize their own history into three epochs, each the subject of a key oral tradition. In our time, the mythic culture history familiar to Iroquois *annalistes* comprises, first, the age of creation (described in the great myth of beginnings mostly recorded around the turn of the twentieth century); second, the age of the Iroquois league (its formation most fully explicated in traditions committed to writing, again, around 1900); and, third, the age of the teachings of Handsome Lake (a Seneca prophet whose visions just prior to 1800 became codified as a new religion by about 1850). Conceiving of the past as sequent eras, this emic perspective shares with scholarly history an insistence that past time is structured linearly, and time's arrow must proceed from oldest to most recent.

Cusick's history features the same tripartite chronological structure but not precisely the same three historical epochs. As Handsome Lake's contemporary, Cusick could not have imagined the Seneca prophet as the subject of a past age. Consequently, Cusick described two of the eras familiar today (creation and the Iroquois league) but, in lieu of Handsome Lake, his third period is one not mentioned in later sources. It takes place along the St. Lawrence River—after the age of creation and before the time of the Iroquois league.

Cusick's second epoch opens with a body of *Ukwehu:wé* (the Iroquois term for themselves, in Oneida) "encamped on the St. Lawrence" (Beauchamp 1892, 5). Beset by various difficulties including an invasion of giants from the north, "a convention were held [*sic*] by the chieftains in order to take some measures to defend their country." Later, "the [same] northern nations formed a confederacy and seated a great council fire on river St. Lawrence." Evidently, this pre-league alliance came to a bad end, for its chapter concludes with a description of the St. Lawrence collapse:

> About this time a great horned serpent appeared on Lake Ontario, the serpent produced diseases and many of the people died, but by the aid of

thunder bolts the monster was compelled to retire. A blazing star fell into a fort situated on the St. Lawrence and destroyed the people; this event was considered as a warning of their destruction. After a time a war broke out among the northern nations which continued until they had utterly destroyed each other, the island again become in possession of fierce animals. (Beauchamp 1892, 9–11)

Cusick's third epoch details the League of the Iroquois familiar from later sources and brings us into historic time as recognized by European newcomers. In this chapter and time period, we learn the origins of the Mohawk, Oneida, Onondaga, Cayuga, Seneca, and Tuscarora nations (the latter having joined the league in the 1700s) and how their confederacy came to be formed. Nothing is said, in this connection, about the St. Lawrence area or an earlier St. Lawrence alliance.

In sum, Cusick documented an early-nineteenth-century Iroquois belief in a northern confederacy antedating the League of the Iroquois. This historical tradition is in broad agreement with the inference drawn from archaeological evidence: A political union distinct from the historic league may have existed in the St. Lawrence region. However, just as the early league accounts fail to mention the St. Lawrence area, so Cusick's description of a northern confederacy makes no reference to league nations. The fit between tradition and archaeology is, in both cases, equally good and equally imperfect.

Effigy Pipe Meaning

What was so desirable or interesting about the messages shared by the smokers of Jefferson County and the eastern Iroquois area? What did the images mean?

The three pipe compositions have distinctive properties in common. All, for example, share the same presentational format: an essentially two-dimensional plane on the pipe bowl facing the smoker. This feature has long been assumed to be diagnostic inasmuch as examples of all three types have been subsumed under the term *escutcheon pipe* (McGuire 1899, 497; see Pendergast 1992, 54–55; Ritchie 1980, 320; Rutsch 1973, 170). Evidently requiring construction of a plaque or storyboard for proper display, this design layout raises the possibility that all of these pipes were as narratively oriented as the Dougherty type.

Additionally, they share an important feature of content: All present the human face or figure at least partially enclosed by the framing device. Because the three pipes have these points in common, we should consider that they might be related conceptually.

The most obvious entrée into intended meaning is that face within the crescent depicted as leaving the enclosed space of the plane (figs. 2a–c). This unusual convention requires the viewer to take notice of a head exiting the composition. Apparently it is coming out; it is emerging into our world.

This may illustrate an ancient Iroquois belief about human origins—people emerged from the earth. Prior to the early 1800s, the Iroquoians did not attribute the appearance of humans to a divinity's creative act (Wonderley 2001). On the contrary, "when asked concerning their origin, they regularly answer, that they came up out of the ground, in the regions where they now live" (Dwight 1822, 203; and see Klinck and Talman 1970, 85, 110). Thus, Hurons and Wyandots long remembered that their forefathers "first came out of the ground" near Quebec (Hale 1894, 6). Mohawks explained that humans, in animal form, "came out of the earth, stroking themselves in the hot sun their hairs came off and so became men and women" (Andrews 1716, 243). In the early 1740s, another Mohawk stated that "they had dwelt in the earth," and subsequently "concluded it best for them all to come out" (Heckewelder 1991, 251). The corresponding Seneca tradition of the late 1700s was that "they broke out of the earth from a large mountain" near Canandaigua (Seaver 1990, 142). And, as the Oneida creation account of the late 1700s put it: "They came up out of the ground in human form. . . . [And the Oneidas] used to show the precise spot of ground, a small hollow, where they said their ancestors came up" (Lounsbury and Gick 2000, 161).

That is why an Iroquois speaker at the Lancaster Treaty in 1744 said: "You came out of the ground in a country that lies beyond the seas, there you may have a just claim, but here you must allow us to be your elder brethren, and the lands to belong to us" (Jennings 1984, 357). This, as Malinowski (1948, 116) observed, is the literal claim of being autochthonous and the reason for owning the land. The myth of emergence is fairly common in North America (Rooth 1957; Wheeler-Voegelin and Moore 1957), especially among horticulturalists staking claim to their territory (Barnouw 1977, 57, 92; Lankford 1987, 136–39). A story of this sort ranks among a culture's key narratives for it is a myth telling how some things started and came to be as they are now. It accounts for and, at the same time, is an important expression of community identity (see, for example, Urton 1990, 39).

The pipe most closely resembling the Figure-in-Crescent is the Figure-in-Arch. Indeed, the two types may depict the same composition from side and frontal views.[2] What I think is the carved-bone version of the Figure-in-Arch (figs. 1f–g) makes this seem likely because the figure appears to be inside a cave or a hill.

At hand, then, are a theme (emergence) and an interpretive principle (depiction of the theme from different points of view) that make sense of a whole series of similar effigy scenes. For example, the so-called boat pipe (Wonderley 2005a: fig. 11), another elaborate pipe composition linked to Jefferson County, has been interpreted as showing a shaman on a spirit voyage (Mathews 1982). To me, it looks more like a figure coming out of the ground and being depicted from a different perspective. Similarly, the Second Woods pipe (Wonderley 2005a: fig. 12), featuring a scene of three or four human faces in nichelike settings (Lenig 1965, 13–15), falls into place as thematically appropriate to Jefferson County and the eastern Iroquois if considered as an allusion to emergence.

Identifying the same theme on several pipe types clarifies and renders relevant a very different phenomenon: Iroquois origin traditions bow, metaphorically speaking, toward the north. At the beginning of part three of Cusick's 1827 history, ancestors of the league nations emerged from a mountain near Oswego at the southeast corner of Lake Ontario (Beauchamp 1892, 11). An early nineteenth-century tradition held that the Onondagas originated northeast of Oswego on the Salmon River (Klinck and Talman 1970, 98). And, in the late 1750s, Sandy Creek in Jefferson County, north

---

2. Depicting the same subject from different perspectives is recognized by Lankford (2007c, 10, 29) as an important convention of Mississippian art.

of the Salmon River, was "the place from which, according to Iroquois tradition, they all came or rather, in their own conception, they were born" (Pouchot 1994, 392). Such details make sense as acknowledgments of some kind of Jefferson County primacy.

Is the more elaborate Dougherty pipe interpretable in the same frame of reference as a theme of emergence? I think so but suspect it also illustrates aspects of what, later in time, was a famous monster tale. The first documented Seneca account of emergence (Seaver 1990) was told in conjunction with a story about a huge snake. "They originated and lived on a well known hill . . . where they were put in eminent peril of utter destruction by a monstrous serpent, which circled itself about the fort and lay with its mouth open at the gate" (Schoolcraft 1975, 60). Confounded by its noxious breath, the villagers fled to their doom through the gate and into the serpent's open maw. Finally slain by a young survivor with a magical weapon, the snake rolled downhill, discharging human heads as it tumbled into a lake. The conclusion to this curious tale is that the Indians gathered at this "sacred place, to mourn the loss of their friends, and to celebrate some rites that are peculiar to themselves" (Seaver 1990, 143).

There seem to be two separate stories here: "Emerging-from-the-earth" and the "Snake-who-swallowed-a-village." Though linked in the telling, their only apparent connection is that they occurred in the same place. Yet, one would suspect a closer relationship in content on the basis of comparative mythology. Elsewhere, snakes play a prominent role in accounting for ancestral and tribal beginnings; so much so that "it is impossible to overstate the importance of the association of the serpent with human origins" (Drummond 1981, 658).

The "Snake-who-swallowed-a-village" was one of the more popular Iroquois narratives during the nineteenth and early twentieth centuries (Beauchamp 1892, 20–21; 1922, 110; Hewitt 1918, 106, 420–21; Klinck and Talman 1970, 110; Morgan 1962, 159–60; Randle 1953, 623; Severance 1904, 80–81). The story also is notable for the attention it has drawn from non-Iroquois analysts who see in it an allegory about the formation of the League of the Iroquois (Hamell 1979, fig. 17 caption; Schoolcraft 1975, 61).

For Marius Barbeau (1951, 85; 1952, 116), the act of entering the serpent's mouth as described in the narrative signified dying and being buried in the ground. Hence, the snake is the earth. On the basis of ethnographic testimony, Barbeau claimed the "Snake-who-swallowed-a-village" was the origin myth of the *Ohgi:we* ceremony—an annual or semiannual feast held to placate spirits of a community's dead. While that specific assertion has never been confirmed, other ethnographers concede *Ohgi:we* implies some invocation of chthonic powers and seems to be of great antiquity (Fenton and Kurath 1951). The dance patterns of *Ohgi:we,* suggestive of coiling and uncoiling, "may echo a half-forgotten myth about an all-devouring earth-serpent" (Kurath 1952, 129).

Attributable to the late 1700s, the "Snake-who-swallowed-a-village" also happens to be one of the oldest stories documented. Indeed, its presence among the Oklahoma Wyandots (Barbeau 1915, 146–48), descendants of Huron and Petun people, implies an age at least 150 years earlier. The reasoning here is homologous to identifying languages that are genetically related. Wyandot and Iroquois folklore similarities are so detailed and pervasive that they are unlikely to be due to chance, independent development, or recent borrowing from each other or from an unknown common source. In all probability, they are cognate beliefs derived from a stock of oral tradition held in common by early-seventeenth-century ancestors of Iroquois and Wyandots (Wonderley 2004, 104–7).

Simply because it is a story of such extraordinary age and interest, we should consider the possibility that the "Snake-who-swallowed-a-village" is referenced on the Dougherty pipe. By this reading, the two prominent circles of the third register would be the serpent's eyes. The lowest register, as shown on the comb illustrated in fig. 3d, would depict skulls of people swallowed by the snake.

The theme of emerging from the earth may occur on the Dougherty pipe's top register in the form of several human faces resting on the square-shaped bracket element. In the early versions of the league tradition, the chief personified his settlement/tribe in such a way that leader and people were metaphorically synonymous. Each head may stand for a community or a community's mythological beginning. In this depiction of emergence, three or four communities would be linked together through ascription of common origin.

Possibly, then, the Dougherty pipe provides visual evidence that the "Snake-who-swallowed-a-village" and "Emerging-from-the-earth" were closely related as components of the same story. If so, the theme of emergence becomes a more encompassing narrative alluding to death as well as birth. This must have been a myth of substantial ideological/religious importance, a story largely lost to us today.

What would be the purpose of such reified narrative? Were these images intended to serve as mnemonic devices to jog the memory in the course of formal declamation? Although men were smoking as ritual recitations took place, no theme of emergence is documented in such speeches as the Greeting at the Woods Edge. The "Snake-who-swallowed-a-village" could well relate to the Death Feast ceremony. Yet, even if that were certain, it is unclear why the performance of *Ohgi:we* would require a pipe alluding to that story. Foreigners never documented the use of effigy pipes as ceremonial objects and never wrote about representational imagery evoking oral narrative. But it must also be said that visitors scarcely mentioned effigy pipes at all.

What is probably Iroquoian testimony bearing on the subject of pipe use is simply that they created imagery good to think about. It was noted early in the seventeenth century that the Hurons rendered pictures of men, animals, birds, and other subjects on their pipes because they enjoyed looking at them (Wrong 1939, 98). We have already noted, later in the century, the Seneca sentiment that "Good thoughts come while smoking" (Fenton 1998, 2). It appears, therefore, that smoking really was regarded as "a mental device used by the smoker to concentrate his thoughts upon a given subject" (Brasser 1980, 96).

Evidently cogitated were origin accounts reified in objects made of a freely available material requiring no specialized knowledge or skill to work. However, as a substance easy to manipulate and durable when fired, clay is an ideal medium for expressing cultural meaning in an egalitarian setting. Such meaning is often "fixed" in ritualistic contexts (Hodder 1986, 151). Further, new social circumstances may require the materialization of new symbols identifying, authorizing, and reinforcing those conditions

(Earle 2004). In this case, the establishment of alliance through political ritual is the altered social state expressed materially. As Iroquois men employed these pipes in diplomatic settings to foster a climate of peace, they also were creating a common political culture surely expressed in the idiom of close kinship and shared origin (see, for example, Ray 1987). The latter found mythic expression agreed upon and, perhaps, codified in compositions rendered on these pipes. "Visible to all, material symbols are used to define moments of social change and to make those moments permanent through the life of the symbols" (Earle 2004, 123).

Effigy Pottery

Archaeology of Pottery

During the last several centuries of indigenous pottery-making in the Northeast, humanlike faces adorn pottery vessels (the pots typically six to eleven inches high) in several regions, chiefly along the St. Lawrence River on both the Canadian and American sides, in upstate New York, in the Susquehanna and upper Delaware River valleys of Pennsylvania, and in southern New England.[3] Stylistically diverse, the images range in depiction from geometric to realistic, from conventionalized to naturalistic. But, nearly everywhere across this apparent horizon, the effigy faces occurred at or directly underneath a castellation—the upward flaring point at the top of a vessel's collar (Rayner-Herter 2001, 168). Agreement on this point was nearly universal: Additive imagery belonged only at this location.

---

3. In present Canada, such faces are reported east of the Georgian Bay (Curtis and Latta 2000), along the St. Lawrence River (for example, Wintemberg 1936, Pls. V, VIII–IX), and, sporadically, elsewhere. In the United States, they occur in western (Rayner-Herter 2001, 169) and central upstate New York, in the Susquehanna River Valley of southern Pennsylvania (Kent 1984), in the upper Delaware River region of Pennsylvania and New York (Kraft 1975), in southeastern New York (Funk 1978, Pl. 22; Lopez and Wisniewski 1972, Pl. 2), and in southern New England (Fowler 1959; Grumet 1995, 143; Snow 1978: Fig. 7; Willoughby 1935, 197).

The latest of these regional effigy traditions developed during the mid-1600s in southern New England (Goodby 1998). Among the earliest is that of the St. Lawrence Iroquoians, whose distinctive tripunctate faces are dated to the 1300s (Clermont, Chapdelaine, and Barré 1983). The St. Lawrence Iroquoian designs may have inspired the later Iroquois tradition of effigies (fig. 4a).

Speakers of several languages made effigy pottery although the more elaborate developments were associated with Iroquoians who, over time, transformed depictions of the face into a complete humanoid figure. Among the Iroquois proper of present upstate New York, this effigy tradition centered among the Oneidas and Onondagas (Bradley 1987, 38, 55, 122; MacNeish 1952, 68–69; Gibson 1963; Tuck 1971, 155, 164, 173).

In the better-known Oneida sequence (Bennett and Clark 1978; Whitney 1971; Wonderley 2002), an effigy art of anthropomorphic faces first appeared around A.D. 1500 at the Buyea and Brunk sites (Bennett 2006, 86; Pratt 1976, 100). Most early faces were realistic in appearance with well-defined facial features (fig. 5a). Eyes tended to be indicated by two horizontally parallel incisions. Although some faces were modeled out of the vessel's fabric, most were separately sculpted on a piece of clay subsequently applied to the pot. Faces range in length from about 0.5 to 2 inches.

4. Plastic decoration on Iroquoian pottery (after Wonderley 2005b, figs. 2, 6): (a) St. Lawrence Iroquoian pot with tri-punctate face at castellation; (b) St. Lawrence Iroquoian corn-ear pot; (c) Seneca pot with ladder effigy.

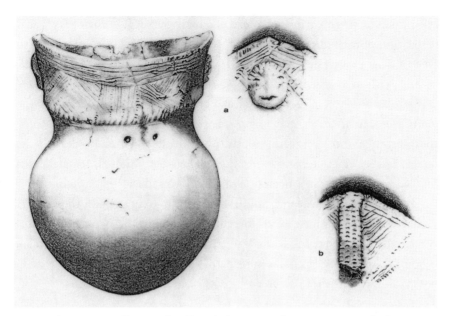

5. Oneida ceramic effigies (after Wonderley 2004, figs. 15, 17; 2005b, fig. 4): (a) pot from the Vaillancourt site with detail of face (A.D. 1525–55); (b) apparent corn cob from the Olcott site (ca. 1520).

Depictions of possible arms and legs appeared early in the sixteenth century (especially the Olcott site, ca. 1515–25) in the form of applied bands of clay marked with parallel indentations or hash marks. At the Vaillancourt site (1525–55), such appliquéd ribbons were occasionally attached, in anatomically correct fashion, to create the first full-figure depictions in Oneida ceramic art. Also present in appreciable amounts at Vaillancourt was a distinctive type of pottery called corn-ear, characteristic of the St. Lawrence Iroquoians to the north, and a decorative element called the ladder effigy, which occurred in a number of places. These additional plastic designs, in other words, were in the working vocabulary of potters who created the first full-figure depictions.

Never entirely out of style, isolated heads continued to occur from the mid–sixteenth century on. However, at sites later than Vaillancourt, the developmental emphasis in effigies was in the direction of clarifying the anthropomorphic figure and homogenizing its depiction. The figure effigies became more standardized in posture (fig. 6a), eventually achieving a full-frontal look with arms outspread at a forty-five-degree angle. Technical realization of the figure also moved toward uniformity. By 1630, the torso area of most effigy figures was indicated by means of two vertically parallel and hash-marked appliquéd bands (figs. 6b–d). Often, an open space was left between them. Below the torso area, the ribbons resolved into the figure's legs. In addition, many figures have what look like wavy or possibly spiky protuberances projecting outward from the exterior borders of the image. Sexual characteristics were not emphasized although femaleness is implied by the occasional depiction of what looks like a cleft crotch.

Impressionistically, humanoid effigies occur frequently in the Oneida archaeological record. At a late-fifteenth-century site, perhaps 2 percent of rim sherds bear effigy faces. At Vaillancourt, the figure may be 6 percent (two of thirty-four classifiable rim sherds). Percentages range from 5 to 14 at two sites of the early seventeenth century.

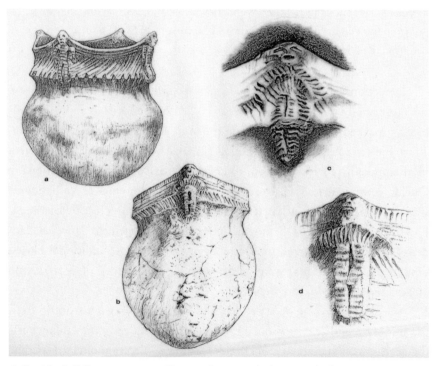

6. Oneida full-figure ceramic effigies (after Wonderley 2005b, fig. 5): (a) ca. 1620; (b–d) ca. 1635.

Throughout the Oneida sequence, effigy pottery derives mostly from the debris of living village life—from habitation areas and middens. It seems to have belonged to the basic domestic ceramic complex that primarily—in our terms and so far as we can tell—was utilitarian in character.[4]

Effigies disappear with the demise of the native-made ceramic industry about 1660. The tradition, therefore, lasted for over 150 years as a coherent representational theme. Its development followed an internal logic progressively clarifying a humanoid subject. The tradition was realistic in essence although verisimilitude, in the sense of photorealism, was never its point.

What does the full-figure effigy depict? Are we looking at an example of split representation or an x-ray perspective meant to emphasize the being's innards? Is the humanoid meant to be understood as skeletal or winged? Could the hash marks represent the wounds of a torture victim in the process of being flayed alive?

Perhaps. A reservation I have with such purely formal interpretations is that most ignore the evidence of developmental sequence to focus on the stylized end product. If the referent was the same throughout (as seems probable to me), any reading of the figure should accord with earlier treatments of it. Thus, if upper limbs are depicted as arms (fig. 6a), then, later in time, they are more likely to be conventionalized arms than wings.

More importantly, any interpretation of the figure should be consistent with the meaning of its primary decorative constituent: the hash marks. Is it likely these denoted bones or wounds? My answer—no—is based on assessment of social context and regional iconography.

Contextual Clues and Suggested Historical Identification

Effigies on pots have attracted little scholarly interest beyond the suggestion that they might represent masks that, in turn, would imply the existence of the Haduwi (False Face) medicine society (Ritchie and Funk 1973,

---

4. Effigy pots, identical to those occurring in village debris, also were placed in graves dating to about 1620–55. In all likelihood, such vessels held food intended to sustain the souls of the dead. Hence, the effigy pottery of the departed was used in much the same fashion as that of the living (Wonderley 2002, 38–39).

367; Tuck 1971, 213). In contrast, amateur archaeologist Ted Whitney suggested (1974, 9) that the effigies invoked "the good will and protection of the spirits entrusted with the feeding of the people." Whitney's reading is likely to be correct because it was based on his understanding that effigy symbolism had something to do with how effigy pottery was employed in daily life. In archaeology, how meaning was constituted requires looking at how the objects were situated in social practice (Hodder 1986, 1987). Who, therefore, made the pottery, and how was it used?

Visiting the Hurons in 1623, the Recollect missionary Gabriel Sagard observed that it was the women who made the pottery (Wrong 1939, 109). Sagard's description apparently is the only first-hand testimony that pottery making was women's work. Yet, it is a sound assumption that women were the potters among the Iroquois also. Both Hurons and Iroquois rigorously maintained a division of labor along gendered or sexual lines and both assigned the same complex of related tasks to the domain of women. For Hurons and Iroquois, making pots was a logical and integral part of female tasks, including food preparation and cooking (Allen 1992, 135, 141).

Ceramic vessels were placed over the fire primarily to boil water used in the preparation or cooking of corn (Allen 1992, 137; Biggar 1929, 126; Harrington 1908, 581–82). The most common dish was a corn soup, a mush or gruel the Jesuits called *sagamité*, brought to a boil in the pot (Waugh 1916, 90–95, 116). "The ordinary sagamité," said Sagard in a passage describing the Hurons but equally applicable to the Iroquois, "is raw maize ground into meal . . . with a little meat or fish if they have any. . . . It is the soup, meat, and dessert of every day, and there is nothing more" (Wrong 1939, 107). "Every morning," according to Lafitau, "the women prepare this sagamité and bring it to a boil for the nourishment of the family" (Fenton and Moore 1977, 60).

Hence, Iroquois pottery vessels, including those bearing effigies, were almost certainly made by women who employed them as cooking pots on their home hearths. Far more than anything else, pots with effigies were used for boiling corn gruels and soups. The most likely connotations of effigy vessels, therefore, were maize, femaleness, and domestic setting (Wonderley 2002, 37–39).

No extant writing and no recorded tradition makes explicit reference to ceramic effigies. One can, however, survey the substantial corpus of

Iroquois ethnography, folklore, and myth hoping to find some indication of a being or belief related to corn, but also in conformity with commensality, femaleness, and perhaps even full-figure imagery.

The subject most clearly satisfying those criteria is a race of beings responsible for the present-day Husk Face medicine society among the Iroquois, mythological cornhusk people for whom great antiquity is suspected (Tooker 1970, 152). Diminutive beings personifying plant fertility, cornhusk people are an industrious agricultural folk "associated with planting and cultivating of prodigious food crops" (Fenton 1987, 490). They are especially concerned with growing corn, and it is cooked corn food that they crave. Today, cornhusk people are regarded as messengers of the Three Sisters (corn, beans, squash) who prophesy—quickly because they must return home to tend crying babies—bountiful crops and many children (Fenton 1987, 383–404, 444; Shimony 1994, 142–56; Speck 1995, 88–96). Cornhusk folk are imbued with feminine associations (Fenton 1987, 105, 408; Fogelson and Bell 1983; Kurath 1968, 49, 182; Tooker 1970, 63, 72).

Stories about cornhusk people specify an appearance completely covered over by corn tassels or husks. These beings "dress in cornhusks" (Fenton 1987, 399), a characteristic still specified in the origin myths for the Husk Face Society collected at the turn of the twentieth century. Husk-face knowledge in such tales derived from a hunter's encounter with a cornhusk person dressed up in corn tassels (Speck 1995, 96). The hunter was informed, "You must tell your people that you and they must prepare something with cornhusks which shall resemble the form of my body" (Fenton 1987, 387).

Identifying archaeological effigies with cornhusk people has the obvious virtue of clarifying the logic behind effigy development. Over time, ceramic imagery increasingly defined the anatomical details of the complete figure—an evolution accomplishing exactly what the hunter was told to do.[5]

5. But if mythical cornhusk people were covered by husk material and humans were supposed to imitate that look, why would their depictions resemble *ears* of corn? Ethnographically, people impersonating the cornhusk folk wear (in addition to masks fashioned

A Regional Iconography of Plastic Decorative Elements

The anthropomorphic effigy figure was not the only form of plastic decoration applied to pottery across the greater Northeast. Archaeologists recognize at least two other forms of design in relief contemporaneous with humanoid effigies: the ladder effigy and the corn-ear motif.

The ladder effigy consists of a vertically oriented ridge with ladderlike markings at or below a castellation (fig. 4c). The raised ridge results from pinching the clay together or from application of a clay strip to the vessel's surface. The ladder's rungs are created by "several short horizontal markings which are cut, stamped or gouged into the thickened area, and are lined up vertically one above the other from the top to the bottom of the effigy" (Wray et al. 1987, 79). While the ladder effigy occurs sporadically over an enormous area, it seems to be most characteristic of Seneca country and the northern zone of the Niagara region in western New York, and possibly the land of the Neutrals in southwestern Ontario (Fitzgerald 2001, 43; White 1961, 89; Wray et al. 1991, 273–74, 499, 508).

Among the Susquehannocks, Iroquoian speakers of southcentral Pennsylvania, the ladder effigy came into widespread use (on a type of pottery called Strickler Cord–marked) during the seventeenth century. Because this was after the heyday of anthropomorphic effigies (on Washington Boro Incised), Barry Kent (1984, 144) reasoned the hash-marked ladders were "very stylized representations" of earlier full-figure effigies decorated in the same hash-marked fashion. The same resemblance was noted in the context of Seneca pottery by Gian Carlo Cervone (1991, 274), who added

---

from braided husks of corn) normal clothing, although it is often old and assembled in odd-looking combinations (Fenton 1987, 404–5). In the recent past, human masqueraders may have dressed in faun-skin mantles and garters. While this (also) does not clarify why the actual appearance of husks was ignored, it does direct us toward metaphorical thinking. The point of the deerskin was "to make the impersonator a swift runner" (Fenton 1987, 390). Such logic is key to understanding the stylized effigies placed on pottery vessels. Corn husks would have been relatively difficult to depict naturalistically. However, the potters had available, in the ear of the corn, a symbolic element that was easily fashioned in clay, recognizable to all, and capable of standing for a larger whole—a visual synechdoche.

that the ladder effigy also resembles an ear of corn removed from the corn-ear type of pottery.

The corn-ear is a distinctive kind of ceramic vessel (a type) characterized by a series of raised, vertically oriented ridges applied around a vessel's exterior rim (figs. 4b and 7g–i). Each ridge is indented with stamped horizontal lines, incised slashes, or punctates most frequently lined up in a single column resembling the rungs of a ladder. Each vertical ridge is one corn-ear motif. Obviously, the name derives from a perceived resemblance to "ears of corn, the rows of transverse linear impressions being intended to represent the kernels" (Wintemberg 1936, 113). This design (type and motif), in other words, is widely, though informally, regarded as naturalistic. It is diagnostic of the late-period St. Lawrence Iroquoian region and especially the Hochelaga province between Prescott and Montreal (Chapdelaine 2004, 65, 68–70).

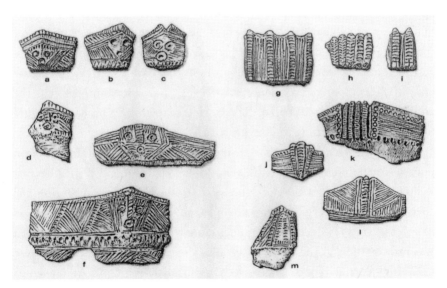

7. Plastic decoration from the Hochelaga Province of the St. Lawrence Iroquoian Area (after Wonderley 2005b, fig. 8): (a–c) tri-punctate faces; (d–f) faces with ladder-like elements; (g–i) corn-ear motifs; (j–m) corn-ear motifs at castellations. These sherds are from the Glenbrook and Roebuck sites, Ontario (Pendergast 1980; Wintemberg 1936).

The ladder and the corn-ear look the same because, physically, they usually are identical, both being a strip of clay with parallel indentations. The difference between them is partly a matter of emphasis. The corn-ear is presented repeatedly around the rim, the ladder effigy only once at a castellation—that is, at a vessel's effigy position. The ladder and corn-ear, in turn, look like the body of the full-figure humanoid effigy in that all bear identical hash-mark decoration. This resemblance is especially strong in the fully evolved Oneida figure, whose body literally consists of what could be called two ladders or corn-ears (figs. 6b–d).

If they all look the same, they could have been related in meaning, and the meaning of one, if known, might reasonably attach to the others. Corn-ears look like corn and sometimes ladder effigies do, too. Or, perhaps more accurately, one occasionally sees an apparent representation of corn placed at a castellation where a ladder effigy would be expected. A good example of this is known from Olcott, the site (fig. 5b) adjacent to and immediately preceding Vaillancourt in the Oneida sequence.

At the Oneida Vaillancourt site and at precisely the same time the hash-marked appliquéd band was being combined with the effigy face, the other two plastic designs of the Northeast also were present, a circumstance suggesting that all were involved in the synthesis that gave rise to the full-figure effigy. The comparative evidence of corn-ear and ladder implies that the addition of the indented strip of clay to the face to create a humanoid figure may have had something to do with corn.

Much the same conceptual synthesis may have been taking place on pottery to the north around the year 1550 (Abel 2001, 129; Pendergast 1980). Among the St. Lawrence Iroquoians of the Hochelaga subregion, the corn-ear motif (figs. 7g–i) apparently was moved to the castellated position of a vessel (figs. 7j–l). Instead of encircling the rim repetitively, the motif was now featured at the effigy position as a ladderlike effigy. Some of these new effigy corn-ears look suggestively naturalistic (fig. 7m). And, even as the corn-ear motif became an effigy, it also became part of the effigy face. Here, the hash-marked linear element was not limblike but fused into the visage itself (figs. 7d–f).

Among both Iroquois and St. Lawrence Iroquoians, a corn-ear/ladder design with effigy associations was joined to an anthropomorphic face and synthesized in the same or homologous fashion. This remarkable parallel development implies the emergence, among both central peoples of similar beliefs, possibly pertaining to corn.

And it suggests we should visualize another interaction sphere, this one defined on the basis of distinctive effigies on domestic pottery. In contrast to the interaction sphere of pipes, this one involved information exchange among pottery makers of the Oneida-Onondaga and Hochelaga–St. Lawrence Iroquoian areas. What behavior would account for this phenomenon?

In Iroquoian archaeology, pottery identified in one region as stylistically indicative of another is frequently interpreted in terms of the "captive bride" hypothesis (Engelbrecht 1974, 61), which holds that women, the potters, were more likely than men to be captured in the warfare regarded as endemic to Iroquoian peoples. Taken back to the raiders' home village for adoption, these women would continue to make the pottery familiar to them in the new setting. Such an interpretive tack is inadequate for envisioning women in different communities engaged in the ceramic expression of similar ideas. While one can never rule out the existence of captive brides, the idea-sharing behind these effigies implies more than the prisoner making an occasional pot. This interaction must have included a more active, willing, and routine component. Possibly it was a result of communities exchanging marriage partners over time. Possibly women visited one another in other communities as travelers or even as traders (Engelbrecht 1985, 178–79).

How did Iroquois people of long ago relate to imagery on their pottery? How were these things *used?* Possibly they were sacred objects of worship or paraphernalia employed in some sort of ritual. This seems unlikely because publicly enacted ceremonialism is and was mostly a men's show in Iroquois society. Men superintend relations with the supernatural by directing the rites, delivering the public speeches, and burning the tobacco. Men even perform the ritual roles of women in ceremony, as when they masquerade as female husk faces. In general, women's ceremonial roles are limited to preparing the food and rather passive participation.

As objects of routine domestic life for upwards of 150 years, the Iroquois effigies bespeak a more meditative function and private realm. I speculate that Iroquois people of long ago regarded these images within the terms of what is expressed today in the Thanksgiving Address, an all-purpose and probably ancient ritual speech (Chafe 1961; Shimony 1994, 140). In this oration, humans announce that they are still performing their ordained duty: to acknowledge and give thanks for the cosmos. By so doing, humans encourage supernaturals to continue their functions in maintaining the universal order. In the terms of this conceptual framework, ceramic effigies may attest to Iroquois people holding up their end of the cosmos-maintaining pact. Given the probable content and context of the imagery, I think the effigies imply prayers of gratitude offered by women food-providers to nonhuman beings (very possibly cornhusk people) in fulfillment of such mythic contract.

Summary and Discussion

Beginning about 1450, several types of effigy pipes bearing humanoid imagery cluster in Jefferson County but consistently show up in smaller numbers among the Mohawks, Oneidas, and Onondagas. The distributional data are suggestive of an interaction sphere, centered in New York's St. Lawrence region. Historic sources indicate some pipes were employed in collective male settings of formal deliberation and diplomacy. The pipes featured here probably were so used, their symbolically prominent compositions being congruent with display in public settings. Therefore, the interaction sphere of pipes reflects the peaceful interaction of pipe-smoking representatives of several communities over a significant length of time.

These pipes might correlate with an early stage of the League of the Iroquois begun by its eastern nations, or they might relate to an earlier confederacy of the St. Lawrence region described in the earliest Iroquois history, published in the 1820s. In either case, the existence of such an alliance suggests the process of Iroquois confederation was a more complex phenomenon than previously imagined, and that its precedents date to pre-European times and non-European circumstances.

I also propose that these pipes illustrate or allude to certain topics of Iroquois oral narrative. If so, the meaning(s) of the objects obviously should be sought in their own context. At least initially, one must seek clarification within Iroquois culture rather than drawing on distant comparisons.

The oral narratives cited in this study are, of course, culturally appropriate because they are Iroquois. But these are not run-of-the-mill folktales, indistinguishable from any other of the hundreds recorded around the turn of the twentieth century. All appear to have been major topics in the oral tradition, and all are among the earliest documented.

The most important of these narratives for my interpretation is the theme of emergence that provides a unifying thread to a series of Jefferson County effigy pipes. This reading posits a close conceptual relationship among several similar types of objects from the same place and time while clarifying a seemingly unrelated phenomenon—allusions to northern origin. This interpretation seems plausible because it makes consistent sense of the pipes and suggests new relationships congruent with culturally specific belief and practice (Preucel and Hodder 1996, 306).

A different art of humanoid effigies developed on the pottery of the Oneida and Onondaga Iroquois of upstate New York between the late 1400s and the mid-1600s. Theirs was a naturalistic tradition in which an anthropomorphic subject received increasing elaboration over time, most obviously by adding bodies to faces. Postcranial body parts were represented by indented clay ribbons, limblike elements resembling two other forms of plastic decoration in the Northeast: the ladder effigy and the corn-ear motif. Since both were present as the face became a figure, both may have contributed to that symbolic synthesis. One of them, the corn-ear, probably denoted an ear of corn. Its incorporation into the effigy figure suggests the latter may have carried corn-related connotations.

Archaeologically, pots bearing effigy depictions are indistinguishable from the rest of the utilitarian pottery of village life. They appear to have been employed in the same fashion as noneffigy vessels. Projecting historical evidence into the past yields the same result. Ceramic vessels probably were made by women who used them in the home, mostly for cooking maize-based dishes. Assuming that meaning was appropriate to contexts in which material symbols were created and used, the most likely connotations of effigy vessels would have been corn, domesticity, and femaleness. Within the corpus of historically attested ethnology and oral narrative, the subject most obviously answering to those criteria is a mythological race of cornhusk people associated with agricultural bounty.

Much the same iconographic process may have been occurring in ceramics of the St. Lawrence Iroquoians around 1550. Those potters, evidently working from the conceptual baseline of their own corn-ear decoration, promoted that motif to effigy status while, at the same time, adding it to their effigy faces. Evidently, similar beliefs pertaining to corn found material expression in both the central Iroquois and the St. Lawrence Iroquoian areas.

The perception of pipe and pottery interaction spheres alerts us to previously unrecognized ties between the eastern Iroquois and the St. Lawrence Iroquoians. The pipes speak to frequent diplomatic interaction between the two areas. The depictions on pots attest to the expression of similar religious impulses in two areas. Together, the similar imagery in two mediums imply that St. Lawrence Iroquoians and eastern Iroquois shared fundamental concepts about the world as well, probably including some of the key oral narratives. Very possibly, the St. Lawrence Iroquoians contributed to Oneida, Onondaga, and Mohawk traditions in interesting and important ways.

In addition, the pottery effigies may clarify an intriguing dichotomy in Iroquois culture. A number of scholars have sensed a fundamental division in Iroquois thinking, which seems to hold ideas about game and the forest separate from beliefs having to do with crops and village life. Early on in his career, Fenton (1940, 164) contrasted the "group religious system, dominated by the idea of renewal and characterized by an annual cycle of first-fruits ceremonies marking crises in maize cultivation" to the "shamanistic fraternities derived from earth-bound animals and peculiarly northern."

Others discern the split more clearly in the contrast between two types of ceremonial masks, each possessing a distinctive set of symbolic associations. Masks made from cornhusk material denote femininity, agriculture, fertility, renewal, the clearing and the village, and warm weather. Those of wood, the so-called False Face masks, in contrast, are correlated with men, with shamanic curing, the forest and the hunt, and with cold weather (Fenton 1987, 105, 481–82; Fogelson and Bell 1983, 54–57; Krusche 1986, 8; Kurath 1968, 49). I have noted aspects of this disjunction in the older creation accounts that contrast the agriculturalist Sky Holder to the hunter Flint (chapter 4) and in a story reflecting feminine concerns as opposed to the largely male orientation of most Iroquois oral narrative (chapter 6). However the dichotomy is described, it looks as though ideas reflecting horticulture and corn came to be grafted on to a Woodland outlook of "untold antiquity" (Kurath 2000, 61–62). Chafe (1964, 284), in fact, found that the vocabulary of shamanic activities is far older than words associated with agriculturally oriented ceremonies.

Possibly, then, we are privileged to witness, in the ceramic effigies, the emergence of corn as symbolically important in Iroquois life. Perhaps the ceramic effigies even signal the development of a horticultural ideology with a recognizably modern flavor, something that accords with attitudes of respect and sacredness for the Three Sisters and for the productive role of women in Iroquois life.

Afterword

THESE ESSAYS collectively argue for the importance of oral narrative in understanding the Native American past in four ways.

First, oral narrative provides one of the few roads to apprehending the conceptual world of the ancient Northeast. Although one cannot assume antiquity of any specific story, it is reasonable to suppose age is indicated roughly by a tale's wide distribution. Accordingly, I infer some oral narrative is likely to be very old. Aspects of stories about the stars must go back thousands of years (chapter 1). Such tales of marvel as "Snake-man" and "Crossing-water-on-a-serpent" are likely to be well over a millennium in age. Pieces of old thinking probably are preserved in them, and it may well be, as George Lankford argues, that these are fragments or vestiges of ancient cosmologies (chapter 3).

Though we cannot predict it, it would hardly be surprising to find important concepts reflected in material culture, especially when dealing with representational art in the archaeological record evocative of metaphor. When we have material symbolism, it is surely worth the effort to unite evidence from oral narrative with the testimony of the object in hopes of shedding light on both. This is what I proposed in the instance of the Dougherty pipe, characteristic of certain St. Lawrence Iroquoians and Eastern Iroquois some five hundred years ago (chapter 7). Later oral narratives speak of birth from the ground and death into the jaws of a monstrous snake, ideas applicable to interpreting what survives in the archaeological record. In contrast, what is physically depicted on the pipes implies a larger primordial myth encompassing both themes.

As material preserving something of older beliefs, oral narrative is a key source for understanding Iroquois religion in historic perspective. If religion is defined as a system of belief in a superhuman presence creating or superintending the universe, then Sky Holder—who he was and what he became—was surely the central figure of Iroquois religion in centuries past (chapter 4). If one regards religion more broadly as a spiritual frame of mind recognizing the existence of greater-than-human presence, the study of stories about cannibal giants and stars (chapters 1, 5, and 6), of depictions on pottery evoking maize traditions, and of portal-like imagery on pipes possibly illustrating myths of emergence (chapter 7) are inquiries into northeastern and Iroquois religion.

Second, oral narrative testifies to movements of ideas over considerable distances. On the one hand, "Killer Lizards" (chapter 3), a story known in two widely separated regions, probably came north in the minds of Tuscarora people emigrating from North Carolina to New York in the early 1700s. The Friendly Visitor story type, on the other hand, is a plot that may have spread outward from an Iroquois hearth at the time of Iroquois military incursions to the north, west, and south (chapter 6). Sharing a complicated and psychologically nuanced plot implies communication at the individual level—frequent, intimate, and peaceful interchange as tangible as the better-documented violence.

Third, oral narrative informs about cultural distinctiveness and ethnic boundedness. Seneca and Tuscarora versions of the Kahkwa War were very different (chapter 2). And, while there was considerable variation in story preferences, Algonquian speakers agreed who windigo was and who he was not. Windigo was not, for example, an Iroquois stone giant (chapters 5 and 6).

Fourth, oral narrative is itself an object of study about change over time. Myths, like the people who tell them, have their own histories and, when the evidence exists, it is important to know how the myths developed. I explored this topic in connection with origin accounts of the League of the Iroquois (chapter 7), with Sky Holder in the Iroquois myth of beginnings (chapter 4), and with the manner in which Kahkwa War stories developed over time (chapter 2). The conclusions I reached are, admittedly, the poor man's version of functionalism (stories expressed and reinforced identity) and, perhaps, of structuralism (Sky Holder's victory symbolized the dominance of agriculture).

Being simple, however, does not bother me so much as being circular. I assume an extensive distribution indicates antiquity, then conclude antiquity from extensive distribution. I describe gender distinctions as historically important, then discover the same in the archaeological record. I posit the importance of myth as group charter and as a means to render a group's past meaningful, then—*mirabile dictu*—the evidence suggests precisely that.

Well. Oral narrative is rich but is also richly ambiguous. Not infrequently, it eludes practical reason. I have tried to indicate throughout this work that I understand stories are multivalent and may convey different messages to different people. I look forward to seeing better interpretations—fuller readings that more compellingly explain this badly neglected material.

References | Index

References

Aarne, Anti. 1930. *Die magische Flucht: Eine Märchenstudie*. Folklore Fellows Communications 92. Helsinki: Academia Scientiarum Fennica.

Abel, Timothy J. 2001. "The Clayton Cluster: Cultural Dynamics of a Late Prehistoric Village Sequence in the Upper St. Lawrence Valley." Ph.D. diss., State Univ. of New York at Albany.

Abler, Thomas S., and Michael H. Logan. 1988. "The Floresence and Demise of Iroquoian Cannibalism: Human Sacrifice and Malinowski's Hypothesis." *Man in the Northeast* 35:1–26.

Ahenakew, E. 1929. "Cree Trickster Tales." *Journal of American Folklore* 42:309–53.

Allen, Kathleen Mae Sydor. 1988. "Ceramic Style and Social Continuity in an Iroquois Tribe." Ph.D. diss., State Univ. of New York at Buffalo.

———. 1992. "Iroquois Ceramic Production: A Case Study of Household-Level Organization." In *Ceramic Production and Distribution: An Integrated Approach*, edited by George J. Bey III and Christopher A. Pool, 133–54. Boulder: Westview.

Andrews, William. 1716. Letter to the Society, October 11. Records of the Society for the Propagation of the Gospel, Letter Books Series A, vol. 12, 239–43. London.

Bahr, Donald. 1998. "Mythologies Compared: Pima, Maricopa, and Yavapai." *Journal of the Southwest* 40, no. 1:25–66.

Barbeau, C. Marius. 1914. "Supernatural Beings of the Huron and Wyandot." *American Anthropologist* 16:288–313.

———. 1915. *Huron and Wyandot Mythology*. Canada Department of Mines, Geological Survey, Memoir 80, Anthropological Series 11. Ottawa: Government Printing Bureau.

———. 1951. "The Dragon Myth and Ritual Songs of the Iroquoians." *Journal of the International Folk Music Council* 3:81–85.

———. 1952. "The Old-World Dragon in America." In *Indian Tribes of Aboriginal America: Selected Papers of the XXIXth International Congress of Americanists,* edited by Sol Tax, 115–22. Chicago: Univ. of Chicago Press.

———. 1994. *Mythologie huronne et wyandotte: avec un annexe les textes publiés antérieurement.* Translated by Stephen Dupont. Montreal: Les Presses de l'Université de Montréal.

Barnouw, Victor. 1977. *Wisconsin Chippewa Myths and Tales and Their Relation to Chippewa Life.* Madison: Univ. of Wisconsin Press.

Beauchamp, William M. 1892. *The Iroquois Trail; or, Foot-Prints of the Six Nations.* Fayetteville, N.Y.: H. C. Beauchamp.

———. 1897. "The New Religion of the Iroquois." *Journal of American Folklore* 8:169–89.

———. 1900. "Onondaga Tale of the Pleiades." *Journal of American Folklore* 13:281–82.

———. 1922. *Iroquois Folklore, Gathered from the Six Nations of New York.* Syracuse: Onondaga Historical Association.

Beck, Horace P. 1947. "Algonquin Folklore from Maniwaki." *Journal of American Folklore* 60:259–64.

Benn, Carl. 1998. *The Iroquois in the War of 1812.* Toronto: Univ. of Toronto Press.

Bennett, Monte R. 2006. "A Brief Look at the Brunk Site, a Mid to Late Prehistoric Oneida Village: Fieldwork Report 1997–2001." *Chenango Chapter Bulletin* (New York State Archaeological Association, Norwich) 29, no. 1:79–109.

———, and Douglas Clark. 1978. "Recent Excavations on the Cameron Site (Ond 8–4)." *Chenango Chapter Bulletin* (New York State Archaeological Association, Norwich) 17, no. 4.

Bierhorst, John. 1985. *The Mythology of North America.* New York: William Morrow.

———. 1995. *Mythology of the Lenape: Guide and Texts.* Tucson: Univ. of Arizona Press.

Biggar, Henry P., ed. 1929. *The Works of Samuel de Champlain.* Vol. 3. Toronto: Champlain Society.

Bishop, Charles A. 1975. "Northern Algonkian Cannibalism and Windigo Psychosis." In *Psychological Anthropology,* edited by Thomas R. Williams, 237–48. The Hague: Mouton.

Blackwood, Algernon. 1964. "The Wendigo." In *Selected Tales of Algernon Blackwood,* by Algernon Blackwood, 253–304. London: John Baker.

Blau, Harold. 1964. "The Iroquois White Dog Sacrifice: Its Evolution and Symbolism." *Ethnohistory* 11:97–119.

Bloomfield, Leonard. 1928. *Menomini Texts.* Publications of the American Ethnological Society, vol. 12. New York: G. E. Stechert.

———. 1934. *Cree Texts.* Publications of the American Ethnological Society, vol. 16. New York: G. E. Stechert.

Boas, Franz. 1914. "Mythology and Folk-Tales of the North American Indians." *Journal of American Folklore* 27:374–410.

———. 1916. "Tsimshian Mythology." In *Thirty-first Annual Report of the Bureau of American Ethnology to the Secretary of the Smithsonian Institution, 1909–1910,* 27–1037. Washington, D.C.: Government Printing Office.

———. 1940. *Race, Language, and Culture.* New York: Macmillan.

Bourgeois, Arthur P., ed. 1994. *Ojibwa Narratives of Charles and Charlotte Kawbawgam and Jacques LePique, 1893–1895.* Detroit: Wayne State Univ. Press.

Boyce, Douglas W. 1973. "A Glimpse of Iroquois Culture History through the Eyes of Joseph Brant and John Norton." *Proceedings of the American Philosophical Society* 117, no. 4:286–94.

Bradley, James W. 1987. *Evolution of the Onondaga Iroquois: Accommodating Change, 1500–1655.* Syracuse: Syracuse Univ. Press.

Brandão, José António, ed. 2003. *Nation Iroquoise: A Seventeenth-Century Ethnography of the Iroquois.* Translated by José António Brandão with Janet Ritch. Lincoln: Univ. of Nebraska Press.

Brasser, Ted J. 1980. "Self-Directed Pipe Effigies." *Man in the Northeast* 19:95–104.

Bricker, Victoria Reifler. 1981. *The Indian Christ, the Indian King: The Historical Substrata of Maya Myth and Ritual.* Austin: Univ. of Texas Press.

Brightman, Robert A. 1988. "The Windigo in the Material World." *Ethnohistory* 35:337–79.

Brotherston, Gordon. 1992. *Book of the Fourth World: Reading the Native Americans through Their Literature.* New York: Cambridge Univ. Press.

Brown, Jennifer S. H. 1971. "The Cure and Feeding of Windigos: A Critique." *American Anthropologist* 73:20–22.

Brown, Jennifer S. H., and Robert Brightman. 1988. *"The Orders of the Dreamed": George Nelson on Cree and Northern Ojibwa Religion and Myth, 1823.* Manitoba Studies in Native History III. Winnipeg: Univ. of Manitoba Press.

Brown, Judith K. 1970. "Economic Organization and the Position of Women among the Iroquois." *Ethnohistory* 17:151–67.

Bryden, Sherry. 1995. "Ingenuity in Art: The Early 19th Century Works of David and Dennis Cusick." *American Indian Art Magazine* 20, no, 2:60–69, 85.

Caldwell, Joseph R. 1964. "Interaction Spheres in Prehistory." In *Hopewellian Studies,* edited by Joseph R. Caldwell and Robert L. Hall, 133–43. Scientific Papers 12. Springfield: Illinois State Museum.

Canfield, William W. 1902. *The Legends of the Iroquois, Told by "The Cornplanter."* New York: A. Wessels.

Cantine, John, and Simeon DeWitt. ca. 1793. Report of a Council Held to Purchase Lands, undated (ca. November). Assembly Paper (Petitions, Correspondence and Reports Relating to Indians, 1783–1831), vol. 40, 119–48. Albany: New York State Archives.

Carrington, Henry B. 1892. "Condition of the Six Nations of New York." In *Extra Census Bulletin: The Six Nations of New York,* by Thomas Donaldson, 19–82. Washington, D.C.: United States Census Printing Office.

Caswell, Harriett S. 1892. *Our Life among the Iroquois Indians.* Boston: Congregational Sunday-School and Publishing Society.

Ceci, Lynn. 1978. "Watchers of the Pleiades: Ethnoastronomy among Native Cultivators in Northeastern North America." *Ethnohistory* 25, no. 4:301–17.

Cervone, Gian Carlo. 1991. "Native Ceramic Vessels." In *Tram and Cameron: Two Early Contact Era Seneca Sites,* edited by Charles F. Hayes III, 84–103, 258–92. Research Record 21. Rochester: Rochester Museum and Science Center.

Chafe, Wallace L. 1961. *Seneca Thanksgiving Rituals.* Bureau of American Ethnology, Bulletin 183. Washington, D.C.: Smithsonian Institution.

———. 1963. *Handbook of the Seneca Language.* New York State Museum and Science Service, Bulletin 388. Albany: State Univ. of New York.

———. 1964. "Linguistic Evidence for the Relative Age of Iroquois Religious Practices." *Southwestern Journal of Anthropology* 20, no. 3:278–85.

Chapdelaine, Claude. 1990. "The Mandeville Site and the Definition of a New Regional Group within the Saint Lawrence Iroquoian World." *Man in the Northeast* 39:53–63.

———. 2004. "A Review of the Latest Developments in St. Lawrence Iroquoian Archaeology." In *A Passion for the Past: Papers in Honour of James F. Pendergast,* edited by James V. Wright and Jean-Luc Pilon, 63–75. Mercury Series Archaeology Paper 164. Hull: Canadian Museum of Civilization.

Clark, Joshua V. H. 1849. *Onondaga; Or, Reminiscences of Earlier and Later Times.* 2 vols. Syracuse: Stoddard and Babcock.

Clermont, Norman, Claude Chapdelaine, and Georges Barré. 1983. *Le site Iroquoien de Lanoraie: témoignage d'une maison-longue.* Montreal: Recherches amérindiennes au Québec.

Connelley, William E. 1899. "Notes on the Folk-Lore of the Wyandots." *Journal of American Folklore* 12:116–25.

Converse, Harriet Maxwell. 1908. *Myths and Legends of the New York Iroquois.* Edited by Arthur Caswell Parker. New York State Museum, Bulletin 125. Albany: State Univ. of New York.

Cooper, John M. 1933. "The Cree Witiko Psychosis." *Primitive Man* 6, no. 1:20–24.

Cornplanter, Jesse J. 1986. *Legends of the Longhouse.* 1938. Reprint. Ohswekon, Ontario: Irocrafts.

Cruikshank, Julie. 1994. "Oral Tradition and Oral History: Reviewing Some Issues." *Canadian Historical Review* 75:403–18.

———. 1998. *The Social Life of Stories: Narrative and Knowledge in the Yukon Territory.* Lincoln: Univ. of Nebraska Press.

Curtin, Jeremiah. 2001. *Seneca Indian Myths.* 1922. Reprint. Mineola, N.Y.: Dover.

Curtis, Jenneth E., and Martha A. Latta. 2000. "Ceramics as Reflectors of Social Relationships: The Auger Site and Ball Site Castellations." *Ontario Archaeology* 70:1–15.

Davidson, D. S. 1928a. "Folk Tales from Grand Lake Victoria, Quebec." *Journal of American Folklore* 41:275–92.

———. 1928b. "Some Tête-de-Boule Tales." *Journal of American Folklore* 41:262–74.

Dorsey, George A. 1904. *The Mythology of the Wichita.* Carnegie Institution of Washington, Publication 21. Washington, D.C.

———. 1997a. *The Pawnee Mythology.* Introduction by Douglas R. Parks. 1906. Reprint. Lincoln: Univ. of Nebraska Press.

———. 1997b. *Traditions of the Caddo.* Introduction by Wallace L. Chafe. 1905. Reprint. Lincoln: Univ. of Nebraska Press.

———, and Alfred L. Kroeber. 1997. *Traditions of the Arapaho.* Introduction by Jeffrey D. Anderson. 1903. Reprint. Lincoln: Univ. of Nebraska Press.

Draper, Lyman C. n.d. Draper's Notes. Series 4, vol. 4. Wisconsin Historical Society, Archives Division, Madison.

Drummond, Lee. 1981. "The Serpent's Children: Semiotics of Cultural Genesis in Arawak and Trobriand Myth." *American Ethnologist* 8:633–60.

Dundes, Alan. 1965. *The Study of Folklore*. Englewood Cliffs, N.J.: Prentice-Hall.

———. 1967. "North American Indian Folklore Studies." *Journal de la Société des Américanistes 56*, no. 1:53–79.

Dunn, Shirley W. 2000. *The Mohican World, 1680–1750*. Fleischmanns, N.Y.: Purple Mountain Press.

Dwight, Timothy. 1822. *Travels in New-England and New-York*. Vol. 4. New Haven: the author.

Earle, Timothy. 2004. "Culture Matters in the Neolithic Transition and Emergence of Hierarchy in Thy, Denmark." *American Anthropologist* 106:111–25.

Edmonson, Munro S. 1971. *Lore: An Introduction to the Science of Folklore and Literature*. New York: Holt, Rinehart, and Winston.

Engelbrecht, William. 1974. "The Iroquois: Archaeological Patterning on the Tribal Level." *World Archaeology 6*, no. 1:52–65.

———. 1985. "New York Iroquois Political Development." In *Cultures in Contact: The Impact of European Contacts on Native American Cultural Institutions, A.D. 1000–1800*, edited by William H. Fitzhugh, 163–83. Washington, D.C.: Smithsonian Institution Press.

———. 1991. "Erie." *Bulletin: Journal of the New York State Archaeological Association* 102:2–12.

———. 1995. "The Case of the Disappearing Iroquois: Early Contact Period Superpower Politics." *Northeast Anthropology* 50:35–59.

———. 2003. *Iroquoia: The Development of a Native World*. Syracuse: Syracuse Univ. Press.

———, and Lynne P. Sullivan. 1996. "Cultural Context." In *Reanalyzing the Ripley Site: Earthworks and Late Prehistory on the Lake Erie Plain*, edited by Lynne P. Sullivan, 14–27. New York State Museum, Bulletin 489. Albany: New York State Education Department.

Erickson, Kirstin C. 2003. "'They Will Come from the Other Side of the Sea': Prophecy, Ethnogenesis, and Agency in Yaqui Narrative." *Journal of American Folklore* 116:465–82.

Fenton, William N. 1940. "Problems Arising from the Historic Northeastern Position of the Iroquois." In *Essays in Historical Anthropology of North America*, edited by Julian H. Steward, 159–251. Smithsonian Miscellaneous Collections 100. Washington, D.C.

———. 1949. "Seth Newhouse's Traditional History and Constitution of the Iroquois Confederacy." *Proceedings of the American Philosophical Society 93*, no. 2:141–58.

———. 1962. "This Island, the World on Turtle's Back." *Journal of American Folklore* 75:283–300.

———. 1978. "Northern Iroquoian Culture Patterns." In Trigger, *Handbook of North American Indians* 15:296–321.

———. 1985. "Structure, Continuity, and Change in the Process of Iroquois Treaty Making." In Jennings et al., *The History and Culture of Iroquois Diplomacy: An Interdisciplinary Guide to the Treaties of the Six Nations and Their League,* 3–36.

———. 1987. *The False Faces of the Iroquois.* Norman: Univ. of Oklahoma Press.

———. 1991. *The Iroquois Eagle Dance: An Offshoot of the Calumet Dance.* 1953. Reprint. Syracuse: Syracuse Univ. Press.

———. 1998. *The Great Law and the Longhouse: A Political History of the Iroquois Confederacy.* Norman: Univ. of Oklahoma Press.

———. 2002. *The Little Water Medicine Society of the Senecas.* Norman: Univ. of Oklahoma Press.

———, and Gertrude P. Kurath. 1951. "The Feast of the Dead, or Ghost Dance at Six Nations Reserve, Canada." In *Symposium on Local Diversity in Iroquois Culture,* edited by William N. Fenton, 143–65. Bureau of American Ethnology, Bulletin 149. Washington, D.C.: Smithsonian Institution.

———, and Elizabeth L. Moore, eds. and trans. 1974, 1977. *Customs of the American Indians Compared with the Customs of Primitive Times by Father Joseph François Lafitau.* 2 vols. Toronto: Champlain Society.

Fewkes, J. Walter. 1890. "A Contribution to Passamaquoddy Folk-Lore." *Journal of American Folklore* 11:256–80.

Finlayson, William D. 1998. *Iroquoian Peoples of the Land of Rocks and Water, A.D. 1000–1630: A Study in Settlement Archaeology.* 4 vols. Special Publication 1. London, Ontario: London Museum of Archaeology.

Fisher, Margaret W. 1946. "The Mythology of the Northern and Northeastern Algonkians in Reference to Algonkian Mythology as a Whole." In *Man in Northeastern North America,* edited by Frederick Johnson, 226–62. Papers of the Robert S. Peabody Foundation for Archaeology, vol. 3. Andover, Mass.: Phillips Academy.

Fitzgerald, William R. 2001. "Contact, Neutral Iroquoian Transformation, and the Little Ice Age." In *Societies in Eclipse: Archaeology of the Eastern Woodlands Indians, A.D. 1400–1700,* edited by David S. Brose, C. Wesley Cowan, and Robert C. Mainfort, Jr., 37–47. Washington, D.C.: Smithsonian Institution Press.

Flannery, Kent V., and Joyce Marcus. 1996. "Cognitive Archaeology." In *Contemporary Archaeology in Theory,* edited by Robert Preucel and Ian Hodder, 350–63. Cambridge, Mass.: Blackwell.

Flannery, Regina, Mary Elizabeth Chambers, and Patricia A. Jehle. 1981. "Witiko Accounts from the James Bay Cree." *Arctic Anthropology* 18, no. 1:57–77.

Fletcher, Alice C., assisted by James R. Murie. 1996. *The Hako: Song, Pipe, and Unity in a Pawnee Calumet Ceremony.* Introduction by Helen Myers. 1904. Reprint. Lincoln: Univ. of Nebraska Press.

Fogelson, Raymond D. 1965. "Psychological Theories of Windigo 'Psychosis' and a Preliminary Application of a Models Approach." In *Context and Meaning in Cultural Anthropology: In Honor of A. Irving Hallowell,* edited by Melford E. Spiro, 74–99. New York: Free Press.

———. 1980. "Windigo Goes South: Stoneclad among the Cherokees." In Halpin and Ames, *Manlike Monsters on Trial: Early Records and Modern Evidence,* 132–51.

———, and Amelia R. Bell. 1983. "Cherokee Booger Mask Tradition." In *The Power of Symbols: Masks and Masquerade in the Americas,* edited by N. Ross Crumrine and Marjorie Halpin, 48–69. Vancouver: Univ. of British Columbia Press.

Foster, Michael K. 1974. *From the Earth to the Sky: An Ethnographic Approach to Four Longhouse Iroquois Speech Events.* Canadian Ethnology Service, Mercury Series Paper 20. Ottawa: National Museum of Man.

———. 1985. "Another Look at the Function of Wampum in Iroquois-White Councils." In *The History and Culture of Iroquois Diplomacy: An Interdisciplinary Guide to the Treaties of the Six Nations and Their League,* edited by Francis Jennings et al., 99–114. Syracuse: Syracuse Univ. Press.

———, Jack Campisi, and Marianne Mithun, eds. 1984. *Extending the Rafters: Interdisciplinary Approaches to Iroquoian Studies.* Albany: State Univ. of New York Press.

Fowler, William S. 1959. "New England Ceramics." *Pennsylvania Archaeologist* 29, no. 1:18–27.

Funk, Robert E. 1978. "Hudson Valley Prehistory: Current Status, Problems, Prospects." In *Neighbors and Intruders: An Ethnohistorical Explanation of the Indians of Hudson's River,* edited by Laurence M. Hauptman and Jack Campisi, 1–87. Canadian Ethnology Service, Mercury Series Paper 39. Ottawa: National Museum of Man.

———, and Robert D. Kuhn. 2003. *Three Sixteenth-Century Mohawk Iroquois Village Sites.* New York State Museum, Bulletin 593. Albany: New York State Education Department.

Gibbon, William B. 1964. "Asiatic Parallels in North American Star Lore: Ursa Major." *Journal of American Folklore* 77:236–50.

Gibson, Stanford J. 1963. "Iroquois Pottery Faces and Effigies." *Chenango Chapter Bulletin* (New York State Archaeological Association, Norwich) 4, no. 8.

Glassie, Henry. 1988. "Meaningful Things and Appropriate Myths: The Artifact's Place in American Studies." In *Material Life in America, 1600–1800,* edited by Robert Blair St. George, 63–92. Boston: Northeastern Univ. Press.

Goddard, Ives. 1984. "Agreskwe, a Northern Iroquoian Deity." In Foster et al., *Extending the Rafters: Interdisciplinary Approaches to Iroquoian Studies,* 229–35.

Goldenweiser, Alexander A. 1914, "On Iroquois Work, 1913–1914." In *Summary Report of the Geological Survey Branch of the Canadian Department of Mines for the Calendar Year 1913,* 365–72. Ottawa: Canadian Department of Mines.

Goldschmidt, Walter. 2000. "A Perspective on Anthropology." *American Anthropologist* 102:789–807.

Goodby, Robert C. 1998. "Technological Patterning and Social Boundaries: Ceramic Variability in Southern New England, A.D. 1000–1675." In *The Archaeology of Social Boundaries,* edited by Miriam T. Stark, 161–82. Washington, D. C.: Smithsonian Institution Press.

Gossen, Gary H. 1986. "Mesoamerican Ideas as a Foundation for Regional Synthesis." In *Symbol and Meaning Beyond the Closed Community: Essays in Mesoamerican Ideas,* edited by Gary H. Gossen, 1–8. Studies on Culture and Society. Vol. 1. Albany: Institute for Mesoamerican Studies, Univ. at Albany, State Univ. of New York.

Grantham, Bill. 2002. *Creation Myths and Legends of the Creek Indians.* Gainesville: Univ. Press of Florida.

Graulich, Michel. 1983. "Myths of Paradise Lost in Pre-Hispanic Central Mexico." *Current Anthropology* 24:575–88.

Graymont, Barbara, ed. 1973. *Fighting Tuscarora: The Autobiography of Chief Clinton Rickard.* Syracuse: Syracuse Univ. Press.

Grumet, Robert S. 1995. *Historic Contact: Indian People and Colonists in Today's Northeastern United States in the Sixteenth through Eighteenth Centuries.* Norman: Univ. of Oklahoma Press.

Guinard, Joseph E. 1930. "Witiko among the Tête-de-Boule." *Primitive Man* 3, nos. 3–4:69–71.

Hagar, Stansbury. 1900. "The Celestial Bear." *Journal of American Folklore* 13:92–103.

———. 1906. "Cherokee Star-Lore." In Anthropological Papers Written in Honor of Franz Boas, no editor cited, 35–66. New York: G. E. Stechert.

Hale, Horatio. 1885. "The Iroquois Sacrifice of the White Dog." *American Antiquarian* 7:7–14.

———. 1888. "Huron Folk-Lore." *Journal of American Folklore* 1:177-83.

———. 1889. "Huron Folk-Lore." *Journal of American Folklore* 2:249–54.

———. 1891. "Huron Folk-Lore." *Journal of American Folklore* 4:289–94.

———. 1894. "The Fall of Hochelaga: A Study of Popular Traditions." *Journal of American Folklore* 7:1–14.

———. 1969. *The Iroquois Book of Rites.* 1883. Reprint. New York: AMS Press.

Hall, Robert L. 1997. *An Archaeology of the Soul: North American Indian Belief and Ritual.* Urbana: Univ. of Illinois Press.

Hallowell, A. Irving. 1926. "Bear Ceremonialism in the Northern Hemisphere." *American Anthropologist* 28:1–175.

———. 1934. "Culture and Mental Disorder." *Journal of Abnormal and Social Psychology* 29:1–9.

———. 1967. "Fear and Anxiety as Cultural and Individual Variables in a Primitive Society." In *Culture and Experience,* by A. Irving Hallowell, 250–65. New York: Schocken Books. First published in 1938 in the *Journal of Social Psychology* 9, 25–47.

Halpin, Marjorie W., and Michael M. Ames, eds. 1980. *Manlike Monsters on Trial: Early Records and Modern Evidence.* Vancouver: Univ. of British Columbia Press.

Hamell, George R. 1979. "Of Hockers, Diamonds, and Hourglasses: Some Interpretations of Seneca Archaeological Art." Paper delivered at the Annual Conference on Iroquois Research, Albany.

———. 1998. "Long-tail: The Panther in Huron-Wyandot and Seneca Myth, Ritual, and Material Culture." In *Icons of Power: Feline Symbolism in the Americas,* edited by Nicholas J. Saunders, 258–91. London: Routledge.

Hamilton, Milton W. 1953. "Guy Johnson's Opinions on the American Indians." *The Pennsylvania Magazine of History and Biography* 77:311–27.

Harrington, M. R. 1908. "Some Seneca Corn-Foods and Their Preparation." *American Anthropologist* 10:875–90.

Hay, Thomas H. 1971. "The Windigo Psychosis: Psychodynamic, Cultural, and Social Factors in Aberrant Behavior." *American Anthropologist* 73:1–19.

Heckewelder, John. 1991. *History, Manners, and Customs of the Indian Nations Who Once Inhabited Pennsylvania and the Neighboring States.* 1876. Reprint. Salem, N.H.: Ayer.

Helm, June, ed. 1981. *Handbook of North American Indians.* Vol. 6, *Subarctic.* Washington, D.C.: Smithsonian Institution.

Hewitt, J. N. B. 1895. "The Iroquois Concept of the Soul." *Journal of American Folklore* 8:107–16.

———. 1910. "Teharonhiawagon." In *Handbook of American Indians North of Mexico.* Part 2, edited by Frederick Webb Hodge, 718–23. Bureau of American Ethnology, Bulletin 30. Washington, D.C.: Smithsonian Institution.

———. 1918. "Seneca Fiction, Legends, and Myths: Collected by Jeremiah Curtin and J. N. B. Hewitt." In *Thirty-second Annual Report of the Bureau of American Ethnology, 1910–1911,* 37–819. Washington, D.C.: Smithsonian Institution.

———. 1974. *Iroquoian Cosmology, Parts I and II.* 1903 and 1928. Reprint. New York: AMS Press.

Hill, Jonathan D. 1988. "Introduction: Myth and History." In *Rethinking History and Myth: Indigenous South American Perspectives on the Past,* edited by Jonathan D. Hill, 1–17. Urbana: Univ. of Illinois Press.

Hodder, Ian. 1986. *Reading the Past: Current Approaches to Interpretation in Archaeology.* Cambridge: Cambridge Univ. Press.

———. 1987. "The Contextual Analysis of Symbolic Meanings." In *The Archaeology of Contextual Meanings,* edited by Ian Hodder, 1–10. Cambridge: Cambridge Univ. Press.

Hoffman, Bernard C. 1964. *Observations on Certain Ancient Tribes of the Northern Appalachian Province.* Bureau of American Ethnology, Bulletin 191, Anthropological Paper 70. Washington, D.C.: Government Printing Office.

Honigman, John J. 1953. "European and Other Tales from the Western Woods Cree." *Journal of American Folklore* 66:309–31.

Hough, Franklin B., ed. 1861. *Proceedings of the Commissioners of Indian Affairs, Appointed by Law for the Extinguishment of Indian Titles in the State of New York.* Albany: Munsell.

Hultkrantz, Åke. 1981. *Belief and Worship in Native North America.* Edited by Christopher Vecsey. Syracuse: Syracuse Univ. Press.

Hymes, Dell. 1981. *"In Vain I Tried to Tell You"*: *Essays in Native American Ethnopoetics*. Lincoln: Univ. of Nebraska Press.

Ireland, Emilienne. 1988. "Cerebral Savage: The Whiteman as Symbol of Cleverness and Savagery in Waurá Myth." In *Rethinking History and Myth: Indigenous South American Perspectives on the Past*, edited by Jonathan D. Hill, 157–73. Urbana: Univ. of Illinois Press.

Jack, Edward. 1895. "Maliseet Legends." *Journal of American Folklore* 8:193–208.

Jameson, J. Franklin, ed. 1909. *Narratives of New Netherland, 1609–1664*. New York: Charles Scribner's Sons.

Jamieson, James Bruce. 1990a. "The Archaeology of the St. Lawrence Iroquoians." In *The Archaeology of Southern Ontario to A.D. 1650*, edited by Chris J. Ellis and Neal Ferris, 385–404. Occasional Publications of the London Chapter, Ontario Archaeological Society, no. 5. London.

———. 1990b. "Trade and Warfare: The Disappearance of the Saint Lawrence Iroquoians." *Man in the Northeast* 39:79–86.

Jennings, Francis. 1984. *The Ambiguous Iroquois Empire: The Covenant Chain Confederation of Indian Tribes with English Colonies from Its Beginnings to the Lancaster Treaty of 1744*. New York: W. W. Norton.

———, William N. Fenton, Mary A. Druke, and David R. Miller, eds. 1985. *The History and Culture of Iroquois Diplomacy: An Interdisciplinary Guide to the Treaties of the Six Nations and Their League*. Syracuse: Syracuse Univ. Press.

Johnson, Crisfield. 1876. *Centennial History of Erie County, New York*. Buffalo: Matthews and Warren.

Johnson, Elias. 1881. *Legends, Traditions, and Laws of the Iroquois; or, Six Nations and History of the Tuscarora Indians*. Lockport, N.Y.: Union Printing and Publishing.

Jones, William. 1911. "Algonquian (Fox)." In *Handbook of American Indian Languages*, Part 1, edited by Franz Boas, 735–873. Bureau of American Ethnology, Bulletin 40. Washington, D.C.: Smithsonian Institution.

Judkins, Russell A. 1987. "David Cusick's 'Ancient History of the Six Nations': A Neglected Classic." In *Iroquois Studies: A Guide to Documentary and Ethnographic Resources from Western New York and the Genesee Valley*, edited by Russell A. Judkins, 26–40. Geneseo: Department of Anthropology, State Univ. of New York.

Kapches, Mima. 2003. "Invisible Women." *Rotunda* 35, no. 3:12–19. Toronto: Royal Ontario Museum.

Kearsley, Ronald Glenn. 1997. "Pinched-Face Human Effigy Pipes: The Social Mechanisms that Conditioned Their Manufacture and Use in Seventeenth Century Iroquoia." M.A. thesis, Trent Univ., Peterborough, Ontario.

Kent, Barry C. 1984. *Susquehanna's Indians*. Anthropological Series 6. Harrisburg: Pennsylvania Historical and Museum Commission.

Kinietz, Vernon, and Erminnie W. Voegelin, eds. 1939. *Shawnese Traditions: C. C. Trowbridge's Account*. Original Contributions from the Museum of Anthropology 9, Univ. of Michigan. Ann Arbor: Univ. of Michigan Press.

Kinsey, W. Fred, III. 1989. "Susquehannock Zoomorphic Images: Or Why the Seasons Changed." In *New Approaches to Other Pasts*, edited by W. Fred Kinsey III and Roger W. Moeller, 71–88. Bethlehem, Conn.: Archaeological Services.

Klinck, Carl F., and James J. Talman, eds. 1970. *The Journal of Major John Norton, 1816*. Toronto: Champlain Society.

Kohl, Johann Georg. 1985. *Kitchi-Gami: Life among the Lake Superior Ojibway*. Translated by Lascelles Wraxall. 1860. Reprint. St. Paul: Minnesota Historical Society Press.

Kraft, Herbert C. 1975. "The Late Woodland Pottery of the Upper Delaware Valley: A Survey and Reevaluation." *Archaeology of Eastern North America* 3:101–40.

Krupp, E. C. ca. 1993. *Echoes of Ancient Skies: The Astronomy of Lost Civilizations*. Rev. ed. Old Saybrook, Conn.: Konecky and Konecky.

Krusche, Rolf. 1986. "The Origin of the Mask Concept in the Eastern Woodlands of North America." *Man in the Northeast* 31:1–47.

Kuhn, Robert D. 1985. "Trade and Exchange among the Mohawk-Iroquois: A Trace Element Analysis of Ceramic Smoking Pipes." Ph.D. diss., State Univ. of New York at Albany.

———, and Robert E. Funk. 2000. "Boning Up on the Mohawk: An Overview of Faunal Assemblages and Subsistence Patterns." *Archaeology of Eastern North America* 28:29–62.

———, Robert E. Funk, and James F. Pendergast. 1993. "The Evidence for a Saint Lawrence Iroquoian Presence on Sixteenth-Century Mohawk Sites." *Man in the Northeast* 45:77–86.

———, and Martha L. Sempowski. 2001. "A New Approach to Dating the League of the Iroquois." *American Antiquity* 66:301–14.

Kurath, Gertrude Prokosch. 1952. "Matrilineal Dances of the Iroquois." In *Indian Tribes of Aboriginal America: Selected Papers of the XXIXth International*

Congress of Americanists, edited by Sol Tax, 123–30. Chicago: Univ. of Chicago Press.

———. 1968. *Dance and Song Rituals of the Six Nation Reserve, Ontario.* Folklore Series 4, Bulletin 220. Ottawa: National Museum of Man.

———. 2000. *Iroquois Music and Dance: Ceremonial Arts of the Seneca Longhouses.* 1964. Reprint. Mineola, N.Y.: Dover.

Landes, Ruth. 1938. *The Ojibwa Woman.* New York: Columbia Univ. Press.

Landy, David. 1958. "Tuscarora Tribalism and National Identity." *Ethnohistory* 5:250–84.

———. 1978. "Tuscarora among the Iroquois." In Trigger, *Handbook of North American Indians* 15:518–24.

Lankford, George E. 1987. *Native American Legends; Southeastern Legends: Tales from the Natchez, Caddo, Biloxi, Chickasaw, and Other Nations.* Little Rock: August House.

———. 2007a. "The Great Serpent in Eastern North America." In Reilly and Garber, *Ancient Objects and Sacred Realms: Interpretations of Mississippian Iconography,* 107–35.

———. 2007b. "The 'Path of Souls': Some Death Imagery in the Southeastern Ceremonial Complex." In Reilly and Garber, *Ancient Objects and Sacred Realms: Interpretations of Mississippian Iconography,* 174–212.

———. 2007c. "Some Cosmological Motifs in the Southeastern Ceremonial Complex." In Reilly and Garber, *Ancient Objects and Sacred Realms: Interpretations of Mississippian Iconography,* 8–38.

Leach, Maria, ed. 1949–50. *Funk and Wagnalls Standard Dictionary of Folklore, Mythology and Legend.* 2 vols. New York: Funk and Wagnalls.

Leland, Charles G. 1992. *Algonquin Legends.* 1884. Reprint. Mineola, N.Y.: Dover.

Lenig, Donald. 1965. *The Oak Hill Horizon and Its Relation to the Development of Five Nations Iroquois Culture.* Researches and Transactions 15. Buffalo: New York State Archaeological Association.

Lévi-Strauss, Claude. 1963. "The Structural Study of Myth." In *Structural Anthropology,* by Claude Lévi-Strauss, 206–31. Translated by Claire Jacobson and Brooke Grundfest Schoepf. New York: Basic Books.

———. 1983. *The Raw and the Cooked: Mythologiques.* Vol. 1. Translated by John and Doreen Weightman. Chicago: Univ. of Chicago Press.

———. 1987. *Anthropology and Myth: Lectures, 1951–1982.* Translated by Roy Willis. New York: Basil Blackwell.

———. 1990a. *The Naked Man: Mythologiques.* Vol. 4. Translated by John and Doreen Weightman. Chicago: Univ. of Chicago Press.

———. 1990b. *The Origin of Table Manners: Mythologiques.* Vol. 3. Translated by John and Doreen Weightman. Chicago: Univ. of Chicago Press.

Long, Charles H. 1963. *Alpha: The Myths of Creation.* New York: George Braziller.

Lopez, Julius, and Stanley Wisniewski. 1972. "The Ryders Pond Site II." *Bulletin: Journal of the New York State Archaeological Association* 55:6–20.

López Austin, Alfredo. 1996. *The Rabbit on the Face of the Moon: Mythology in the Mesoamerican Tradition.* Translated by Bernard R. Ortiz de Montellano and Thelma Ortiz de Montellano. Salt Lake City: Univ. of Utah Press.

Lounsbury, Floyd G. 1978. "Iroquoian Languages." In Trigger, *Handbook of North American Indians* 15:334–43.

———, and Bryan Gick, trans. and eds. 2000. *The Oneida Creation Story: Demus Elm and Harvey Antone.* Columbia, S.C.: Yorkshire Press.

Lowie, Robert H. 1908. "The Test-Theme in North American Mythology." *Journal of American Folklore* 21:97–148.

MacNeish, Richard S. 1952. *Iroquois Pottery Types: A Technique for the Study of Iroquois Prehistory.* National Museum of Canada Bulletin 124, Anthropological Series 31. Ottawa: Canada Department of Resources and Development.

Malinowski, Bronislaw. 1948. "Myth in Primitive Psychology." In *Magic, Science and Religion, and Other Essays,* by Bronislaw Malinowski, 93–148. Boston: Beacon.

———. 1984. "The Role of Myth in Life." In *Sacred Narrative: Readings in the Theory of Myth,* edited by Allen Dundes, 193–206. Berkeley and Los Angeles: Univ. of California Press.

Mann, Barbara Alice. 2000. *Iroquoian Women: The Gantowisas.* New York: Peter Lang.

Marano, Lou. 1982. "Windigo Psychosis: The Anatomy of an Emic-Etic Confusion." *Current Anthropology* 23:385–412.

Margry, Pierre, ed. 1876. *Découvertes et établissements des Français dans l'ouest et dans le sud de l'Amérique septentrionale, 1614–1754: Mémoires et documents originaux.* Vol. 1. Paris: D. Jouast.

Mathews, Zena Pearlstone. 1976. "Huron Pipes and Iroquoian Shamanism." *Man in the Northeast* 12:15–31.

———. 1981. "Janus and Other Multiple-Image Iroquoian Pipes." *Ontario Archaeology* 35:3–22.

———. 1982. "On Dreams and Journeys: Iroquoian Boat Pipes." *American Indian Art Magazine* 7, no. 3:46–51, 80.

McCallum, James Dow, ed. 1932. *The Letters of Eleazar Wheelock's Indians.* Hanover, N.H.: Dartmouth College.

McElwain, Thomas. 1992. "Asking the Stars: Seneca Hunting Ceremonial." In *Visions of the Cosmos in Native American Folklore,* edited by Ray A. Williams and Claire R. Farrer, 260–77. Albuquerque: Univ. of New Mexico Press.

McGee, Harold Franklin, Jr. 1972. "Windigo Psychosis." *American Anthropologist* 74:244–46.

———. 1975. "The Windigo Down-East or, The Taming of the Windigo." In *Proceedings of the Second Congress, Canadian Ethnology Society.* Vol. 1, edited by Jim Freedman and Jerome H. Barkow, 110–32. Canadian Ethnology Service, Mercury Series Paper 28. Ottawa: National Museums of Canada.

McGuire, J. D. 1899. "Pipes and Smoking Customs of the American Aborigines, Based on Material in the United States Museum." In *Annual Report of the Board of Regents of the Smithsonian Institution, 1897,* 351–645. Washington, D.C.: Government Printing Office.

Michelson, Truman, ed. 1917. *Ojibwa Texts, Collected by William Jones.* Publications of the American Ethnological Society, vol. 7, pt. 1. Leyden: E. J. Brill.

———. 1919. *Ojibwa Texts, Collected by William Jones.* Publications of the American Ethnological Society, vol. 7, pt. 2. New York: G. E. Stechert.

Miller, Dorcas S. 1997. *Stars of the First People: Native American Star Myths and Constellations.* Boulder: Pruett.

Mindlin, Betty. 2002. *Barbecued Husbands, and Other Stories from the Amazon.* Translated by Donald Slatoff. London: Verso.

Momaday, N. Scott. 1969. *The Way to Rainy Mountain.* Albuquerque: Univ. of New Mexico Press.

Monroe, Jean Guard, and Ray A. Williamson. 1987. *They Dance in the Sky: Native American Star Myths.* Boston: Houghton Mifflin.

Mooney, James. 1995. *Myths of the Cherokee.* 1900. Reprint. Mineola, N.Y.: Dover.

Morgan, Lewis Henry. 1962. *League of the Iroquois.* 1851. Reprint. Secaucus, N.J.: Citadel Press.

Morrison, Kenneth M. 1979. "Towards a History of Intimate Encounters: Algonkian Folklore, Jesuit Missionaries, and Kiwakwe, the Cannibal Giant." *American Indian Culture and Research Journal* 3, no. 4:51–80.

Myrtle, Minnie. 1855. *The Iroquois; or, the Bright Side of Indian Character.* New York: D. Appleton.

Nabokov, Peter. 2002. *A Forest of Time: American Indian Ways of History.* New York: Cambridge Univ. Press.

Noble, William C. 1979. "Ontario Iroquois Effigy Pipes." *Canadian Journal of Archaeology* 3:69–90.

Norman, Howard A., trans. *Where the Chill Came From: Cree Windigo Tales and Journeys.* San Francisco: North Point Press.

O'Callaghan, Edmund B., ed. 1853–87. *Documents Relative to the Colonial History of the State of New York, Procured in Holland, England and France, by John R. Brodhead.* 15 vols. Albany: Weed, Parson.

Olcott, William Tyler. 2004. *Star Lore: Myths, Legends, and Facts.* 1911. Reprint. Mineola, N.Y.: Dover.

Opler, Morris Edward. 1994. *Myths and Tales of the Jicarilla Apache Indians.* Introduction by Scott Rushforth. 1938. Reprint. Lincoln: Univ. of Nebraska Press.

Overholt, Thomas W., and J. Baird Callicott. 1982. *Clothed-in-Fur and Other Tales: An Introduction to an Ojibwa World View.* Washington, D.C.: Univ. Press of America.

Paredes, J. Anthony. 1972. "A Case Study of 'Normal' Windigo." *Anthropologica* 14, no. 2:97-116.

Parker, Arthur C. 1913. *The Code of Handsome Lake, the Seneca Prophet.* New York State Museum, Bulletin 163. Albany: State Univ. of New York.

———. 1916. *The Constitution of the Five Nations.* New York State Museum, Bulletin 184. Albany: State Univ. of New York.

———. 1919. *The Life of General Ely A. Parker: Last Grand Sachem of the Iroquois and General Grant's Military Secretary.* Buffalo: Buffalo Historical Society.

———. 1928. *Rumbling Wings and Other Indian Tales.* Garden City, N.Y.: Doubleday, Doran.

———. 1989. *Seneca Myths and Folk Tales.* 1923. Reprint. Syracuse: Syracuse Univ. Press.

———. 1994. *Skunny Wundy: Seneca Indian Tales.* 1926. Reprint. Syracuse: Syracuse Univ. Press.

Parker, Seymour. 1960. "The Witiko Psychosis in the Context of Ojibwa Personality and Culture." *American Anthropologist* 62:603–23.

Parks, Douglas R. 1985. "Interpreting Pawnee Star Lore: Science or Myth?" *American Indian Culture and Research Journal* 9, no. 1:53–72.

———. 1996. *Myths and Traditions of the Arikara Indians.* Lincoln: Univ. of Nebraska Press.

Parsons, Elsie Clews. 1925. "Micmac Folklore." *Journal of American Folklore* 38:55–133.

Pearson, Bruce L., ed. and trans. 2001. *Huron-Wyandotte Traditional Narratives: Told by Catherine Johnson, Smith Nichols, John Kayrahoo, Star Young, Mary McKee; Collected by Marius Barbeau.* Columbia, S.C.: Yorkshire Press.

Pendergast, James F. 1980. "Ceramic Motif Mutations at Glenbrook." In *Proceedings of the 1979 Iroquois Pottery Conference,* edited by Charles F. Hayes III et al., 133–45. Research Record 13. Rochester: Rochester Museum and Science Center.

———. 1990. "Emerging Saint Lawrence Iroquoian Settlement Patterns." *Man in the Northeast* 40:17–30.

———. 1991a. *The Massawomeck: Raiders and Traders into the Chesapeake Bay in the Seventeenth Century.* Transactions of the American Philosophical Society, vol. 81, pt. 2. Philadelphia.

———. 1991b. "The St. Lawrence Iroquoians: Their Past, Present, Immediate Future." *Bulletin: Journal of the New York State Archaeological Association* 102:47–74.

———. 1992. "Some Notes on Ceramic Smoking Pipes from St. Lawrence Iroquoian Archaeological Sites." In *Proceedings of the 1989 Smoking Pipe Conference: Selected Papers,* edited by Charles F. Hayes III, Connie Cox Bodner, and Martha L. Sempowski, 51–70. Research Records 22. Rochester Museum and Science Center.

———. 1994. "The Kakouagoga or Kahkwas: An Iroquois Nation Destroyed in the Niagara Region." *Proceedings of the American Philosophical Society* 138, no. 1:96–144.

———. 1996. "High Precision Calibration of the Radiocarbon Time Scale: CALIB 3.0.3 (Method 'A') in a St. Lawrence Iroquoian Context." *Bulletin: Journal of the New York State Archaeological Association* 111–12:35–62.

———. 1999. "The Ottawa River Algonquin Bands in a St. Lawrence Iroquoian Context." *Canadian Journal of Archaeology* 23:63–136.

———, and Bruce G. Trigger. 1972. *Cartier's Hochelaga and the Dawson Site.* Montreal: McGill-Queen's Univ. Press.

Peterson, James B., John C. Crock, Ellen R. Cowie, Richard A. Boisvert, Joshua R. Toney, and Geoffrey Mandel. 2004. "St. Lawrence Iroquoians in Northern New England: Pendergast Was 'Right' and More." In *A Passion for the Past: Papers in Honour of James F. Pendergast,* edited by James V. Wright and Jean-Luc Pilon, 87–123. Mercury Series Archaeology Paper 164. Hull: Canadian Museum of Civilization.

Pilkington, Walter, ed. 1980. *The Journals of Samuel Kirkland: 18th-Century Missionary to the Iroquois, Government Agent, Father of Hamilton College.* Clinton, N.Y.: Hamilton College.

Podruchny, Carolyn. 2004. "Werewolves and Windigos: Narratives of Cannibal Monsters in French-Canadian Voyageur Oral Tradition." *Ethnohistory* 51:677–700.

Pouchot, Pierre. 1994. *Memoirs on the Late War in North America between France and England.* Edited by Brian Leigh Dunnigan. Translated by Michael Cardy. Youngstown, N.Y.: Old Fort Niagara Association.

Powers, Mabel. 1923. *Around an Iroquois Story Fire.* New York: Frederick A. Stokes.

Pratt, Peter Paul. 1976. *Archaeology of the Oneida Iroquois.* Vol. 1. Occasional Publications in Northeastern Anthropolgy 1. George's Mills, N.H.: Man in the Northeast.

Preston, Richard J. 1978. "Ethnographic Reconstruction of Witiko." In *Papers of the Ninth Algonquian Conference,* edited by William Cowan, 61–67. Ottawa: Carleton Univ.

———. 1980. "The Witiko: Algonkian Knowledge and Whiteman Knowledge." In Halpin and Ames,*Manlike Monsters on Trial: Early Records and Modern Evidence,* 111–31.

Preucel, Robert, and Ian Hodder. 1996. "Material Symbols." In *Contemporary Archaeology in Theory,* edited by Robert Preucel and Ian Hodder, 299–307. Oxford: Blackwell.

Prince, John Dyneley. 1921. *Passamaquoddy Texts.* Publications of the American Ethnological Society, vol. 10. New York: G. E. Stechert.

Ramsden, Peter G. 1990a. "The Hurons: Archaeology and Culture History." In *The Archaeology of Southern Ontario to* A.D. *1650,* edited by Chris J. Ellis and Neal Ferris, 361–84. Occasional Publications of the London Chapter, Ontario Archaeological Society 5. London.

———. 1990b. "Saint Lawrence Iroquoians in the Upper Trent River Valley." *Man in the Northeast* 39:87–95.

Ramsey, Jarold. 1983. *Reading the Fire: Essays in the Traditional Indian Literatures of the Far West.* Lincoln: Univ. of Nebraska Press.

Rand, Silas Tertius. 1894. *Legends of the Micmac.* New York: Longmans Green.

Randle, Martha Champion. 1953. "The Waugh Collection of Iroquois Folktales." *Proceedings of the American Philosophical Society* 97:611–33.

Rands, Robert L. 1954. "Horned Serpent Stories." *Journal of American Folklore* 67:79–81.

Ray, Keith. 1987. "Material Metaphor, Social Interaction and Historical Reconstruction: Exploring Patterns of Association and Symbolism in the Igbo-Ukwu Corpus." In *The Archaeology of Contextual Meanings*, edited by Ian Hodder, 66–77. Cambridge: Cambridge Univ. Press.

Rayner-Herter, Nancy Lynn. 2001. "The Niagara Frontier Iroquois: A Study of Sociopolitical Development." Ph.D. diss., State Univ. of New York at Buffalo.

Recht, Michael. 1995. "The Role of Fishing in the Iroquois Economy, 1600–1792." *New York History* 76:5–30.

Reilly, F. Kent, III, and James F. Garber, eds. 2007. *Ancient Objects and Sacred Realms: Interpretations of Mississippian Iconography.* Austin: Univ. of Texas Press.

Renfrew, Colin. 1986. "Introduction: Peer Polity Interaction and Socio-Political Change." In *Peer Polity Interaction and Socio-Political Change*, edited by Colin Renfrew and John F. Cherry, 1–18. Cambridge: Cambridge Univ. Press.

Richter, Daniel K. 1992. *The Ordeal of the Longhouse: The Peoples of the Iroquois League in the Era of European Colonization.* Chapel Hill: Univ. of North Carolina Press.

Ridington, Robin. 1976. "Wechuge and Windigo: A Comparison of Cannibal Belief among Boreal Forest Athapaskans and Algonkians." *Anthropologica* 18, no. 2:107–29.

Ritchie, William A. 1980. *The Archaeology of New York State.* 2nd rev. ed. Harrison, N.Y.: Harbor Books.

———, and Robert E. Funk. 1973. *Aboriginal Settlement Patterns in the Northeast.* New York State Museum and Science Service, Memoir 20. Albany: Univ. of the State of New York.

Robertson, David A., and Ronald F. Williamson. 1998. "The Archaeology of the Parsons Site: Summary and Conclusions." *Ontario Archaeology* 65–66:146–50.

Rohrl, Vivian J. 1970. "A Nutritional Factor in Windigo Psychosis." *American Anthropologist* 72:97–101.

Rooth, Anna Birgitta. 1957. "Creation Myths of North America." *Anthropos* 52:497–508.

Rudes, Blair A. 1994. "Two Tuscarora Legends." In *Coming to Light: Contemporary Translations of the Native Literatures of North America*, edited by Brian Swann, 464–75. New York: Random House.

————, and Dorothy Crouse. 1987. *The Tuscarora Legacy of J. N. B. Hewitt.* 2 vols. Canadian Ethnology Service, Mercury Series Paper 108. Ottawa: Canadian Museum of Civilization.

Rustige, Rona. 1988. *Tyendinaga Tales.* Kingston and Montreal: McGill-Queen's Univ. Press.

Rutsch, Edward S. 1973. *Smoking Technology of the Aborigines of the Iroquois Area of New York State.* Rutherford, N.J.: Fairleigh Dickenson Univ. Press.

Saindon, J. E. 1933. "Mental Disorders among the James Bay Cree." *Primitive Man* 6, no. 1:10–20.

Sapir, Edward. 1994. "Time Perspective in Aboriginal American Culture: A Study in Method" (originally published 1916). In *The Collected Works of Edward Sapir.* Vol. 4, *Ethnology,* edited by Regna Darnell and Judith Ivine, 31–120. Berlin: Mouton de Gruyter.

Schoolcraft, Henry Rowe. 1975. *Notes on the Iroquois; or, Contributions to the Statistics, Aboriginal History, Antiquities, and General Ethnology of Western New-York.* 1846. Reprint. Millwood, N.Y.: Krauss Reprint.

————. 1999. *Algic Researches: North American Indian Folktales and Legends.* 1839. Reprint. Mineola, N.Y.: Dover.

Scott, Duncan C., ed. 1912. "Traditional History of the Confederacy of the Six Nations, Prepared by a Committee of the Chiefs." *Transactions of the Royal Society of Canada,* 3rd ser., 5, no. 2:195–246. Ottawa.

Seaver, James E. 1990. *A Narrative of the Life of Mrs. Mary Jemison . . . Carefully Taken from Her Own Words, Nov. 29th, 1823.* 1823. Reprint. Syracuse: Syracuse Univ. Press.

Sempowski, Martha L. 2004. "Spiritual Transformation as Reflected in Late Prehistoric Human Effigy Pipes from Western New York." In *A Passion for the Past: Papers in Honour of James F. Pendergast,* edited by James V. Wright and Jean-Luc Pilon, 263–81. Mercury Series Archaeology Paper 164. Hull: Canadian Museum of Civilization.

————, and Lorraine P. Saunders. 2001. *Dutch Hollow and Factory Hollow: The Advent of Dutch Trade among the Seneca.* Research Records 24. Rochester: Rochester Museum and Science Center.

Severance, Frank H., ed. 1904. *Journals of Henry A. S. Dearborn.* Publications of the Buffalo Historical Society 7:35–228.

Shea, John Gilmary, trans. 1881. *First Establishment of the Faith in New France by Father Christian Le Clerq, Recollect Missionary.* Vol. 1. New York: the author.

Shimony, Annemarie Anrod. 1994. *Conservatism among the Iroquois at the Six Nations Reserve.* Rev. ed. Syracuse: Syracuse Univ. Press.

Skinner, Alanson. 1911. *Notes on the Eastern Cree and Northern Saulteaux.* Anthropological Papers of the American Museum of Natural History, vol. 9, pt. 1. New York.

———. 1921. *Notes on Iroquois Archaeology.* Museum of the American Indian, Heye Foundation, Indian Notes and Monographs. New York.

———. 1928. "Sauk Tales." *Journal of American Folklore* 41:147–71.

———, and John V. Satterlee. 1915. *Folklore of the Menomini Indians.* Anthropological Papers of the American Museum of Natural History, vol. 13, pt. 3. New York.

Smith, Erminnie A. 1983. *Myths of the Iroquois.* 1883. Reprint. Ohsweken, Ontario: Irocrafts.

Smith, James G. E. 1976. "Notes on the Witiko." In *Papers of the Seventh Algonquian Conference,* edited by William Cowan, 18–34. Ottawa: Carleton Univ.

Smith, Harlan I. 1897. "The Monster in the Tree: An Ojibwa Myth." *Journal of American Folklore* 10:324–25.

Smith, Theresa S. 1995. *The Island of the Anishnaabeg: Thunders and Water Monsters in the Traditional Ojibwa Life-World.* Moscow: Univ. of Idaho Press.

Snow, Dean R. 1978. "Late Prehistory of the East Coast." In Trigger, *Handbook of North American Indians* 15: 58–69.

———. 1994. *The Iroquois.* Oxford: Blackwell.

Snyderman, George S. 1948. "Behind the Tree of Peace: A Sociological Analysis of Iroquois Warfare." *Pennsylvania Archaeologist* 8, nos. 3–4:2–93.

Speck, Frank G. 1925. "Montagnais and Naskapi Tales from the Labrador Peninsula." *Journal of American Folklore* 38:1–32.

———. 1931. *A Study of the Delaware Indian Big House Ceremony.* Publications of the Pennsylvania Historical Commission 2. Harrisburg.

———. 1935a. "Penobscot Tales and Religious Beliefs." *Journal of American Folklore* 48:1–107.

———. 1935b. *Naskapi: The Savage Hunters of the Labrador Peninsula.* Norman: Univ. of Oklahoma Press.

———. 1995. *Midwinter Rites of the Cayuga Long House.* 1949. Reprint. Lincoln: Univ. of Nebraska Press.

———, and Jesse Moses. 1945. *The Celestial Bear Comes Down to Earth: The Bear Sacrifice Ceremony of the Munsee-Mahican in Canada as Related by Nekatcit.* Scientific Publications 7. Reading, Penn.: Reading Public Museum and Art Gallery.

Steckley, John. 1985. "A Tale of Two Peoples." *Arch Notes* 85, no. 4:9–15. Toronto: Ontario Archaeological Society.

———. 1992. "The Warrior and the Lineage: Jesuit Use of Iroquoian Images to Communicate Christianity." *Ethnohistory* 39:478–509.

Steward, Julian H. 1942. "The Direct Historical Approach to Archaeology." *American Antiquity* 7:337–43.

Strong, William Duncan. 1942. "Historical Approach in Anthropology." In *Anthropology Today,* edited by Alfred L. Kroeber, 386–97. Chicago: Univ. of Chicago Press.

Sturtevant, William C. 2006. "David and Dennis Cusick: Early Iroquois Realist Artists." *American Indian Art Magazine* 31, no. 2:44–55, 95.

Swanton, John R. 1929. *Myths and Tales of the Southeastern Indians.* Bureau of American Ethnology, Bulletin 88. Washington, D.C.: Smithsonian Institution.

Taggart, James M. 1983. *Nahuat Myth and Social Structure.* Austin: Univ. of Texas Press.

Tehanetorens. 1998. *Legends of the Iroquois.* Summerstown, Tenn.: Book Publishing.

Teicher, Morton I. 1960. *Windigo Psychosis: A Study of a Relationship between Belief and Behavior among the Indians of Northeastern Canada.* Proceedings of the 1960 Annual Spring Meeting of the American Ethnological Society, edited by Verne F. Ray. Seattle: American Ethnological Society.

Thompson, Stith. 1929. *Tales of the North American Indians.* Cambridge, Mass.: Harvard Univ. Press.

———. 1946. *The Folktale.* New York: Holt, Rinehart, and Winston.

———. 1955–1958. *Motif-Index of Folk-Literature: A Classification of Narrative Elements in Folktales, Ballads, Myths, Fables, Mediaeval Romances, Exempla, Fabliaux, Jest-Books and Local Legends.* 6 vols. Rev. ed. Bloomington: Indiana Univ. Press.

———. 1965. "Myth and Folktales." In *Myth: A Symposium,* edited by Thomas A. Sebeok, 169–80. 1955. Reprint. Bloomington: Indiana Univ. Press.

Thwaites, Reuben Gold, ed. 1896–1901. *The Jesuit Relations and Allied Documents.* 73 vols. Cleveland: Burrows Bros.

———. 1903. *A New Discovery of a Vast Country in America by Father Louis Hennepin.* Vol. 2. Chicago: A. C. McClurg.

Tiro, Karim M. 1999. "James Dean in Iroquoia." *Ethnohistory* 80:391–422.

Tooker, Elisabeth. 1970. *The Iroquois Ceremonial of Midwinter.* Syracuse: Syracuse Univ. Press.

———. 1978. "The League of the Iroquois: Its History, Politics, and Ritual." In Trigger, *Handbook of North American Indians* 15: 418–41.

———. 1984. "Women in Iroquois Society." In Foster et al., *Extending the Rafters: Interdisciplinary Approaches to Iroquoian Studies,* 109–23.

———. 1991. *An Ethnography of the Huron Indians, 1615–1649.* 1964. Reprint. Syracuse: Syracuse Univ. Press.

Trigger, Bruce G. 1969. *The Huron: Farmers of the North.* New York: Holt, Rinehart, and Winston.

———, ed. 1978. *Handbook of North American Indians.* Vol. 15, *Northeast.* Washington, D.C.: Smithsonian Institution.

———. 2001. "The Liberation of Wendake." *Ontario Archaeology* 72:3–14.

Tuck, James A. 1971. *Onondaga Iroquois Prehistory: A Study in Settlement Archaeology.* Syracuse: Syracuse Univ. Press.

Turner, D. H. 1977. "Windigo Mythology and the Analysis of Cree Social Structure." *Anthropologica* 19, no. 1:63–73.

Turner, Glen D., and Harold Hickerson. 1952. Field Report (Sept.–Oct. 1950). Thirty-five-page typescript comprising pp. 7–41 (handwritten pagination) of the manuscript accompanying "Testing Procedures for Estimating Transfer of Information among Iroquois Dialects and Languages," Freeman Guide no. 1835. Philadelphia: American Philosophical Society.

Turner, O. 1849. *Pioneer History of the Holland Purchase of Western New York.* Buffalo: Jewett, Thomas.

Urton, Gary. 1985. Introduction to *Animal Myths and Metaphors in South America,* edited by Gary Urton, 3–10. Salt Lake City: Univ. of Utah Press.

———. 1990. *The History of a Myth: Pacariqtambo and the Origin of the Inkas.* Austin: Univ. of Texas Press.

Vecsey, Christopher. 1983. *Traditional Ojibwa Religion and Its Historical Changes.* Philadelphia: American Philosophical Society.

———. 1984. "Midewiwin Myths of Origin." In *Papers of the Fifteenth Algonquian Conference,* edited by William Cowan, 445–67. Ottawa: Carleton Univ.

———. 1988. *Imagine Ourselves Richly: Mythic Narratives of North American Indians.* New York: Crossroad.

Voegelin, Erminnie W. 1984. "Lodge-Boy and Thrown-Away." In *Funk and Wagnalls Standard Dictionary of Folklore, Mythology, and Legend,* edited by Maria Leach, 2:642. 1949–50. Reprint. San Francisco: Harper and Row.

von Gernet, Alexander D. 1992. "Hallucinogens and the Origins of the Iroquoian Pipe/Tobacco/Smoking Complex." In *Proceedings of the 1989 Smoking Pipe*

Conference: Selected Papers, edited by Charles F. Hayes III, Connie Cox Bodner, and Martha L. Sempowski, 171–85. Research Record 22. Rochester: Rochester Museum and Science Center.

Waisberg, Leo G. 1975. "Boreal Forest Subsistence and the Windigo: Fluctuation of Populations." *Anthropologica* 17, no. 2:169–85.

Wallace, Anthony F. C. 1958. "Dreams and the Wishes of the Soul: A Type of Psychoanalytic Theory among the Seventeenth Century Iroquois." *American Anthropologist* 60:234–48.

———. 1972. *The Death and Rebirth of the Seneca.* New York: Vintage Books.

———. 1978. "Origin of the Longhouse Religion." In Trigger, *Handbook of North American Indians* 15: 442–48.

Wallis, Wilson D., and Ruth Sawtell Wallis. 1955. *The Micmac Indians of Eastern Canada.* Minneapolis: Univ. of Minnesota Press.

Waterman, T. T. 1914. "The Explanatory Element in the Folk-Tales of the North-American Indians." *Journal of American Folklore* 27:1–54.

Waugh, Frederick W. 1916. *Iroquois Foods and Food Preparation.* Canada Department of Mines, Geological Survey, Memoir 86, Anthropological Series 12. Ottawa: Government Printing Bureau.

———. n.d. Iroquois Folklore Papers. Canadian Museum of Civilization, Library, Archives, and Documentation. Hull, Quebec.

Weaver, Sally M. 1984. "Seth Newhouse and the Grand River Confederacy at Mid–Nineteenth Century." In Foster et al., *Extending the Rafters: Interdisciplinary Approaches to Iroquoian Studies,* 165–82.

Wheeler-Voegelin, Erminnie, and Remedios W. Moore. 1957. "The Emergence Myth in Native North America." In *Studies in Folklore: In Honor of Distinguished Service Professor Stith Thompson,* edited by W. Edson Richmond, 66–91. Bloomington: Indiana Univ. Press.

Whipple, J. S., et al. 1889. *Report of Special Committee to Investigate the Indian Problem of the State of New York, Appointed by the Assembly of 1888.* Assembly Document 51. Albany: Troy Press.

White, Marian E. 1961. *Iroquois Culture History in the Niagara Frontier Area of New York State.* Museum of Anthropology, Anthropological Paper 16. Ann Arbor: Univ. of Michigan.

———. 1971. "Ethnic Identification and Iroquois Groups in Western New York and Ontario." *Ethnohistory* 18, no. 1:19–38.

———. 1978a. "Neutral and Wenro." In Trigger, *Handbook of North American Indians* 15: 407–11.

———. 1978b. "Erie." In Trigger, *Handbook of North American Indians* 15:412–17.

Whitney, Theodore. 1971. "The Olcott Site, Msv-3." *Chenango Chapter Bulletin* (New York State Archaeological Association, Norwich) 12, no. 3.

———. 1974. "Aboriginal Art and Ritual Objects." *Chenango Chapter Bulletin* (New York State Archaeological Association, Norwich) 15, no. 1.

Williamson, Ray A. 1984. *Living with the Sky: The Cosmos of the American Indian*. Boston: Houghton Mifflin.

———. 1992. "The Celestial Skiff: An Alabama Myth of the Stars." In *Earth and Sky: Visions of the Cosmos in Native American Folklore*, edited by Ray A. Williamson and Claire R. Farrer, 52–66. Albuquerque: Univ. of New Mexico Press.

Willoughby, Charles C. 1935. *Antiquities of the New England Indians*. Cambridge: Peabody Museum of American Archaeology and Ethnology, Harvard, Univ.

Wintemberg, W. J. 1936. *Roebuck Prehistoric Village Site, Grenville County, Ontario*. Canada Department of Mines, National Museum of Canada, Bulletin 83, Anthropological Series 19. Ottawa: J. O. Patenaude.

Wissler, Clark. 1938. *The American Indian: An Introduction to the Anthropology of the New World*. 3rd ed. 1917. Reprint. New York: Oxford Univ. Press.

———, and D. C. Duvall. 1995. *Mythology of the Blackfoot Indians*. Introduction by Alice Beck Kehoe. 1908. Reprint. Lincoln: Univ. of Nebraska Press.

Wonderley, Anthony. 2001. "The Iroquois Creation Story Over Time." *Northeast Anthropology* 62:1–16.

———. 2002. "Oneida Ceramic Effigies: A Question of Meaning." *Northeast Anthropology* 63:23–48.

———. 2004. *Oneida Iroquois Folklore, Myth, and History: New York Oral Narrative from the Notes of H. E. Allen and Others*. Syracuse: Syracuse Univ. Press.

———. 2005a. "Effigy Pipes, Diplomacy, and Myth: Exploring Interaction between St. Lawrence Iroquoians and Eastern Iroquois in New York State." *American Antiquity* 70:211–40.

———. 2005b. "Iroquois Ceramic Iconography: New Evidence from the Oneida Vaillancourt Site." *Ontario Archaeology* 79–80:73–87.

———. 2006a. "Archaeological Research at the Oneida Vaillancourt Site." *Bulletin: Journal of the New York State Archaeological Association* 122:1–26.

———. 2006b. "Sky Dancers and Bear Chasers: What (If Anything) Does Haudenosaunee Star Lore *Mean?*" *Northeast Anthropology* 71:9–21.

Woodbury, Hanni, ed. and trans., in collaboration with Reg Henry and Harry Webster. 1992. *Concerning the League: The Iroquois League Tradition as Dictated in Onondaga by John Arthur Gibson.* Memoir 9, Algonquian and Iroquoian Linguistics. Winnipeg.

Wray, Charles F., Martha L. Sempowski, and Lorraine P. Saunders. 1991. *Tram and Cameron: Two Early Contact Seneca Sites.* Research Records 21. Rochester: Rochester Museum and Science Center.

Wray, Charles F., Martha L. Sempowski, Lorraine P. Saunders, and Gian Carlo Cervone. 1987. *The Adams and Culbertson Sites.* Research Records 19. Rochester: Rochester Museum and Science Center.

Wright, Roy A. 1974. "The People of the Panther: A Long Erie Tale (An Ethnohistory of the Southwestern Iroquoians)." In *Papers in Linguistics from the 1972 Conference on Iroquoian Research,* edited by Michael K. Foster, 47–118. National Museum of Man Mercury Series, Ethnology Division Paper 10. Ottawa: National Museums of Canada.

Wrong, George M., ed. 1939. *The Long Journey to the Country of the Hurons by Father Gabriel Sagard.* Translated by H. H. Langton. Toronto: Champlain

Index